Leadership for Educational Psychologists

BPS Textbooks in Psychology

BPS Wiley presents a comprehensive and authoritative series covering everything a student needs in order to complete an undergraduate degree in psychology. Refreshingly written to consider more than North American research, this series is the first to give a truly international perspective. Written by the very best names in the field, the series offers an extensive range of titles from introductory level through to final year optional modules, and every text fully complies with the BPS syllabus in the topic. No other series bears the BPS seal of approval!

Many of the books are supported by a companion website, featuring additional resource materials for both instructors and students, designed to encourage critical thinking and providing for all your course lecturing and testing needs.

For other titles in this series, please go to http://psychsource.bps.org.uk

Leadership for Educational Psychologists

Principles & Practicalities

Edited by Julia Hardy, Charmian Hobbs and Mohammed Bham

Registered Offices
John Wiley & Sons, Inc., 111 River Street, Hoboken, NJ 07030, USA
John Wiley & Sons Ltd, The Atrium, Southern Gate, Chichester, West Sussex, PO19 8SQ, UK

Editorial Office
111 River Street, Hoboken, NJ 07030, USA

For details of our global editorial offices, customer services, and more information about Wiley products visit us at www.wiley.com.

Wiley also publishes its books in a variety of electronic formats and by print-on-demand. Some content that appears in standard print versions of this book may not be available in other formats.

Library of Congress Cataloging-in-Publication Data

Names: Hardy, Julia, editor. | Hobbs, Charmian, editor. |
    Bham, Mohammed, editor.
Title: Leadership for educational psychologists : principles &
    practicalities / edited by Julia Hardy, Charmian Hobbs,
    and Mohammed Bham.
Description: Hoboken, NJ : Wiley-Blackwell, 2020. | Series: BPS textbooks
    in psychology | Includes bibliographical references.
Identifiers: LCCN 2019029948 (print) | ISBN 9781119628606 (Paperback) |
    ISBN 9781119628620 (ePDF) | ISBN 9781119628651 (epub)
Subjects: LCSH: Educational psychologists–Professional relationships. |
    Educational psychology. | Educational leadership.
Classification: LCC LB3013.6 .L43 2020 (print) | LCC LB3013.6 (ebook) |
    DDC 370.15–dc23
LC record available at https://lccn.loc.gov/2019029948
LC ebook record available at https://lccn.loc.gov/2019029949

Cover Design: Wiley
Cover Image: © Jose A. Bernat Bacete/Getty Images

Set in 9.5/12.5pt STIXTwoText by SPi Global, Pondicherry, India

10 9 8 7 6 5 4 3 2 1

Contents

About the Contributors

Mohammed Bham completed the University of Southampton 4-year Integrated Postgraduate Master of Science Professional Qualification in Educational Psychology in 1999. He has applied educational psychology in the public sector for the past 20 years, taking up his first promoted post in 2004 as a senior EP with Leicestershire County Council. In 2008, as a Principal EP with Solihull Council, Mohammed also joined the National Association of Principal Educational Psychologists (NAPEP-UK), started organising EP leadership courses and served as chair from 2011 to 2013. Since 2013, Mohammed is the British Psychological Society's Division of Educational & Child Psychology representative and deputy chair of the BPS Ethics Committee (www.bps.org.uk) communicating the guidance available from the society on ethical matters and assisting members in resolving ethical dilemmas. Since 2016, Mohammed has been the PEP and head of learning support and schools wellbeing services for Brighton & Hove City Council.

Poppy Chandler trained as an educational psychologist at Birmingham University in 1990 and her first post was secured in Staffordshire. She then shared the role of Principal Educational Psychologist in Telford. Alongside her colleagues they have built a robust traded service. As PEP for Shropshire, from December 2015, she has focussed on and developed a model for delivering therapeutic mental health support to schools at a systemic, group and individual level. Her professional interest continues to centre on families and joint working across services to apply psychology to make the difference for children and young people.

Dr Janet Crawford has over 25 years of operational, strategic leadership and management experience working as a Local Authority educational psychologist. She is currently Principal Educational Psychologist for Durham County Council managing a number of diverse teams who provide specialist SEND Support in a variety of contexts and supporting strategic developments across the Local Area. She has held specialist and senior educational psychologist (SEP) roles in a number of areas including literacy, speech and language and autism. Currently she is closely involved with a number of large-scale development projects where the process of change and evaluation of change in complex systems is required.

Ffion Edwards Ellis joined the Gwynedd and Anglesey EPS in 2006 as a Senior Educational Psychologist. During 2015–2017 she was seconded to work on the Strategic Review of Additional Learning Needs (ALN) and Inclusion Provision in Gwynedd and Anglesey, which contributed to the formation of a new ALN and Inclusion Service across both LAs in September 2017. Since September 2017 she has been Principal Educational Psychologist, and since December 2018 senior manager for ALN and Inclusion.

Dr James Gillum is Principal Educational Psychologist for Coventry Educational Psychology Service. He has published articles in a range of journals, with a particular focus on the use of labels with children and young people and mathematical difficulties.

Dr Julia Hardy works as an associate educational psychologist through Psychologicalservices.gb ltd, having previously been a Principal Educational Psychologist in Lambeth and more recently in Kingston Upon Thames and Richmond. Julia has interests in consultation, qualitative research, deafness, and cognitive behaviour therapy (CBT) and after undertaking an MBA with the Open University she has facilitated numerous leadership courses for SEPs and PEPs.

Dr Charmian Hobbs has worked as an educational psychologist in Local Authorities across England and as an academic and professional tutor at Newcastle University. She is committed to developing narrative therapy as a practitioner and trainer in educational psychology practice and beyond.

Dr Rhona Hobson has worked as an educational psychologist, senior educational psychologist and Principal Educational Psychologist for 13 years becoming the PEP for Halton Borough Council in 2015. Rhona has interests that include the use of narrative therapy within the EP role as well as developing the use of Video Interaction Guidance and other therapeutic interventions. She is passionate about the application of psychology to create positive change for children, young people, families and communities.

Dr Vikki Jervis is Principal Educational Psychologist in Bristol. She is part of the strategic leadership team for Trading With Schools (the trading arm of Bristol City Council) and the education directorate management team. She also leads the Inclusion Service across Bristol. Vikki has 12 years experience working as a senior educational psychologist and is in her fifth year of working as a principal educational psychologist. Vikki has recently completed her doctoral studies at University College London and has spent the past 4 years reading, researching and writing about leadership generally and more specifically about the leadership of psychological services. She is committed to the development of evidence informed leadership of psychological services and strengthening the profession for the future.

Dr Anna Lewis is Acting Principal Educational Psychologist for East Sussex EPS. She has worked as a senior educational psychologist in Kent and as an educational psychologist in Medway and Worcestershire. She completed both her professional doctorate in educational psychology and her initial master's in educational psychology at the University of

Birmingham. Prior to being an EP, she worked as an advisory teacher for maths and a primary school teacher in Oxfordshire and Herefordshire. She completed a BSc honours degree in psychology at the University of St Andrews and a Postgraduate Certificate in Education and DipEd at the University of Dundee. She is a Chartered Psychologist with the British Psychological Society and a member of the Division of Educational and Child Psychology (DECP).

Dr Harriet Martin worked as a Principal Educational Psychologist and senior manager in Local Authorities for 15 years. She has had experience of leading a wide variety of teams other than educational psychologists, including advisory teachers, early years, behaviour support, children in care education team, post-16 transition and special education needs assessment team. She is now retired from Local Authority work but continues to write and be involved in the DECP, British Psychological Society.

Dr Melernie Meheux is a senior educational psychologist working within a Local Authority. She is also a play therapist and works one day a week as an academic tutor at University College London, Institute of Education. Her professional interests include attachment; the social, emotional and mental health of children; and supporting children who have been excluded or are at risk of permanent school exclusion.

Dr Tara Midgen joined Wandsworth Council as Principal Educational Psychologist in 2015. She has worked for 30 years in education, initially as a primary school teacher. Tara is interested in childhood development, looked after and adopted children, loss and bereavement and mental health and well-being.

Joy Mitchell began her career in educational psychology in Derbyshire and has worked in a number of local authorities throughout Wales. She is now Principal Educational Psychologist for Wrexham Educational Psychology Service in North Wales.

Mandy Owen is currently the head of Children's Psychology Services/Principal Educational Psychologist in Cornwall and leads a number of teams which are line managed by educational and clinical psychologists. She previously worked as an educational psychologist in Southampton and Northamptonshire. She has a particular interest in solution focused practice and in creating new opportunities to use psychology to improve outcomes for children and young people.

Dr Kevin Rowland has held leadership roles in six Local Authorities as senior educational psychologist, Deputy Principal Educational Psychologist, twice as a PEP and assistant director. He appeared before the Commons Select Committee for the DECP and led a secondary special school out of special measures in Worcestershire. KR was part of the Department for Education (DfE) working party for Mental Health and Behaviour in Schools and is currently working for the DfE as an adviser for SEND and Alternative Provision.

Ms. Theodora Theodoratou was born and grew up in Athens, Greece. She started working as an educational psychologist in Wandsworth in September 2003, where she still practises, becoming a senior EP in November 2016. She completed the 2-year Systemic Family Therapy diploma in May 2016 and her practice as well as style of supervision has been strongly influenced by systemic approaches and tools.

Dr Juliet Whitehead was the chair of the BPS's Division of Educational and Child Psychology in 2018 and is the current vice-chair. Juliet is Assistant Principal Educational Psychologist in Coventry Educational Psychology Service. She has published articles and research studies in a range of publications and journals.

Glossary

Academy Chains: An academy chain is a partnership between a group of academies (schools).

AI: Appreciative inquiry, a solution-focused approach to organisational change.

ALN: Additional Learning Needs is a term used within the Welsh legislative framework.

ALNCo: Additional Learning Needs Co-ordinator used within Welsh schools.

AEP: Association of Educational Psychologists is the professional body and trade union for registered EPs practicing in the UK.

BME: Black and Minority Ethnic. A number of terms have been used, by government and more generally, to refer to the collective ethnic minority population.

BPS: British Psychological Society is a registered charity which acts as the representative body for psychologists and psychology in the UK.

BSI: British Standards Institute is the business standards company that 'helps organizations make excellence a habit'.

CAMHS: Child and Adolescent Mental Health Service is used as a term for all services that work with children and young people who have difficulties with their emotional or behavioural well-being.

CBT: Cognitive behaviour therapy is a talking therapy that can help people manage problems by changing the way they think and behave.

CCG: Clinical Commissioning Groups are responsible for implementing the commissioning roles as set out in the Health and Social Care Act 2012.

CIC: A community interest company is a type of company introduced by the United Kingdom government in 2005 under the Companies (Audit, Investigations and Community Enterprise) Act 2004, designed for social enterprises that want to use their profits and assets for the public good.

CPD: Continuing professional development.

CQC: The Care Quality Commission is an executive nondepartmental public body of the Department of Health and Social Care of the United Kingdom. It was established in 2009 to regulate and inspect health and social care services in England.

DECP:	Division of Educational and Child Psychology – a division within the BPS that supports the practice and professional development of its members (mostly educational psychologists) in England, Wales and Northern Ireland.
DfE:	Department for Education is responsible for children's services and education, including early years, schools and higher and further education policy.
DfEE:	Department for Employment and Education from 1995 to 2001.
ECHA:	Educational, Health and Care Needs Assessments undertaken as part of the Children and Families Act 2014.
EFQM:	European Foundation of Quality Management.
EHCP:	An Education Health Care Plan is required as a part of the Children and Families Act (2014) and is required for children and young people aged up to 25 who need more support than is available through special educational needs support.
ELSA:	Emotional literacy support assistant.
EP:	Educational psychologist.
EPNET:	An online discussion forum for EPs.
EPS:	Educational Psychology Service that provides a dedicated educational psychology input to a local area, usually an LA.
FE:	Further education institutions, usually colleges providing educational and training courses for those over 16 years of age.
HCPC:	The Health & Care Professions Council.
HR:	Human resources departments which are responsible for ensuring employer and employee rights and responsibilities.
IiP:	Investors in People is a standard for people management, offering accreditation to organisations that adhere to the Investors in People Standard.
KPI:	Key Performance Indicators are a measurable value that demonstrates how effectively a company is achieving key business objectives.
LA:	Local Authority – responsible for providing a range of services including education to a prescribed geographical area.
Local Area:	The local area includes the local authority, health commissioners and providers.
MBA:	Master of business administration.
NAPEP:	National Association of Principal Educational Psychologists – promotes the professional development of leaders and managers of EPSs.
NAPEP-L:	National Association of Principal Educational Psychologists online forum.
NHS:	National Health Service.
Ofsted:	Ofsted is the Office for Standards in Education, Children's Services and Skills.
PEP:	Principal Educational Psychologist – the leader and manager of an EPSs who may also manage other services such as specialist support teams.
SDT:	Self-Determination Theory is a macro theory of human motivation and personality that concerns people's inherent growth tendencies and innate psychological needs.

SENCo: Special Educational Needs Co-ordinator.

SEND: Special educational needs and disability. The term was first used when the Department for Education (DfE) published a new SEND Code of Practice, which came into effect in 2019.

SEP: Senior educational psychologist – an educational psychologist with management responsibilities for a group of EPs within their service or a specialist responsibility for an area of service delivery or both.

SFBT: Solution-focussed brief therapy is future focussed, goal directed and focusses on solutions, rather than on the problems that bring people to seek help.

SLA: Service level agreement.

SLT: Senior Leadership Team.

SPA Points: Structured Professional Assessment is part of a system for pay progression for EPs in England and Wales.

SWOT: Strengths, Weaknesses, Opportunities and Threats analysis.

TEP: Trainee educational psychologist who is undertaking a doctoral training programme.

Third Sector
Organisations: They include voluntary and community organisations (both registered charities and other organisations such as associations, self-help groups and community groups), social enterprises, mutual and co-operatives. Third sector organisations (TSOs) generally are independent of government.

TOM: Therapy Outcome Measures, a tool which provides a framework for measuring effectiveness of intervention.

VIG: Video Interaction Guidance is an intervention through which a practitioner aims to enhance communication within relationships.

Section 1

Reflections

1

Introduction to Leadership: The Context of Managing Educational Psychology Services (EPSs)

Julia Hardy, Charmian Hobbs and Mohammed Bham

This book is written by educational psychologists (EPs) for EPs in leadership positions. It offers a combination of reflections from practitioners past and present combined with a range of practical exemplars pertinent to key themes that current and prospective Educational Psychology Service (EPS) leaders are interested in debating.

This text is inspired by the absence of evidence-informed guidance and literature for EPs aspiring to join the leadership of educational psychology; and we are appreciative of some of the EPs in leadership positions for their commitment to share with you some of the principles and practicalities in the UK context. The importance of experienced EPs providing informed and resilient leadership in every Local Authority (LA) ensures the highest quality of service for the community. Using the British Psychological Society Quality Standards Framework as summarised by Gillum and Whitehead (Chapter 13) enables EPS leaders and service stakeholders to reflect upon and continually improve the quality of an EPS.

Whilst inequalities and disadvantage remain, radical recalibration of the mindset that created the problem in the first place is the only way to limit the damage of some of the current public sector policies. In Chapter 9, Bham and Owen discuss issues relating to recruitment and retention and Jervis and Hardy (Chapter 2) discuss the development of leaders to consider collaborative approaches in leadership. Both chapters touch on the importance of interdependence. Global leadership paradigms have influenced how leadership is being interpreted and enacted in the UK as well as elsewhere. A term from the Bantu languages of Southern Africa that is difficult to translate exactly into English in summary offers a rich idea:

> Ubuntu: I am because of you, or I am because you are[1]

Essentially, Ubuntu offers the alternative to the inspirational leader or hero innovator and speaks of the interdependence of humankind. It is only through a spirit of collaboration that the leaders will be able to thrive; in particular through professional networks, supervision and coaching and continuous professional leadership development. In Chapter 7, Hardy and Bham write about the importance of relationships and in Chapter 14 they discuss support mechanisms and ways to manage the well-being of leaders.

---

[1] https://medium.com/thrive-global/ubuntu-i-am-because-you-are-66efa03f2682

Leadership for Educational Psychologists: Principles & Practicalities, First Edition.
Edited by Julia Hardy, Charmian Hobbs and Mohammed Bham.
© 2020 John Wiley & Sons Ltd. Published 2020 by John Wiley & Sons Ltd.

Some of the leadership-speak that we come across in our work within LAs will be familiar from your general reading and specific knowledge of psychology. In this book we will not debate at length recurring topics, such as the differences between leadership and management. Certainly we will not be coming to simple conclusions, such as how leadership is about coping with change while management is about coping with complexity (Kotter, 2006), the well-known phrase attributed to Peter Drucker and Warren Bennis that 'management is doing things right, leadership is doing the right things' nor will we address what typifies the behaviour of 'good leaders' (George, 2003). It does aim to provide models and creative ways of thinking that can enable Principal Educational Psychologists (PEPs), both those new to their post and those who are more established, to develop and support their EPs and as importantly themselves.

There are a number of cross-cutting themes that run throughout the chapters. Firstly there is context. Although there have been pressures from national policy, local practice and finance in the past, EPSs are now working in times of great austerity when all the services available to children and families are severely stretched or even absent. Given this climate, EPSs are challenged by a fragmented education system, an impoverished LA, cash-strapped schools and at least within England an increasing pressure from changes in legislation which have led to a high demand for statutory work in many LAs. Leaders in EPSs are further asked to 'market' their services to schools and communities such that they provide an income for their EPS and the continuation of their service. This need to 'trade to survive' sits very uncomfortably with professional practice centred on equity and inclusion. Alongside this are societal pressures which draw in an increasing emphasis on 'othering' and segregation rather than a willingness to foster and promote inclusive practice. To take one example the exclusion of children as young as two is now being reported in the national press (*The Guardian*, 2019). Given this background, becoming a leader within an EPS can be a daunting task.

Secondly is the nature of leadership. Rowland and Chandler (Chapter 6) remind us that both leadership and change have produced a continual debate within educational psychology almost from the beginning of the profession within the UK. There are many theories and understandings of leadership within the literature. Some chapters (Hardy and Jervis, Chapter 2) refer to current and also long-lasting leadership theorists, for instance Covey (2004) who uses the ladder-climbing metaphor when thinking of management as being efficiency in climbing the ladder of success; whereas leadership determines whether the ladder is leaning against the right wall. There is, however, consistency in the way the authors see leadership. Leadership is viewed as participatory. It is about engaging with all members of the EPS and beyond (when PEPs manage a number of teams) to develop a shared understanding of the aims and purpose of the EPS. It involves listening to and enabling members of the service to speak about what is important to them as educational psychologists; how they wish to practice in the best interests of children, families and communities; to share ideas they have about effective service delivery and be open about the challenges and difficulties experienced in day-to-day work. A key to developing this approach is to understand the organisation within which you and your colleagues work (see Hardy and Bham, Chapter 7).

Thirdly is equity in practice. There is acknowledgement that there has always been a concern that children who may be the most in need of support were not accessing the help of an educational psychologist; however, this concern is heightened by the marketisation of education. This hangs heavily over leaders who are charged with delivering educational psychology services as fairly as possible alongside the need to maintain a steady income to ensure EPs continue to be employed. Ways of addressing this tension are discussed by Hardy, Braithwaite and Hobson (Chapter 12) with the suggestion that trading can provide opportunity as well as challenge and EPs need to reflect on how to be entrepreneurial within a LA context.

Fourthly there is ethics. As practitioners we need to continually reflect on and revisit our practice, not only our activities and actions but also the many taken for granted ways of working that can remain unexamined and out of kilter with what we would want to achieve. This match or mismatch between espoused values and practice is considered in depth by Midgen and Theodoratou (Chapter 3). Crawford (Chapter 4) also examines this when discussing how her EPS began to explore what EPs really meant by 'inclusion' and how their understanding could be translated into everyday work with schools. Hobbs and Owen (Chapter 5) bring to the forefront the way women have been portrayed in leadership literature and how this affects selection for leadership positions and the way women may view themselves and be viewed by others.

Fifthly, inevitably in a book by psychologists, relationships are referred to in most chapters. Positive relationships within a team are crucial. Tuckman's (1965) forming–storming–norming–performing model of group development focussing on the improvements in team effectiveness over time, with a dip in functioning after the forming stage, when there are inevitable conflicts before moving on to accepting norms of the group and then reaching the peak in performance. Martin and Meheux (Chapter 11) consider how to create team working which as far as possible avoids conflict alongside providing ways of addressing difficult situations if they do occur. Beckhard (1972) wrote about team development and at the same time the diagnosis of issues, whether they are about goals, roles, procedures or/ and interpersonal relationships. Lewis (Chapter 8) examines appreciative inquiry (AI) as an approach to rebuilding teams in challenging times. Relationships also need to be outward facing when developing, maintaining and evaluating educational psychology services. Hardy, Braithwaite and Hobson (Chapter 12) emphasise the importance of hearing the views of 'customers' (these are the children, young people and families we work with as well as schools and other commissioners) and Gillum and Whitehead (Chapter 13) acknowledge the need to work closely with 'stakeholders' in establishing a sound process of evaluation.

All the authors in this book have experience of educational psychology leadership in the public sector context and all share the obligation to get engaged with the leadership challenges in the climate of austerity and marketisation of education services. Waterman and Peters (1982) wrote about the 'Eight Attributes' of management excellence, including a bias for action. The bias for action is a hidden thread throughout this book, with an emphasis by EPS leaders on prioritising their actions within a system that will benefit all children, young people and their parents/carers and staff in education settings. They are all involved in designing and sustaining high-quality EPSs. Now that we have again secured government funding for training educational psychologists in England and Wales, these prestigious professional doctoral qualifications with the highest qualified practitioners in LAs, bring an obligation to work for the public sector and its community to try to fix the broken system and the way in which the system functions – what happens in our communities impacts on us. In Chapter 9, Bham and Owen discuss recruitment and retention and nothing matters unless we recruit the best staff, offer the range of professional practice opportunities and keep them engaged on the key issues: that everyone is entitled to an education and to have their special educational, disability and well-being needs met. We have been a profession of optimists and scientist-practitioners; we must get engaged in the civil rights struggle, the human right for an inclusive education and well-being of all.

We are training our psychologists to be fully capable and better equipped for the challenges that lie ahead. We are certain that the current and future generations of leaders in EPSs will also be able, through peer support, supervision, coaching and professional leadership development, to capably lead the profession in the public sector for our community.

There are many metaphors within leadership texts and we are attracted towards Senge's (1990). He sees the gap between vision and current reality as a source of energy. If there were no gap, there would be no need for any action to move towards the vision. This gap is 'creative tension'. It is hoped that this book brings together many ideas for taking action towards the vision.

References

Beckhard, R. (1972). Organizational issues in the delivery of comprehensive health care. *The Milbank Memorial Fund Quarterly, 50*(3), 287–316

Covey, S. (2004). *The 7 habits of highly effective people* (2nd ed). London: FranklinCovey.

George, B. (2003). *Authentic leadership: Rediscovering the secrets to creating lasting value.* San Francisco: Jossey-Bass.

Kotter, J. P. (2006). Leadership versus management: What's the difference? *Journal for Quality and Participation, 29*(2), 13–17.

Senge, P. M. (1990). *The fifth discipline. The art and practice of the learning organisation.* New York: Random House.

The Guardian. (2019, 1 April). The Guardian view on school exclusion: The wrong answer. *The Guardian.*

Tuckman, B. W. (1965). Developmental sequence in small groups. *Psychological Bulletin, 63*(6), 384–399.

Waterman, R. H., & Peters, T (1982). *In search of excellence.* New York: HarperCollins Publishers.

2

Leadership Frameworks

Models Past, Present and Hopes for the Future

Vikki Jervis and Julia Hardy

Contextual Introduction

Effective leadership within Educational Psychology Services (EPSs) is crucial to the success of our profession. There is an inevitable movement of educational psychologists (EPs) into leadership positions, given there are approximately 344 EPSs in England and Wales. EPs have written about the rapid changes within EPSs, from the turn of the century with Sharp, Fredrickson and Laws (2000) observing 'Educational psychology services are entering a period of unprecedented change' (p. 98), to Booker (2013) arguing for adaptive leadership within the growing culture of budget cuts and rapid change to services.

Rowland (2002) asserted that EPSs need to modernise and demonstrate quality or they will be privatised. Whilst relevant in 2002 given the changes in the current context where many services are traded, this assertion is somewhat out of date. However, perhaps more importantly, Rowland also suggested a possible way forward was to use and apply information from leadership studies to develop an evidence-based model of leadership for psychology services. This is still relevant; however, there is little evidence that such a model has been developed and the question was posed 11 years later by Booker (2013) as to whether leadership in educational psychology services was *fit for purpose*.

Not long ago, the educational psychology profession celebrated the centenary of the appointment of the first EP in England. An understanding and celebration of the development of the profession are perhaps now essential for reflection and planning for the future. However, until the relatively recent publication of *British Educational Psychology: The First Hundred Years* (Arnold & Hardy, 2013), it had been argued that the profession lacked an authoritative account of its history (Stringer, Dunsmuir, & MacKay, 2013). In addition to the previous lack of a historical perspective, the profession was criticised for a lack of a coherent account of the role and function of EPs (Stringer, Burton, & Powell, 2006).

> In other words there is no strong narrative about the profession of educational psychology. (Stringer et al., 2013, p. 7)

Leadership for Educational Psychologists: Principles & Practicalities, First Edition.
Edited by Julia Hardy, Charmian Hobbs and Mohammed Bham.

This argument can be extended to leadership in EPSs. There is a scarcity of literature about leadership written by EPs for EPs and the question of what the leaders in EPSs do has been largely ignored. The central theme here is that the educational psychology literature lacks a dominant leadership discourse and leadership narrative.

The profession has come a long way in its first centenary (Arnold & Hardy, 2013). However, the environment for EPs is rapidly changing and the profession needs to respond to this. Economic austerity measures have had an impact on EPs from personal perspectives to professional experiences, the economic effects being evident in families, schools and communities (Gibbs & Lauchlan, 2015). Significant organisational developments such as trading services, changes in employers and changes in training are being rapidly implemented (Midgen, 2015).

Changes in technology have also had an impact on working practices with offices becoming paperless and computers and mobile technology challenging the traditional view of a team and office-based working. Remote and home working has become a reality as expensive offices are closed as the result of austerity measures. The benefits and issues of these technological and locational changes are mentioned further (see Chapters 9 and 10). Principal Educational Psychologists (PEPs) need to consider how to keep the service communications about its vision, mission, values and strategy accessible to the whole service, with a transparent and inclusive approach to reviewing these aspects and keeping the service as a whole engaged in and owning its strategy over time.

For the profession to survive, rapid changes need to be embraced. For the profession to thrive, thoughtful and passionate beliefs and values are essential (Allen & Hardy, 2013). In addition to this, we suggest that pragmatic and effective evidence-informed leadership is crucial.

New Leaders Feeling Unprepared

For new leaders into the profession, both PEPs and senior educational psychologists (SEPs), there is often a feeling of unpreparedness when taking up a new post. The second author, when first taking up a SEP position was inspired to undertake an Open University master's of business administration in order to fill in the gaps in her knowledge of leadership principles and practice. Following this the second author facilitated a number of 6 to 8-day leadership courses, first at University of East London (UEL) and Warrington and then throughout England, attended by hundreds of EPS leaders from England and Wales.

The first author began a SEP position 4 years after completing EP training. She was appointed into a PEP role after 13 years working as a SEP and started a part-time continuing professional development (CPD) doctorate a year prior to this. She originally began wondering if one day she may wish to apply for a PEP post. Part way through planning her leadership research an opportunity arose and she was appointed as PEP. Following her appointment, she realised that an appropriate induction into service leadership would be possible only if she created it. Her doctoral research provided the opportunity to study leadership in depth. Wondering why other EPs apply for and accept promoted posts and how other promoted post holders achieve their goals, stay resilient and create frames of reference for their work intrigued her.

Being new and feeling unprepared for a PEP role, (and being enrolled on the CPD doctorate), she was keen to investigate all relevant literature and to draw on the wisdom of experienced leaders of psychological services and empirical research. The search for an evidence-informed handbook for leaders of psychological services proved fruitless at the time. This book is therefore filling an important gap in the literature for leaders of EPSs.

What Is Leadership?

There are many definitions of leadership. This debate is extensive and there has not been a definitive resolution. Whilst it is an interesting debate, this book could have focussed on a definition of leadership alone. The authors consider the following to be a useful definition for EPSs. Leadership is purposeful action undertaken

> to create the conditions for people to thrive, individually and collectively and to achieve significant goals. (Pendleton & Furnham, 2012, p. 2)

The words leadership and management are often heard together and are, therefore, frequently confused as having similar meanings or are used as if they are synonymous (Kent, 2005). Northouse (2013) argues that there are as many academic definitions of leadership and management as there are authors who have written on the subject. However difficult it is to define the concepts, it is generally accepted in current literature that it is helpful to make a distinction between the two terms.

Drucker (2001) has written extensively on management and latterly leadership. Many authors have taken his ideas and expanded upon them. Cohen (2010) describes how towards the end of his career, Drucker suggested that management should be considered to be separate and distinct from leadership. Drucker is often credited as being the author of the famous distinction between leadership and management, where management is defined as doing things right and leadership defined as doing the right things.

Kotter (1990) discussed the differences and similarities in the concepts of leadership and management. He suggests that management produces consistency in complex organisations and that leadership produces the movement needed for organisational change and development. He stated that it is possible to manage and not lead, and to lead and not manage. Management was referred to by Kotter as an active process akin to a science, and Grint (2000) referred to leadership as an interactive process more akin to an art.

Leadership can be viewed either as being assigned or emergent (Northouse, 2013). Assigned leadership is based on the appointment to a formal title or position in an organisation. In contrast, emergent leadership results from the actions undertaken by an individual and followers are generated through those actions. Therefore, emergent leaders may not be appointed to a formal leadership role. Managers, however, occupy a formal role in an establishment and are expected to complete discreet tasks assigned to that role. Emergent leadership is an interesting dimension to the leadership and management debate.

Kent (2005) summarises the views of different scholars who have endeavoured to differentiate between leadership and management and to define the characteristics, enabling a greater depth and breadth of understanding. He suggests the following (see table 2.1).

Table 2.1 Characteristics of leadership and management

Characteristics of Managers	Characteristics of Leaders
Managers do things right	Leaders do the right things
Managing is an authority relationship	Leading is an influential relationship
Managing creates stability	Leading creates change

Adapted from Kent (2005).

In 1990, Kotter produced a summary of the functions of leadership and management. Northouse (2013) adapted this summary into Table 2.2.

Table 2.2 Functions and activities of leadership and management

Management Order and Consistency	Leadership Produces Change and Movement
Planning and Budgeting	**Establishing Direction**
Establish agendas	Create a vision
Set timetables	Clarify the big picture
Allocate resources	Set strategies
Organising and Staffing	**Aligning People**
Provide structure	Communicate goals
Make job placements	Seek commitment
Establish rules and procedures	Build teams and coalitions
Controlling and Problem Solving	**Motivating and Inspiring**
Develop incentives	Inspire and energise
Generate creative solutions	Empowering
Take corrective actions	

From Northouse (2013, p. 12).

Goleman (1996) develops the emotional aspect of leadership and management suggesting that to thrive, organisations need to consider the previously ignored emotional aspects of management.

The usefulness of the distinction between assigned leadership and management has been questioned. Booker (2012) questions whether this distinction is useful as any individual in a promoted or formal management role embodies both. Fullan (2001) also suggests that he would not advocate the separation of the two terms as they overlap and the functions and activities associated with both are required to be successful.

For readers wishing to read more about definitions, a comprehensive discussion of definitions of leadership can be found in Northouse (2013). This text also provides a discussion of the differences between leadership and management.

In EPSs, leadership teams typically consist of promoted post holders who have acquired additional managerial and leadership responsibilities. However, there is a strong argument that all EPs are leaders or have the potential to be leaders. Leadership activities are embedded in EP practices yet the EP literature has largely ignored the leadership debate (Rowland, 2005).

Key Concepts: Strategy, Culture, Mission, Vision and Values

Much has recently changed within the context of EP work, due to the Special Educational Needs and Disability Code of Practice (Department for Education & Department of Health, 2015) with the increasing demands for Education, Health and Care Plans and Needs Assessments, following the Children and Families Act (2014). Nevertheless, the language of organisational change has remained consistent for many decades. Schein (1985) in his seminal text wrote about how leaders communicate the organisation's **culture** and **values**. One of the most commonly used terms in discussing '**leadership**' is **strategy**, followed closely by the distinction between **operational** and **strategic** issues. There are other jargon terms used within organisations, including the Local Authorities (LAs) within which most of us work. These include **mission** and **vision** as well as values. There are many tools that PEPs and SEPs have found useful when applying these terms in practice (see Chapter 7).

Strategy

The Oxford Living Dictionary defines strategy as 'a plan of action designed to achieve a long-term or overall aim'.[1] Porter (1996) argues that competitive strategy is about being different'. He adds: 'It means deliberately choosing a different set of activities to deliver a unique mix of value'.

Mintzberg and Waters (1985) wrote about a range of strategies, including planned, deliberate, entrepreneurial, umbrella, ideological, process, unconnected, consensus and imposed. These different approaches to strategic planning are of interest, but what is important for new EPS leaders is the diagram showing how strategic plans and intentions may not always be realised but influenced by unexpected and emergent events (see Figure 2.1).

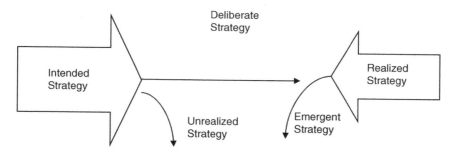

Figure 2.1   A range of strategies (from Minztberg & Waters, 1985).

Culture

There are many definitions of culture. Kostova (1999) describes it as 'particular ways of conducting organizational functions that have evolved over time ... [These] practices reflect

1 https://en.oxforddictionaries.com/definition/strategy

...ou knowledge and competence of the organization' (p. 309). Van den Berg and Wilderom (2004) write about how 'organisational culture forms the glue that holds the organisation together', as well as proposing that the culture 'stimulates employees to commit to the organisation and to perform' (p. 571). Schein (2010) defines culture as 'a pattern of shared basic assumptions learned by a group as it solved its problems of external adaptation and internal integration, which has worked well enough to be considered valid and, therefore, to be taught to new members as the correct way to perceive, think and feel in relation to those problems' (p. 18).

Understanding the organisation's culture is crucial but is also tricky, as EPS leaders are often so accustomed to the way things are done within their LA that it is hard to stand back and reflect on its unique culture. In Chapter 7, Johnson and Scholes' (1988) cultural web will be explained in detail as a tool to help the EPS team reflect on the subtleties of organisational structure.

Mission statement

Throughout the literature describing both public and private sector organisations within the UK, the importance of an agreed mission statement is consistent. The purpose of a mission statement is to describe the organisation's 'core purpose and focus' (see http://www.businessdictionary.com/definition/mission-statement.html).

Usually, EPSs located within a LA adopt their LA's mission statement. However, there may be times, such as when an EPS is marketing its service, that it produces a definition of the core purpose and range of focus of the service.

Vision

In contrast to a mission statement, which would normally remain the same while the organisation has a consistent purpose, the vision is an aspirational description of what an organisation would like to achieve or accomplish in the mid-term or long-term future. It is intended to serve as a clear guide for choosing current and future courses of action. The second author used the need to develop a strategic plan within the service as an opportunity to agree with all the service members where they wished to go in the next three to five years. The processes of agreeing a vision are as important as the product. The act of agreeing on an EPS vision is a fundamental leadership task, with this agreed vision underpinning all the more detailed strategic planning.

Values

Values are the other fundamental aspect that needs agreement. They are about the unseen drivers of our behaviour, based on our deeply held beliefs that drive decision-making. As with the vision, the EPS needs to undertake work together to co-create and agree to its shared values. As indicated in the Francis Report (2013), shared values, as well as agreed objectives and strategy, are the founding pillars of organisations.

Hogan (2013) made the distinction between values and principles. He argued that values are enduring and rarely change whereas principles evolve to your circumstances and can change. So within the educational psychology world, the service may evolve agreed principles about how to undertake trading with schools. When an EPS has a new leadership team, or indeed a significant change to staff within the service, then it is important to revisit the values EPs bring to their work, and where possible exemplify these so that there can be agreement as to which are the shared values.

Leadership within the Context of Being an EP

Leadership is no easy title to enact. By the time EPs move into promoted posts they have already a strongly developed sense of professional identity, informed by both their knowledge base, experience and philosophy. Whilst this is important, it is arguably the starting point for the development of leadership skills and knowledge and further development of leadership understanding is critical. This has however not been easy for PEPs to achieve. Individuals' needs are clearly different as are opportunities and the finances for CPD. The empirical research into leadership in EPSs is also limited and until now, leaders of EPSs have lacked access to a summary of specific leadership information.

So, given this difficult context, why do we become leaders of psychological services? What are our experiences of promoted posts? How do we develop leadership knowledge? How can the leadership of EP services be improved?

The findings from the most recent research (Jervis, 2019) undertaken by the first author are summarised in the following paragraphs under research question headings. The quotes in italics are the words of the participants who took part in the study. Before exploring the findings a summary of the research is presented.

The research described here is based on the assertion that EPs promoted into leadership roles have limited research to inform their work. Leaders of EPSs would benefit from documented experiences and perceptions of current promoted post holders. Therefore, the study aimed to gain an understanding of the experiences and perceptions of leaders in EPSs.

Participants in the study included eight promoted post holders employed in seven local authorities. Eight parallel semistructured interviews were analysed together as a single case. Although gender was not controlled for, four men and four women took part in the study. A schedule was used to guide semistructured interviews and the data were analysed using thematic analysis. The study identified 10 overarching themes and 40 lower level themes that can be used as a framework to understand the experiences and perceptions of leaders in EPSs. The themes are used to enable the reader to see how eight leaders understand their roles, identify the support they consider necessary, identify their knowledge base, explore experiences of starting first promoted posts and consider how leadership in EPSs can be improved.

The answers to the four questions posed here are based on the research findings.

Why do EPs apply for leadership posts and what experiences and perceptions influence their decisions?

Decisions about applying for promoted posts involve considerations of personal factors, interpersonal and organisational factors and professional knowledge and philosophy. Whilst this is not surprising, it is perhaps more surprising that the participants did not discuss factors such as pay and professional status. Rather participants focussed on the application and strengthening of models of psychology at a strategic level and the opportunity to make a greater difference to the lives of children and young people.

What are the experiences of starting first leadership posts and how can this inform us about the support necessary for those embarking on a promoted post?

A large range of negative emotions can be associated with starting in promoted posts. High levels of *anxiety, discomfort, intimidation, pressure, vulnerability, uncertainty, responsibility* and *frustration* were described by experienced practitioners. Some leaders express self-doubt and wonder, *how do I know if I am doing a good job* and also describe *grappling with the expectations of others.* Positive emotions related to decision-making about whether to apply for a promoted post are also evident but to a lesser extent. The type of work available to promoted post holders can be described as *exciting* and *thrilling.*

Starting promoted posts can be daunting and exciting and those new to post would benefit from a sense of belonging to a wider community providing mutual support, which will in turn support leadership development. Experiences and support are variable and there would be benefits in facilitating some consistency of expectations and support. Given the diverse number of employing organisations, differences in the size of EPSs managed, and wide number of different organisational cultures and individuals, it is impossible to create unified experience for all new promoted post holders. However, it is possible to give some generic advice that would enable the profession to support the next generation of leaders. A proposed induction guide and /or CPD guide for leaders of EPSs is included in the appendices.

How do educational psychologists develop a leadership knowledge base and what is the leadership knowledge base amongst promoted post holders?

Some promoted post holders use leadership and management perspectives in addition to their generic psychological skills, some learn through observing leaders around them and some consider wider philosophical views. However, a dominant leadership discourse based on current literature is not evident. Creating a dominant discourse through the identification of a body of theoretical and research literature that relates to educational psychology may address some of the difficult issues leaders face. This point is summarised by the following extract.

> *If you know that this is the model...And you're doing that...If it's not working it's not just because you're rubbish...Actually it's just a difficult situation...And it'll help you... sort of take that meta perspective...on what's going on...and see it in terms of your profession...how well you are carrying out those professional acts...as defined in the models of management and supervision that you're using as well as in in a difficult situation...Rather than just taking on this isn't going very well I must be rubbish.*

How can leadership in educational psychology services be improved?

Participants were asked their views about succession planning for promoted posts in EPSs. More specifically, they were asked how the profession should plan for leaders of the future and what career paths should look like. They had clear views and were able to identify how systems and individual skills could be developed and also identified what stands in the way of making this happen. Three themes were identified: blockers to development, the development of systems and the development of individuals. They are discussed next.

The participants identified that EPSs are restricted by blockers to developing leadership skills. Factors such as pay scales and structures in local authorities were identified as potential blockers. Pay scales can prohibit the opportunity to develop leadership skills as tasks can be deemed as related to a specific pay grade rather than being a development opportunity. Some organisational cultures described a hierarchical model of accountability, which appeared to prohibit enabling colleagues to develop prior to starting a promoted post.

Participants identified that the development of systems could improve leadership and development. Technology is beginning to be used to connect promoted post holders across the country. For example, National Association of Principal Educational Psychologists-L (NAPEP-L, an online discussion forum for mutual support for PEPs) was highlighted as being helpful in connecting PEPs. NAPEP could be strengthened and developed through the further use of shared technology. Participants reported that such support is valuable. For example, one participant commented that:

> You need people that are like, how would I say people supporters you know and they are peer supporters. They mentor colleagues. We could do that as a network of colleagues coming together.

Leadership develops where there is *scaffolded progression* or an *articulated pathway* identifying the types of experiences likely to promote development. Promoted post holders (and those aspiring to promotion) could therefore find a developmental approach helpful. This could identify leadership experiences and responsibilities from training through to applying for a promoted post. This could also include attending national training. For example, one participant commented that:

> I think there needs to be some sort of maybe national training on what being a senior is. I suppose it would be hard to argue to develop it because maybe in each authority it's slightly different but there is still going to be some basics that we all share...line management...budget management...legal responsibilities.

In addition to the preceding comments, some participants suggested that expectations for promotion could follow a certain number of years of experience in a post and a mapped progression. *Clear job descriptions, leadership development programmes, quality standards, or core competencies.* This could be developed by NAPEP, Association of Educational Psychologists (AEP) and the Division of Educational and Child Psychology (DECP) working together. One participant summed up this view by suggesting:

we should plan this...by thinking more systematically about what leadership opportunities are offered within services and what leadership development programmes are offered that are specifically offered to EPs...there probably needs to be a regional response that acknowledges the period we are entering into and what it is going to look like...

One participant suggested the need to consider formalising *quality standards* now for EPSs for future generations. This would enable newly promoted post holders to see clear lines of professional responsibility and standards to aspire to.

Participants identified tasks, experiences, skills and existing strengths as needing attention, to assist individual development. Supervision of trainee educational psychologists (TEPS) was described as the closest experience main grade EPs have to develop line management skills. Discrete skills such as *accountancy* and *HR and business support* were identified as key development areas required for promoted posts. One participant commented even when psychologists have existing strengths:

You know you don't suddenly pop up and you're a senior... it should be something that's a progression based on previous experiences in a supervised way have led you to that direction...

And another suggested:

For the future it would be having a good clear model.

Another participant expanded on this point suggesting:

We need to look at leadership programmes...you know it could be leadership seminars... workshops that could be short and sharp...where people come together across Britain... this can be effective a bit like having ...master classes...saying this is the topic and then we will write it up and share it.

All of these suggestions are practical ways forwards and this publication represents a first step in in enabling leadership in educational psychology services to become 'fit for purpose' (Booker, 2013).

So What Would It Be Helpful for Us All to Know?

The next section of this chapter explores 10 frameworks and concepts that leaders of EPSs may find helpful. The 10 frameworks and concepts are not an exhaustive list, rather they are considered (by the authors) to be helpful ways to think about leadership which can in turn inform action and decision-making. We are able to provide only a brief outline of each and we therefore encourage you to turn to the references if you are inspired to explore the ideas in greater depth. This chapter closes with a summary of key documents that have been published by our professional bodies and a summary of papers written by EPs about leadership.

Useful frameworks and concepts

1) Appreciative inquiry

Appreciative inquiry (AI) is an effective methodology to facilitate change and develop professional practice in an EP service (for a fuller description of AI in practice see Chapter 8). AI is a type of action research with its foundations in social constructionist epistemology (Doggett & Lewis, 2013). The effectiveness of AI is attributed to the motivational effects of engaging participants through four stages (discovery, dream, design and destiny) thus enabling active participation. The solution-focussed approach, emphasis on group agency, shared control and collegiate working is highlighted as playing a role in the effectiveness of the process for EPSs.

Doggett and Lewis (2013) gathered data to elicit views of EPs about the AI process through questionnaires. Seventy-two percent of the sample population returned the questionnaires and the conclusion was drawn that AI was successful in enabling an active learning process. However, it is not clear if the process ensured that change was embedded into practice. Further research is needed for us to be certain about the impact of AI as an approach to lead organisational change in EP services.

2) Results accountability model (Friedman, 2005)

The results accountability framework explores how to identify outcomes to improve performance rather than looking at why services should be concerned with measuring improvements. This model includes a process that promises to move services from discussion to action (Friedman, 2005, p. 11). Articulated simply, the process consists of steps in which questions designed to focus conversation towards outcomes are worked through. The central questions used in this approach to evaluate service effectiveness are:

- How much did we do? (For example, the number of psychological advice reports).
- How well did we do it? (Quality standards question)
- Is anyone better off? (Outcomes and impact question).

Interestingly, a slightly different version of the three questions described here were used by Stobie (2002) and Her Majesty's Inspectorate of Education (HMIe, 2010).

Friedman (2005) cites examples of work in communities (mainly in America) where this approach has made a difference. There is not enough detail in the descriptions to make informed decisions about whether the examples given are reliable and this work is not without its critics. For example, Fortuin and Van Marissing (2009) argue that the model is simplistic in assuming that all community problems are straightforward and lend themselves to logical and rational procedures, thus ignoring within community tension and conflict. However, Pinnock (2012) argues that the results-based accountability model has developed a common language of outcomes thus enabling outcomes work to be accessible and inclusive. In terms of one of the authors' own practice it has been a useful planning tool and has enabled service outcomes to be identified and discussed.

3) Distributed leadership

Distributed leadership suggests that leadership spreads across the organisation and individuals are able to exercise influence regardless of formal roles. There is an expectation that all members of the organisation should have a voice and should lead an aspect of service delivery. This is particularly useful in a profession consisting of highly qualified motivated practitioners.

The concept of distributed leadership is related to the concept of empowerment. Gronn (2000) suggests that distributed leadership offers a possible way to bridge the divide between an emphasis on individual agency and a focus on system design. Distributed leadership is congruent with the perspectives of educational psychology where arguably an emphasis on relationships, interaction and the leadership capacity of all needs to have a central role (Booker, 2013; Day, 2000).

Distributed leadership has developed most widely as a concept in educational leadership in the United Kingdom (Bolden, 2011). However, Bolden highlights the lack of coherence in the leadership literature. He suggests that distributed leadership has also been referred to as shared leadership, collective leadership, co-leadership and emergent leadership. Developing a dominant, shared discourse in educational psychology leadership could prevent confusion such as this where the same idea is referred to in five different ways.

4) Matrix management

Matrix management enables different aspects of line management to be implemented across traditional teams or business groups, irrespective of their functions or geographical location. Therefore, EPs could be managed for some aspects of their work in a locality team by a nonpsychologist, with a psychologist offering part of the management functions, such as professional supervision. Matrix management, however, has been criticised as having the potential for conflict and confusion (Barlett & Ghoshal, 1990). Potentially straightforward solutions to difficult leadership dilemmas such as matrix management should be treated with caution and it is essential to consider the evidence base to inform the introduction of such management structures (Brooks & Kakabadse, 2014). Leaders of EPSs need to be aware of the benefits and drawbacks of such models.

5) Authorising environments

The authorising environment concerns those institutions, groups and individuals to whom the EPSs can be held accountable. These individuals or groups (constituencies) are the source of legitimacy of an EPS range of activities (Moore, 1995).

Generally speaking, the authorising environment for leaders of EPSs starts within their organisational management hierarchy or commissioner. They will have a line manager or commissioners who, in turn, will report to another manager. However, in public sector organisations, accountability will quickly reach a management position outside the organisation that is a political appointment. This concept of authorising environments is linked to the concept of creating public value (Moore, 1995). Creating public value is about ensuring that social goals are delivered in a way that is perceived as legitimate and trusted by the public.

Moore (1995) suggests that in creating a public value vision, those in management positions need to find a way of integrating the three key areas of politics, substance and administrative tasks. By focussing on what is authorised, valuable and done, we are looking at the different systemic influences on our work. Put simply there are two key questions to ask ourselves under three different headings:

Table 2.3 Questions to consider about the authorising environment and public value

In the authorising environment, we need to consider:	In the operation environment we need to consider:	In considering our public value proposition, we need to consider:
1) Do we have permission to exercise leadership? 2) Is the work legitimate and politically sustainable?	1) Is the work operationally and administratively feasible? 2) Can we deliver?	1) What is it that we are trying to achieve? 2) Is the work substantively valuable for the public?

Moore (1995)

6) Personal issues

A significant part of being a leader is dealing with relationships, your emotional reactions to difficulties and successes at work and the tricky issue of looking after yourself while being considerate and thoughtful towards others. A framework for structuring the Leadership task which considers these issues is that of Covey's 7 Habits (1989) – see Figure 2.2.

Although the title is off-putting, his concept is that you have to be aware of the path that others in your teams are moving from: starting with a sense of dependence, moving towards wanting to become independent and finally to the more collaborative stage of interdepend-

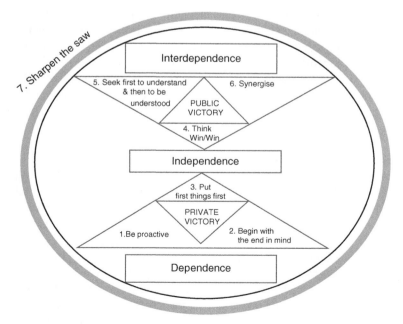

Figure 2.2 Covey's 7 habits.

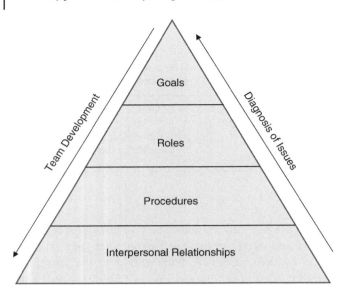

Figure 2.3 GRPI model (Beckhard, 1972).

ence. At the same time leaders must look after themselves with the 'private victory': being proactive, starting with the end in mind (a focus on strategy) and prioritising through putting first things first. The 'public victory' rightly focusses on understanding where others are coming from first before hoping to be understood, it suggests 'think win/win' which implies the corporate-private sector context that Covey is coming from, but it is an important concept in term of the operational and strategic elements being of benefit to all. The sixth habit addresses the need to build on individuals' strengths in order to achieve synergy and the final habit is about paying attention to yourself (physically, emotionally, mentally and spiritually) so that you can work with others to the best effect.

Another useful framework that Beckhard (1972) described states that for teams to be effective they must manage four areas internal to the team: goals, roles, processes and relationships (see Figure 2.3). Further research has identified a fifth factor a performance: how the team manages its interaction with the organisational environment.

7) The Primary Colours Model of Leadership
The Primary Colours model is a recently published framework described by Pendleton and Furnham (2012, p. 54). It neatly reminds us of the three key domains (strategic, operational and interpersonal), with leading being the centre of the model, and with a representation of operational tasks in the present that are specific and also a focus on future aspects that are generic (see Figure 2.4).

There are overlaps with the findings of the first author's research into leadership in EP services and the primary colours model of leadership. The findings from thematic analysis suggest that the primary colours of leadership model has face validity for use in EPSs. This strengthens the argument that EPSs should take into account aspects of the generic leadership literature. In particular, we should consider those aspects with a rigorous review of the existing literature and a strong empirical base such as the primary colours of leadership model.

The Primary Colours Model of Leadership

Figure 2.4 The primary colours model of leadership (from Pendleton & Furnham, 2016).

The model in Figure 2.5 represents the 10 themes from the first author's research that link to the primary colours of leadership model. The 10 themes are all interconnected as represented by the arrows in the diagram. Three themes relating to the individual are presented in the inner circle in black type. Three themes related to working in an organisation are in the outer boxes and two themes related to the specific profession of educational psychology are presented on the right-hand side of the diagram. The remaining two themes can be described as having an overarching impact. These are presented at the top of the diagram with arrows to demonstrate the wider impact.

The 10 themes could be used as areas to facilitate professional dialogue about leadership issues.

8) Learning organisations

Peter Senge's (1990) vision of a learning organisation as a group of people who are continually enhancing their capabilities to create what they want to achieve has been deeply influential in many organisations.

Senge (1990) describes learning organisations as:

> 'organizations where people continually expand their capacity to create the results they truly desire, where new and expansive patterns of thinking are nurtured, where collective aspiration is set free, and where people are continually learning to see the whole together'. (p. 3)

He and his colleagues suggest that 'five learning disciplines' can lead to a new way of looking at the world that emphasises the organisation as a whole rather than emphasising the position of the individual at the expense of the whole (Senge, Ross, Smith, Roberts,

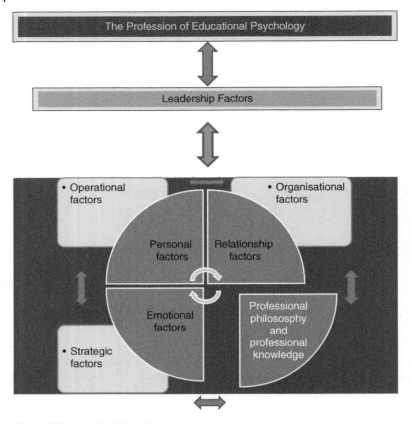

Figure 2.5   Model of the 10 themes.

& Kleiner, 1999). The five learning disciplines are referred to as being lifelong programmes of study. They are:

1) **Personal Mastery**. This is described as the ability to expand personal needs for the
   benefit of the organisation. The organisation will benefit from individuals developing
   themselves towards the goals and aspirations that they choose.
2) **Mental Models**. This discipline stresses the importance of reflection. Reflection on
   internal pictures of the world to see how they can shape decision-making.
3) **Shared Vision**. This could be viewed as having echoes of a simple problem-solving
   model. For example, where are we now, where do we want to be and how will we get
   there (shared vision). A key factor in this discipline is building a sense of commitment
   in the group by developing a shared vision of the future.
4) **Team Learning**. This discipline is based on the assumption that collective thinking
   skills can develop group intelligence that is greater than the sum of the individual members' talents.
5) **Systems Thinking**. This is described as developing a way to think about and a vocabu-
   lary to discuss systems. By understanding the forces and interrelationships that shape
   the behaviour of a system, we can design change processes that are in tune with other
   processes such as the economic world.

9) The incomplete leader

Researching the incomplete leader came as a relief to the first author. Being a complete leader somehow seems like a daunting task whereas being an incomplete leader seems achievable. Ancona, Malone, Orlikowski and Senge (2011) praise leaders who are aware that their skills as a leader are incomplete. They maintain that leadership involves the cultivation and coordination of the work of others at all levels. They identify four key areas of skill on the part of leadership team: sense making, relating, visioning and inventing.

This approach emphasised the move towards the study of leadership as a team endeavour rather than the identification of traits or actions demonstrated by an individual. Leadership teams are discussed as the units of research rather than single leaders. A trend can be identified over time by a move from interpersonal factors and their role in leadership to intrapersonal and contextual factors as units of study. This has some similarities in other areas of psychological thinking, for example, within attachment theories the relationship between parent and child is viewed as the unit of study or intervention rather than a specific focus on the child (Kennedy, Landor, & Todd, 2011).

This can be helpful when thinking about, for example, leadership team recruitment. This approach would suggest that in leadership recruitment, attention should be paid to recruiting into the leadership team those with different and complementary skills.

10) Invitational leadership

Stoll and Fink (2002) suggest that leadership is about creating invitational messages to groups and individuals with whom leaders interact and thus enable a shared vision and joint action to meet shared goals.

They further suggest that invitational leadership is based on:

- Optimism (that people will grow and develop under the right circumstances)
- Respect (invitational leaders respect the individuality of each human being and this is manifested through politeness, courtesy and caring)
- Trust (invitational leaders trust others' judgements and behaviours)
- Intentionality (to create a supportive caring and encouraging climate)

In Halton, Stoll and Fink (2002) worked with over a hundred school leaders and found that there were a significant number of individuals, who senior leaders felt confident in placing in any leadership role, knowing they would thrive. The thing that made these leaders different from others is described as being the clear set of principles and values which underpinned any decisions they made.

Rather than insist that individuals follow their lead through an authoritarian model, invitational leaders invite colleagues to join their creative supportive teams. Stoll and Fink (2002) suggest that invitational leaders:

- Invite themselves personally (to address what they really cherish or value in their lives)
- Invite themselves professionally (to grow and develop by reading, reflecting and researching)
- Invite others personally (to join a team or professional group thus building the kind of relationships required to create supportive communities)
- Invite others professionally (to join a group or working group and to work towards a shared goal)

What Else Would It Be Helpful for Us All to Know?

Juggling the many tasks of leadership in an EPS makes it difficult to find the time to research and locate professional guidance especially if the guidance is historical rather than newly published. The appendices attempt to address this issue and enable professional documents, position papers and research to be located and accessed more readily.

Conclusions

Interest in leadership has been ongoing since the times of Plato 380 BC (Pendleton & Furnham, 2012). Philosophers, psychologists, historians, economists, sociologists and novelists are amongst the groups that have written on this topic. Generic psychological knowledge and understanding give leaders of EPSs good foundations on which to develop their leadership skills and knowledge. For example, there is much that we can learn from behavioural, biological, cognitive, developmental, personality and social psychology that will enhance leadership practices. However, in addition to this, insights from organisational psychology and leadership studies are essential to understanding leadership within the organisations in which we work. Fullan (2001) reminds us that 'the more complex society gets, the more sophisticated leadership must become' (preface, p. 1).

Leadership requires strategic thinking and direction. There is more to leadership than simply writing a vision and mission statement. Tools and approaches from the leadership literature can usefully strengthen and inform leadership of EPSs. By combining our generic psychological knowledge and leadership knowledge and approaches, we can move towards a model of evidence-informed leadership and a dominant educational psychology leadership discourse, and leadership of EPSs services can become 'fit for purpose' (Booker, 2013).

Four hopes for the future

The authors have four main hopes for leadership work in the future. They are discussed in this final section.

PEPs and SEPs tell us they value attending leadership courses. There have been a number on offer in recent years, both whole six-eight day long courses (in Birmingham, Sheffield, Doncaster, Bristol and Cornwall) and the twilight sessions delivered in London. Leadership is an essential theme to the work of NAPEP who run an annual day conference where one main focus is invariably leadership of EPSs. Our first hope is that this work continues to flourish and more SEPs and PEPs will benefit from this training.

The DECP have re-issued the Quality Standards for EPSs (British Psychological Society [BPS] 2019), following a pilot by a number of EPSs in 2018. This document will enable PEPs and their teams to consider the elements of their service functioning and to critique the quality of these 10 standards systematically, using an external peer review process (see Chapter 13). Although this provides a general overview of EPS quality standards in 10 aspects of functioning, it has a more operational perspective and does not reference leadership theories per se. The strengths of this approach are that they can be used to consider the functioning of a service in a systematic way, including covering key aspects that EPS leaders value, such as induction, supervision and the contentious area of EP trading (see

Chapter 12). In this chapter we have mentioned the need for a shared discourse about leadership to apply to EPSs. The elements of consultation, assessment, intervention, training and research set out in the Scottish Executive Report (2002) is certainly one useful approach that EPSs within and beyond Scotland refer to in evaluations of the range of activity that EPSs undertake. Our second hope is that perhaps, in a similar way, the revised DECP Quality Standards will become another essential framework that leaders in educational psychology will use to review their own service effectiveness and to undertake constructive and developmental challenge by peers.

In addition to the revised Quality Standards document, PEPs in the south of England are considering working together to create a developmental model of leadership spanning from initial training through to PEP posts. It is hoped that by identifying key skills and experiences at each professional stage this will encourage future leaders to begin thinking about developing their leadership skills from the start of their careers.

Our final hope is that leaders of EPSs will continue to discuss leadership both in terms of service delivery and development but also to enable all EPs to see themselves as leaders in education; playing a vital role in shaping and developing important work across the geographical area in which they work. The four hopes expressed here could lead to the dominant discourse about leadership in EPSs discussed throughout this chapter.

Appendix 1

What documents have our professional bodies published about leadership?

As discussed earlier in this chapter, there are very few documents published by the professional bodies of EPSs that make specific reference to leadership. The following list of documents has been provided here to enable further reading (full details in the references):

- Department for Education and Employment (DFEE) (2000). *Educational Psychology Services (England) Current Role, Good Practice and Future Directions. The Research Report.*
- BPS: DECP (2002). *Professional Practice Guidelines.*
- BPS: DECP (2006). *Quality Standards for Educational Psychology Services Division of Educational and Child Psychology.*
- AEP (2008) position paper *The Management of Educational Psychology Services and the Role of Principal Educational Psychologist.*
- HMIe (2010). *Educational Psychology in Scotland: Making a Difference. An Aspect Report on the Findings of Inspections of Local Authority Educational Psychology Service.*
- AEP (2011). *The Delivery of Educational Psychology Services.*
- Health and Care Professionals Council (HCPC) (2012). *Standards of Performance Conduct and Ethics.*
- Truong & Ellam (2014). *Educational Psychology Workforce Survey 2013. Research Report.*
- Lyonette et al. (2019). *Research on the Educational Psychologist Work Force.* Government social research
- BPS: DECP (2019). *Quality Standards for Educational Psychology Services Division of Educational and Child Psychology.*

Appendix 2

What have educational psychologists published about leadership?

One of the authors undertook a literature review focussing on research and articles about leadership published by EPs. A systematic literature search was undertaken. Two electronic databases were searched: PsychINFO and ERIC. The key search words used were 'education*' 'and' 'psychology*' 'and' 'leader*'. All identified studies or articles written by educational psychologists about leadership are discussed here.

Eight studies or articles ranging from 2001 to 2015 by three different authors and two coauthors were located. An additional paper was identified following the later replication of the search. All articles with a date earlier than 2001 were excluded from the review. Five of the eight articles are position papers or literature reviews and the remaining four are empirical papers. An analysis of the five position papers and literature reviews is undertaken next and this is followed by an analysis of the four empirical papers.

Position papers and literature reviews

The position papers and literature reviews (Booker, 2012, 2013; Midgen, 2015; Rowland, 2005; Rowland, Traxson, & Roberts, 2010;) differ in their academic rigour and their aims, two being written for a professional newsletter and three for peer reviewed journals. Two have a specific children's services focus (Booker, 2012) and (Rowland, 2005) and one attempts to embed educational psychology in a community psychology perspective (Rowland et al., 2010). The fourth paper aims to define current theories of leadership most relevant to psychological services and to encourage a focus on the leadership capacity of a whole service (Booker, 2013). The fifth paper suggests that educational psychology would benefit from ethical leadership.

The position papers and literature reviews agree that leadership in EPSs is an important area of study given the current climate. They also agree that models and theories of leadership can and should be applied to EPSs although, the papers vary in the model or theory suggested and the emphasis placed on leadership ethics. The papers by Booker (2012, 2013) are comprehensive. He synthesises six strands from recent leadership research (charismatic/transformational leadership, distributed leadership, complexity leadership, authentic leadership, identity-based leadership and the social construction of leadership) and suggests that these six strands could be used to answer the question of whether leadership in EPSs is 'fit for purpose'. A move away from the focus on those at the top of an organisation and a move towards consideration of leadership capacity at all levels of an organisation can be seen in the reviews.

Booker (2013) addresses the question of what areas of leadership studies have particular relevance to leadership of EPS. Rowland et al. (2010) suggest that this can be undertaken through a model of community psychology. However, this seems to complicate the issue rather than enable a clear view of leadership. Booker (2013) suggests that the following areas are particularly relevant for EPS leadership:

- A focus on authenticity and trusting relationships rather than authority
- The ability to read and manage the local and national contexts
- Three key skills of observation, reflection and sound judgement
- A role for creating disequilibrium alongside emotional containment for colleagues in times of change and uncertainty
- Leadership should emerge at all levels of an organisation
- It is crucial for head of service to see leadership as enabling to facilitate strong downwards accountability to all staff together with upwards accountability to line management and commissioners (pp. 203–204)

All the papers reviewed make the distinction between leadership and management as two separate areas and agree that leadership should be a concern at all levels of an organisation. However, Booker (2013) expands on this point suggesting that a focus on leadership needs to begin in core professional training leading to coaching relationships for those in formal positions of authority. The papers all make reference to the importance of ethics in leadership (see Chapter 3 for further consideration of ethical leadership).

Empirical papers

Only four empirical studies were located investigating leadership in EPSs. The studies span from 2002 to 2015 (Rowland, 2002, 2008; Brooks & Kakabadse, 2014; Booker, 2015). The four papers varied in the population studied, methodology and aims; however, they all agree that this is an important topic of study given the current social, political and financial environment.

All highlight the fast pace of change for EPSs and consider how services could respond to the challenges through the development of leadership, management and self-evaluation systems. It is suggested that a school improvement framework could be used in EPSs although the link between leadership and outcomes is difficult to establish (Rowland, 2002).

In one study PEPs were found to have a sophisticated understanding of change, organisations, and the relationship between leadership and management (Rowland, 2008), although they were found to be based on mainstream psychology or popular theories of leadership as opposed to an understanding of the leadership literature.

Knowledge of motivation, systems thinking and leadership were seen to be important but need to be addressed through a lens that recognises that leadership is contextual and that processes are complex and interactional (Booker, 2015). Therefore, possible ways forward should not be seen as solution finding but as applying a possible set of leadership actions to generate capacity to address current and future dilemmas (Booker, 2015). Potentially straightforward solutions to difficult leadership dilemmas such as matrix management should be treated with caution and it is essential to consider the evidence base to inform the introduction of such management structures (Brooks & Kakabadse, 2014).

A key finding of the literature review was the scarcity and variability of leadership research in EPSs. What is required is an increase in both the quantity and quality of what is currently available.

Appendix 3

Suggested Induction Guide for Promoted Post Holders in Educational Psychologist Services

Following the findings of doctoral thesis research that the induction experiences of SEP and PEPs are variable and that coming into a promoted post can be challenging, the following collation of activities and ideas is presented to support induction processes. The list is provided here as an aide memoire rather than an exhaustive to-do list.

Skills and practicalities

1) Arrange a handover conversation or series of conversations if possible.
2) Consider carefully how to introduce yourself to the service (if you are moving into the service). This could include attending a meeting prior to your start date and a series of individual meetings. If you are already part of the service then it will be important to consider how the change in role could/will affect existing relationships.
3) Develop Excel spreadsheet skills or find someone in your organisation who has great Excel skills.
4) Consider and research how your organisation deals with the media.
5) Consider and research how your organisation writes and presents cabinet papers.
6) Consider and research how your organisation manages complaints and how you wish to manage complaints in the service.
7) Consider and research how your organisation manages responses to letters from MPs.
8) Consider observing a cabinet meeting.
9) Consider observing schools forum meetings.
10) Consider how to manage your line manager and how they understand the role of the EP in the LA.
11) Consider finding a report-writing friend — someone you can share reports with and who can share reports with you.

Contacts

1) Compile or locate the most recent list of key LA contacts.
2) Compile or locate the most recent list of key external partner contacts.
3) Walk the corridors and be available for informal discussions with these contacts.
4) Locate a friendly accountant in the LA.
5) Locate a friendly human resources manager in the LA.
6) Locate a friendly member of the legal team.
7) Locate a friendly member of the data and statistics team in your LA.
8) Identify potentially allied professionals and peer groups.

Organisational issues

1) Consider the political environment and arrange a meeting with key councillors.
2) Consider the organisation and how organisational factors have an impact on your work and role.
3) During your first year consider compiling an annual timetable that lists key events such as writing the service plan, agreeing on commissions, setting service dates for next year, when questionnaires for parents/schools are sent out, and when service data are reviewed.

Support and development

1) Look at the NAPEP website.
2) Join the local NAPEP regional meetings.
3) Request a mentor through the regional NAPEP meetings.
4) Attend the NAPEP conferences and courses.
5) Become a member of NAPEP-L (a discussion forum).
6) Prioritise your own supervision from the outset (possibilities: PEP in a neighbouring LA, a retired PEP, a child and adolescent mental health services manager). You may also wish to consider the differences between clinical support and line management support.
7) Spend time researching the leadership courses offered by your organisation for prospective/existing leaders and enrol on them.
8) Locate key documents from NAPEP, DECP, HCPC and AEP to support your work. For example, the code of ethics and conduct, ethical trading document and quality standards for EP work.

Leadership issues

1) Protect some time to consider leadership as a topic. Insights from generic models of leadership are useful in considering leadership in psychological services.
2) Consider whether the wider leadership literature will prove to be a useful resource for you. For example, Harvard business school publications.
3) Consider the benefits of leadership development courses in addition to the application of generic psychology in leadership roles.
4) Create opportunities to explore one's own professional philosophies and those of others to inform service direction and vision.

References

Allen, A., & Hardy, J. (2013). The future of educational psychology. In C. Arnold & J. Harvey (Eds.), *British educational psychology. The first hundred years.* Leicester: BPS.

Ancona, D., Malone, T., Orlikowski, W., & Senge, P. (2011, November). In praise of the incomplete leader. *Harvard Business Review*, 1–10.

Arnold, C., & Hardy, J. (Eds.). (2013). *British educational psychology. The first hundred years.* Leicester: BPS.

Association of Educational Psychologists (AEP). (2008). *The management of educational psychology services and the role of principal educational psychologist: The AEP position.* Durham: AEP.

Association of Educational Psychologists (AEP). (2011). *The delivery of educational psychology Services.* Durham: AEP.

Barlett, C., & Ghoshal, S. (1990). Matrix management: Not a structure, a frame of mind. *Harvard Business Review*, *68*(4), 138–145.

Beckhard, R. (1972). Optimizing team building efforts. *Journal of Contemporary Business*, *1*(3), 23–32.

Bolden, R. (2011). Distributed leadership in organizations: A review of theory and research. *International Journal of Management Reviews*, *13*(3), 251–269.

Booker, R. (2012). Leadership in children's services. *Children & Society*, *26*(5), 394–405.

Booker, R. (2013). Leadership of education psychology services: fit for purpose? *Educational Psychology in Practice*, *29*(2), 197–208.

Booker, R. (2015). Trainee educational psychologists' views of psychological service leadership. *Division of Educational and Child Psychology: Debate, no. 154*, 31–36.

British Psychological Society (BPS). (2002). *Professional practice guidelines for educational psychologists: Division of Education and Child Psychology.* Leicester: BPS.

British Psychological Society (BPS). (2006). *Quality standards for Educational Psychology Services: Division of Educational and Child Psychology.* Leicester: BPS.

British Psychological Society (BPS). (2019). *Quality standards for Educational Psychology Services: Division of Educational and Child Psychology.* Leicester: BPS. Retrieved from https://www.bps.org.uk/member-microsites/division-educational-child-psychology/resources

Brooks, M., & Kakabadse, N. (2014). Introducing matrix management within a children's services setting – personal reflections. *Management in Education, 28*(2), 58–63.

Children and Families Act 2014. Retrieved from http://www.legislation.gov.uk/ukpga/2014/6/contents/enacted

Cohen, W. (2010). *Drucker on leadership. New lessons from modern management.* San Francisco: Wiley.

Covey, S. R. (1989). *The 7 habits of highly effective people.* London: FranklinCovey.

Day, D. (2000). Leadership development: A review in context. *The Leadership Quarterly, 11,* 581–613.

Department for Education & Department of Health. (2015). *Special educational needs and disability code of practice: 0 to 25 Years. Statutory guidance for organisations who work and support children and young people with special educational needs and disabilities.* London: DfE & DoH. Retrieved from https://assets.publishing.service.gov.uk/government/uploads/system/uploads/attachment_data/file/319071/SEND_code_of_practice_0_to_25_years_response.pdf

Department for Education and Employment (DfEE). (2000). *Educational Psychology Services (England): Current role, good practice and future directions. The research report.* London: DfEE.

Doggett, C., & Lewis, A. (2013). Using appreciative inquiry to facilitate organisational change and develop professional practice within an *Educational Psychology Service. Educational and Child Psychology, 30*(4), 124–143.

Drucker, P. (2001). *The essential Drucker. The best sixty years of Peter Drucker's essential writings on management.* New York: Harper.

Friedman, M. (2005). *Trying hard is not good enough. How to produce measurable improvements for customers and communities.* Santa Fe, NM: FPSI.

Fortuin, K., & Van Marrising, E. (2009). Results based accountability. There is more to it than the right tools. *Journal of Social Intervention: Theory and Practice, 18*(3), 81–97.

Francis, R. (2013). *Report of the Mid Staffordshire NHS Foundation Trust Public Inquiry.* London: The Stationery Office.

Fullan, M. (2001). *Leading in a culture of change.* San Francisco: Jossey-Bass.

Gibbs, S., & Lauchlan, F. (2015). Guest editorial: Practicing educational psychology in challenging times. *Educational and Child Psychology, 32*(4), 6–7.

Goleman, D. (1996). *Emotional intelligence. Why it can matter more than IQ.* London: Bloomsbury Publishing PLC.

Grint, K. (2000). *The arts of leadership.* Oxford: Oxford University Press.

Gronn, P. (2000). Distributed properties: a new architecture for leadership. *Education Management and Administration, 28,* 317–338.

Health and Care Professionals Council (HCPC). (2012). *Standards of performance conduct and ethics.* London: HCPC.

Her Majesty's Inspectorate of Education. (2010). *Educational psychology in Scotland: Making a difference. An aspect report on the findings of inspections of Local Authority Educational Psychology Service* 2006–10. Edinburgh: Scottish Executive.

Hogan, M. (2013). The difference between a value and a principle. Retrieved from https://www.smartcompany.com.au/marketing/difference-values-principles/

Jervis, V. (2019). *An exploratory study into the experiences and perceptions of leaders in educational psychology services.* Unpublished thesis. London: University College London.

Johnson, G., & Scholes, K. (1988). *Exploring corporate strategy* (2nd ed.). London: Prentice-Hall.

Kennedy, H., Landor, M., & Todd, L. (2011). *Video interaction guidance. A relationship-based intervention to promote attunement, empathy and wellbeing.* London: Jessica Kingsley Publishers.

Kent, T. (2005). Leading vs management: It takes two to tango. *Management Decision, 43*(7–8), 1010–1017.

Kostova, T. (1999). Transnational transfer of strategic organizational practices: A contextual perspective. *Academy of Management Review, 24,* 308–324.

Kotter, J. (1990). *A force for change. How leadership differs from management.* New York: Free Press.

Lyonette, C., Atfield, G., Baldauf, B., & Owen, D.(2019). *Research on the educational psychologist work force.* London: Department for Education. Retrieved from https://assets. publishing.service.gov.uk/government/uploads/system/uploads/attachment_data/ file/787417/Research_on_the_Educational_Psychologist_Workforce_March_2019.pdf

Midgen, T. (2015). (Un) ethical leadership: What can educational psychology services learn? *Educational and Child Psychology, 32*(4), 81–93.

Moore, M. H. (1995). *Creating public value. Strategic management in government.* London: Harvard University Press.

Mintzberg, H., & Waters, J.A. (1985). Of strategies, deliberate and emergent. *Strategic Management Journal, 6,* 257–272.

Northouse, P. (2013). *Leadership. Theory and practice* (6th ed.). Los Angeles: Sage.

Pendleton, D., & Furnham, A. (2012). *Leadership: All you need to know* (2nd ed.). Palgrave: Macmillan.

Porter, M. (1996, November-December). *What is strategy? Harvard Business Review.*

Pinnock, M. (2012). How outcomes saved my life (or at least my sanity). *Social Work Now, 51,* 22–29.

Rowland, K. (2002). Effective leadership and service improvement in contemporary Educational Psychology Services: The historical context. *Educational Management and Administration, 30*(3), 275–291.

Rowland, K. (2005). 'It's better to have the camel in the tent peeing out...' EPS leadership in children's services: (ECM) Every Camel Matters! *Division of Education and Child Psychology (DECP) Debate,* no. *116,* 25–28.

Rowland, K. (2008). *A study investigating the role of the principal educational psychologist and associated theories of leadership.* Unpublished thesis, University of Birmingham.

Rowland, K., Traxson, S., & Roberts, W. (2010). Community educational psychology and ethical leadership. *Division of Education and Child Psychology (DECP) Debate,* no. 137.

Schein, E. (1985). *Organizational culture and leadership* (4th ed.). San Francisco: Jossey-Bass.

Schein, E. (2010). *Organizational culture and leadership* (5th ed.). San Francisco: Jossey-Bass.

Scottish Executive. (2002). *Review of provision of educational psychology services in Scotland.* Edinburgh: Scottish Executive. Retrieved from http://www.aspep.org.uk/wp-content/ uploads/2014/05/Currie-Report-2002.pdf

Senge, P. (1990). *The fifth discipline: The art and practice of the learning organization.* London: N. Brearley.

Senge, P, Ross, R., Smith, B., Roberts, C., & Kleiner, A. (1999). *The fifth discipline fieldbook.* London: N. Brearley.

Sharp, S., Frederickson, N., & Laws, K. (2000). Changing the profile of an educational psychology service. *Educational and Child Psychology, 17*(1), 98–111.

Stobie, I. (2002). Processes of 'change' and 'continuity' in educational psychology–Part I. *Educational Psychology in Practice, 18*(3), 203–212.

Stoll, L., & Fink, D. (2002). *Changing our schools.* Buckingham: Open University Press.

Stringer, P., Burton, S., & Powell, J. (2006). Developing a community orientation in an educational psychology service. *Educational and Child Psychology, 23*(1), 59–67.

Stringer, P., Dunsmir, S., & MacKay, T. (2013). Guest editorial: Marking a centenary and a quest to restore history. *Educational and Child Psychology, 30*(3), 6–12

Truong, Y., & Ellam, H. (2014). *Educational psychology workforce survey 2013.* Research report. Nottingham: National College for Teaching and Leadership.

Van den Berg, P.T., & Wilderom, C.P.M. (2004). Defining, measuring, and comparing organisational cultures. *Applied Psychology: An International Review, 53*(4), 570–582.

3

Ethical Selfhood and Team Awareness: The Role of Reflexivity in Leadership

Tara Midgen and Theodora Theodoratou

Introduction

Many Educational Psychology Services (EPSs) began to sell services to schools following public spending cuts linked to the 2010 Government Spending Review (HM Treasury, 2010). The public sector reform associated with this review also triggered changes to other services for children with special educational needs and disability (SEND) that were previously delivered at no direct cost to schools. Such change to service delivery has continued with most EPSs now operating in this way nationally. Alongside this, other significant reform of the educational landscape has included the academisation of schools (Department for Education [DfE], 2010), SEND Reform (DfE, 2014) and most recently the arrival of Mental Health Support Teams in Schools (DfE, Department of Health & Social Care [DoH & SC], 2018).

The Children and Families Act (2014), whilst positively strengthening the voice of parents and children with SEND, had the unintended consequence of a national rise in Education, Health and Care Needs Assessments (EHCA), the system that has replaced the previous statutory assessment arrangements for children with SEND. Additionally, it is widely reported in the press that government policy has failed to tackle childhood poverty which has increased over time, that homelessness has increased, that there is an insufficient housing stock for families, and that the number of children in public care and the prevalence of mental health difficulties in children and young people has risen (Bedell, 2016; Lepper, 2018). These circumstances have continued to place significant additional pressures on local authority resources, against a climate of widespread political and financial uncertainty following the public's decision to leave the European Union in the national referendum of 2016.

The Responsibilities and Accountability of Principal Educational Psychology (PEP) Leadership

The primary function of PEPs as leaders is to lead applied psychological services that make a difference to the lives of children and families. When commissioned by local authorities (LAs), we are usually required to deliver a statutory service that fulfils educational

Leadership for Educational Psychologists: Principles & Practicalities, First Edition.
Edited by Julia Hardy, Charmian Hobbs and Mohammed Bham.
© 2020 John Wiley & Sons Ltd. Published 2020 by John Wiley & Sons Ltd.

psychologist (EP) responsibilities in relation to the Children and Families Act (2014) along-side a range of other responsibilities usually including the supervision and management of EPs or other professionals, consideration of staff and team well-being, development and support, financial accounting and work allocation. From the position of financial account-ability, leaders of traded services are in the complex and perhaps unenviable position of ensuring that we simultaneously generate enough income to maintain our services, bal-ance end of year accounts and retain enough staffing to fulfil service demands such as delivering commissioned services to schools and the LA. We need to consider how to max-imise 'best value' service delivery for the greatest public good (Sellick, 2011), which may be more complicated for leaders of traded services owing to the possible inequity caused by differences in the distribution of purchased services. PEPs and senior EPs (SEPs) may also attend Education, Health and/or Care Panels, where complex resourcing decisions draw-ing on public sector funding are made.

Public sector leaders including PEPs are accountable for the spending of public funds. We need to give careful consideration as to how we make decisions in relation to spending. Whether or not we are employed by a LA and regardless of whether a service is traded, EP leaders and private EPs, who are selling or delivering services to maintained schools or academies, are either drawing on public sector funding as income or spending public sector funds through the delivery of a service.

PEPs, as registered practitioner psychologists, must have regard to the professional codes/standards of conduct and ethics (British Psychological Society [BPS], 2009; Health and Care Professions Council, 2012). Working with and striving to navigate the complexi-ties of our professional context and landscape and make decisions that will minimise harm and maximise positive impact call for insight and awareness. When and how often do we, as leaders in this messy world, take the time to pause and carefully consider the ethical dilemmas that face us in relation to our responsibilities and what might be needed to help us make the best possible decisions? Public sector managers face ongoing uncertainty and complexity in their day-to-day management and ethical problem solving (Adriansen & Knudsen, 2013). In the context of organisations that go through persistent change, one aspect of EPS leadership is to continuously reflect on how 'the organisation is created and its relation to the surroundings, the employees, the users, even superiors' (Adriansen & Knudsen, 2013, p.110). Given the polyphony (multiple voices) in LA contexts, EPS leaders needs to deal with multiple narratives and consider multiple factors to inform the choices we make in relation to our responsibilities and ethical decision making.

Ethical Leadership and Ethical Climate

Ethical leadership, a distinct form of leadership in the leadership literature, based primarily on social learning theory developed by Bandura (Brown & Trevino, 2006; Brown, Trevino, & Harrison, 2005) has been characterised by the dimensions of the *moral person* and the *moral manager*. Whilst other forms of leadership (authentic, spiritual, transformational) empha-sise care and concern for others, the moral manager is expected to set clear ethical standards, act as a role model for ethical behaviour, use rewards and sanctions to reinforce ethical standards and hold followers accountable for ethical conduct (Brown & Trevino, 2006)

Ethical climate is a multidimensional construct comprising the ethical characteristics of workplace environments (Shacklock, Manning, & Hort, 2011). Whilst research exploring factors contributing to an ethical climate suggests that the relative importance of the key characteristics of ethical climate varies across organisations, elements such as the genuine caring nature of staff towards one another, the degree to which staff comply with organisational policies and professional codes and 'the degree to which employees are expected to be guided by their personal moral beliefs' (Shacklock et al., 2011, p. 36) have been identified in the literature.

Both ethical leadership and ethical climate have been associated with positive organisational outcomes such as job satisfaction, organisational commitment, staff well-being, reduced employee misconduct and low turnover intentions of staff (Avey, Wernsing, & Palanski, 2012; Brown & Mitchell, 2010; Martin & Cullen, 2006; Shacklock et al., 2011).

Whilst leaders facilitate the cultural tone of an organisation or service and this may vary, as research suggests that cultural differences influence perspectives on ethical and unethical leadership (Eisenbeiss & Brodbeck, 2014; Resick, Martin, Keating, Dickson, & Kwong Kwan, 2011), leaders have a moral responsibility to promote integrity and lead by example. However, leadership as a moral activity is not necessarily and exclusively about having a code of ethics, setting ethical standards and training team members to act in ethical ways, which places ethical responsibility outside of us in what we do (i.e. activities), rather than who we are (Cunliffe, 2009). Similarly, it does not just involve thinking ethically (Muturano, 2005) or problem solving. Responsible and ethical leadership involves continuously reflecting on the actual problem formulation and the effects that are created with any interpretation of a situation.

Moral leadership and moral practice are therefore tied in with who we are in relation to others, our values, beliefs and the will and capacity to empathise with others regardless of potential considerable differences. Ricoeur (1995) situated ethics as interpersonal. EPs' professional morality is essentially shown in 'our attitudes, our behaviour and our relationship with others' (Fox, 2015, p. 394). Ethical selfhood unfolds in a 'reflexive process of recognising we are accountable for our self, our actions and our relationships' (Cunliffe, 2009, p. 97) and professional conscience becomes about how we respond to the voice of the others, with ethical intention to live, operate and work well with others.

Ethical Leadership: What Can Philosophy and Systemic Thinking Offer?

Understanding of the issues and problems addressed by fields outside of educational psychology, such as systemic thinking and philosophy, forms a basis for thinking differently about ourselves and our experience. It is a different way of thinking about social and organisational life as 'emergent, socially constructed, and inherently ideological and political, that encourages us to challenge taken-for-granted organisational realities, places upon us a responsibility for relationships with others and forms the genesis for alternative realities' (Cunliffe, 2009, p. 93). With this position in mind, ethical leadership needs to involve a process of thinking more critically and reflexively about ourselves as leaders and practitioners, our actions and the situations in which we find ourselves (Cunliffe, 2009).

EP leaders and practitioners as active and responsible agents of change

An important example of how philosophy can be useful to the work of EPS leaders and individual EPs, comes from existentialism, which sets out to make every individual aware of what they are and to make the full responsibility of their existence rest on them. According to Sartre when we say, 'that a man is responsible for himself, we do not only mean that he is responsible for his own individuality, but that he is responsible for all men' (Sartre, 1965/1993, p. 36). This position brings the need to accept responsibility for ourselves, for our actions and for others and shifts attention away from forms of leadership that aim to create and transform business (Heifetz, 1994), to the notion of leadership as moral responsibility and ethical choice.

Cunliffe (2009) argues for the need to develop 'philosopher leaders', who can critically view 'social and organisational realities' and use their reflexivity 'to examine strategies, policies, programmes and organisational practices', to understand 'how and why they might impact on people and exclude them from active participation in organisational life' and community life, 'to act in more responsive ways and engage in dialogue that is critical and open' (Cunliffe, 2009, pp. 98–99). However, as Moore (2005) wondered, 'how often do we as applied psychologists [we would add EP leaders] stop and question the legitimacy of our paradigms as expressed through our actual practice?' (p.107) As already mentioned, 'the basic moral problem in life is not what to do, but what kind of person to be' (Shotter & Cunliffe, 2002, p. 20). Knowing who we are means 'recognising that we, with others, are the authors of our social and organisational realities, identities and sense of self'. If we are clear (or at least clearer) about who we want to be as moral and ethical applied psychologists and leaders, then 'what to do falls into place' (Cunliffe, 2009, p. 94).

Given that EPs and EPS leaders are involved in decision-making on a daily basis it is very important for us to be clear, conscious and open about our philosophical stance, our core world beliefs and our positions (both theoretical and in action) with regard to the four core moral principles that underpin the work of all health and care professionals in the UK: autonomy, beneficence, nonmaleficence and social justice (Beauchamp & Childress, 2009; Gillon, 1995) to ensure that we do not fall into ethical traps and perpetuate the power laden status quo. Fox (2015) argued that 'EPs' positioning takes place within a moral and value-laden world, as does the positioning of all professionals' (p. 383). It is important to recognise that 'any change in position at least partially rests in a change in the position of our values and the moral principles which underpin them. Without such a change in moral principles our behaviour in unlikely to change' (Fox, 2015, p. 383).

Social constructionism and the role of language

According to Cunliffe (2009) 'who we are is always open, emergent, imaginative' (p. 90). As the ontological position moved from constructivist (individuals create their own reality) to social constructionism (groups in society create a social reality through the language that they use), it became apparent that the language people use gives meaning to their world. The dominant discourse is the way that a group of people, parts of society and a system create a coherent understanding about their experience. However, the language that groups of people with power use becomes the dominant discourse (for example, medical discourse) and in relation to that, other experiences can become marginalised. It is widely accepted in systemic thinking that when the modernist practitioner ignores (even unconsciously) this feature of social life and uses or leaves unquestioned the discourse of power she/he can without intention maintain the existing relations of power (Goldner, 1985; Hare-Mustin, 1978; Paré, 1996). Awareness of how our language can marginalise, alienate, or even annihilate the experience of minority groups that we work with is crucial.

Social constructionism encourages practitioners to pay attention to the language they use, for example, using diagnostic language in consultations and/or the verb *is* to describe difficulties that an individual may experience. While this may have some benefit of rapid communication between the professionals concerned, when used in conversation with children and families it can shut down the opportunity for them to describe their unique experiences and the path to unique solutions. This would be particularly relevant to educational psychology consultation as a positive change process in any context.

First- and second-order cybernetics

A critical and central shift in systemic thinking was the move from first-order to second-order cybernetics. In first-order modernist positioning, practitioners see themselves as separate from the individual or system (family, school, organisation) they are working with, maintaining the position of the external expert with specialist knowledge, which is used to assess and recommend treatment, whilst remaining untouched by the social, systemic, or organisational dynamics that are at play (Keeney, 2002). However, early systemic writings stressed that 'what we hear in any given communication is in part determined by what we expect and want to hear and by the history of the relationship' (Dallos & Draper, 2015, p. 69).

Second-order cybernetics 'challenged the view that any interpretation of the practitioner was merely an inference in the mind of the practitioner himself/herself' (Dallos & Draper 2015, p. 69). In second-order postmodernist positioning, practitioners' expert role is being challenged, as the focus of the work becomes the quality of listening to the stories people share about their lives with a view to empowering them, honouring their autonomy and facilitating their ability to find their own solutions (Roth & Weingarten, 1995). This position relies on the understanding of the complex 'relationships between knowledge, power and authority' (Moore, 2005, p. 109) as well as the fundamental belief that the experience of being listened to and responded to, within a relationship of care, will help people to find alternatives to their problem-saturated story (White & Epston, 1990).

These two very different approaches (i.e. first- and second-order cybernetics) towards life and positioning in the caring professions come with two distinct ways for practitioners to think about their work: reflection vs. reflexivity/self-reflexivity.

Reflection vs. reflexivity/self-reflexivity: How are they different?

'Reflection is traditionally defined as a mirror image, an objectivist ontology based on the idea that there is an original reality we can think about and separate ourselves from' (Cunliffe & Jun, 2005, p. 226). Reflexivity, by contrast, is 'the process in which practitioners can reflect on the consequences of their reflections and on how articulations create reality'

(Adriansen & Knudsen, 2013, p. 111). Self-reflexivity is about a process that continuously sheds a critical light on our interpretations of the world and our lived experience and 'examines the issues involved in acting responsibly and ethically' (Cunliffe, 2009, p.9 3).

Reflexivity and its relevance to the EP profession

Although 'reflection helps thinking about past work and how this may affect practice in the future' (Pellegrini, 2009, p. 271), reflexivity and self-reflexivity encourage the practitioner not only to monitor his or her perceptions, beliefs and feelings and how these are in turn shaping the system with which they are working (Dallos & Draper, 2015) but also to critically examine 'the assumptions underlying textual, theoretical and ideological positions' that keep the cultural, social and organisational status quo (Cunliffe, 2009, p. 93). In other words, reflexivity refers to 'the regular exercise of the mental ability, shared by all normal people, to consider themselves in relation to their (social) contexts and vice versa' (Archer, 2007, p.4). According to second-order systemic practitioners such as Barry Mason (2012), connections between the personal self and the professional task are very important in our capacity to distinguish and address how our core beliefs might 'helpfully or unhelpfully influence the professional task' (Mason, 2012, p. 177). However, EPs' persistence in distinguishing ourselves from a psychotherapeutic discourse, as well as perhaps our lack of confidence (and explicit training) in placing clear boundaries so that supervision does not turn into therapy, may have limited our reflective conversations and purposefully not included material that can be very useful both in our understanding of our actions and prevention of ethical mistakes.

Practical Applications of Systemic and Existential Ideas in Leadership

Leadership self-care and the prevention of team burnout

Systemic thinkers argue that in the course of our practice, positioning and actions, we also co-create who we are (Lang, Little, & Cronen, 1990). Archer (2007) explained that 'one's internal conversations enable a weighing up of personal desires and motivations with the normalising structures in place to decide on the best action for oneself at this time in this place' (Moffatt, Ryan, & Barton, 2016, p. 30). Her theory of reflexivity helps us to explore how individuals who care for others can also care for themselves in an 'ongoing process of reflexive practice and professional identity building' (p. 30). Archer continued to argue that 'individuals have agency even when social structures seek to normalise or discipline practices and given her assertion that society has no pre-set form or state, actions can be seen as 'morphogenic' if they transform the social structures in which they operate' (p. 32).

This idea offers the practitioner the power to examine and articulate their internal conversations and decision-making through a clear process of reflexivity, leading to intentional actions with the potential to 'transform and transcend the social structures in which they practice' (Moffatt et al., 2016, p. 32). The practitioner can come to address both the unique requirements of their field and their individual experiences, consciously making them active agents in their own professional contexts.

However, as Moffatt et al. (2016) argued, those who facilitate others' well-being and creative solutions to problems, do not always practise their own self-care, potentially leading to physical/mental exhaustion and/or disillusionment.

Alongside all caring professions, EPs often face moments when we feel that we could not listen further or have been overwhelmed with feelings of compassion (Vetere & Stratton, 2016). There are various aspects of the current EP context that can add to feelings of pressure and stress. The consequences of any form of stress in the workplace (not enough/appropriate training due to financial pressures, lack of/poor supervision, burdensome work environments, the impact of teacher stress, organisational anxiety regarding austerity measures, pressures for commissioning of work, overwork) can also lead to feelings of mental/physical exhaustion and disillusionment. In such cases, the EP can become either overactive and overcontrolling, taking on responsibility that does not belong to him/her, or freeze in a state of paralysis. Both scenarios can lead to clouded judgement and ethical errors in the process (Vetere & Stratton, 2016). According to systemic thinkers, burnout happens in a 'complex web of organisational and interpersonal processes' (Vetere & Stratton, 2016, p. 74). This emphasises the importance of empathic and reflective supervision to ameliorate and prevent it.

There is widespread stigma associated with mental health conditions and in many helping professions it may be viewed as a failure if one seeks help personally or requires the involvement of systems such as occupational health to support one's mental health. The role of blame can be significant when people are seen as too weak and unable to cope, or management is perceived as neglectful. Managers of people in the caring professions may also fall victim to stresses that lead to burnout or compassion fatigue. Lamson, Meadors and Mendenhall (2014) warned that one's capacity to care for and support others may be significantly affected if the practitioner does not attend to their own feelings of distress as they emerge from the work they engage with.

Leading by example: The role of relational reflexivity

Brené Brown (2018) in her book *Dare to Lead* unpicks the role of vulnerability in creating meaningful relationships and connections in the workplace and advises that leadership involves remaining curious about blind spots (ours and those that we manage) and bringing those to the surface in supportive and gentle ways. According to current systemic thinkers, in a reflexive and self-reflexive thinking space we can contain pressures, tensions and anxiety as well as help ourselves and team members be accountable for their work and responsible for their ethical decision-making.

Similarly, Mason and Sawyerr (2002) argued that 'to develop intimacy, to develop closeness of whatever kind, one has to be prepared to take chances and risk vulnerability' (p. 164). In order for individual EPs to expose their vulnerabilities and remain curious, creative, resourceful and clear about their ethical and moral responsibilities (within a practice characterised by freedom and autonomy), they need to feel able to trust our ability as leaders to appreciate and acknowledge risk taking, respond to pressures (internal and external) in an equally reflexive and self-reflexive way, model ethical and moral clarity within the complex systems we live and operate in, whilst paying attention to everyone's psychological safety (both in teams and in the communities we serve).

Inevitably, by increasing our reflexivity and emotional clarity we can acknowledge our limitations and the limits of our impact, for example, on local policy and practice and can let ourselves rest in processes of supervision that could 'provide the contact for persistence in the face of disappointment' (Vetere & Stratton, 2016, p. 104).

EP as practitioner: How can reflexivity help our teams further develop ethical practice

As already described, the individual EP as an active agent in shaping social and cultural structures, not only has freedom and autonomy to bring about positive change but also responsibility to position themselves in ways that adhere to the morals of our profession (Fox, 2015).

For example, given there are particular difficulties in addressing challenging topics in light of ongoing austerity measures and the 'natural resistance to changing deeply held beliefs' (Fox, 2015, p. 394), Rogers and O'Bryon (2008) argued that it is easy for leaders and individual practitioners to ignore (consciously or unconsciously) 'the damaging effects of prejudice and oppressive practices, policies and systems' (Fox, 2015, p. 394). Social constructionism calls for 'a more ethical, socio-political awareness of our practice relationships and for expert practice to begin to challenge some of the dominant discourses' (Moore, 2005, p. 111).

Many EPs have long accepted the social constructionist and postmodern view that individuals do not live, act, or develop untouched by the social structures around them. We have collectively adopted many methods and techniques that epistemologically and ontologically belong to postmodern and social constructionist thinking (e.g. consultation, solution-focussed therapy, narrative therapy). Yet, when it comes to our own individual and collective awareness in day-to-day practice, we wonder whether the majority of EPs continue to adopt a modernist expert position of power (both in their work with schools and parents) and EP supervisors continue to favour the practice of reflection as opposed to reflexivity and self-reflexivity, which can often lead to a confused and potentially confusing application of psychology. For example, when parents and schools disagree about the nature of a child's difficulty, whether a child has or does not have a diagnosable problem and where blame is to be placed, it is easily possible that we would engage in an act of 'convincing' parents for the dominant school narrative, in our attempts to be 'helpful' and maintain relationships (and currently business) with schools.

For example, training institutions and qualified EPs would mostly agree with the position that a child's environments play a critical role in the child's development and overall presentation. Yet very few have moved the environment and consideration of social factors into a central part of our role; for example, we still write reports from a within-child expert perspective often with a paternalistic stance, albeit disguised as information giving for parents to make decisions (Fox, 2015).

As Burnham (1992) clarified in writing about the links between an approach, a method and a technique, practitioners may 'choose to use aspects of a model such as technique while continuing to organise their work under the influence of a different approach' (p. 6). For example, we use the miracle question from Solution-Focused Brief Therapy (SPBT) to strategically change a teacher's construct that nothing works with a child. However, it is the incongruence and lack of conscious awareness of our stance/approach whilst using a technique that in our opinion can harm the client and lead the practitioner to ethical mistakes, for example, pushing a parent or teacher to think about exceptions to the rule when they are not ready for this, using aspects of Burnham's (1992) Social Ggrraaacceeesss[1] (e.g. race, religion etc.) to highlight that a parent's choice of school is wrong given that it does not fit with the dominant (school, professional network, LA) discourse or even using dynamic assessment tools but then reporting from an intelligence-is-static position.

Cunliffe (2009) argued that changing our practice happens following an internal critical exploration and not necessarily because of an external critique that can be easily ignored or dismissed. Given Fox's (2015) argument about the need for EPs to be clear about and change how we position ourselves to ensure we develop and maintain our moral professional identities, in our view, practising reflexivity and self-reflexivity is a safer way for us to become responsive to others and critically open to new ways of being and acting. This is particularly pertinent for EPS leaders given the pressures we face when trying to lead teams in the face of austerity whilst acting in morally responsible ways. Moore (2005) stated that our 'conventional understandings of our practice' in how to respond to issues of social injustice, difference and social complexity 'may not only have failed to prepare us', but our efforts to address them may be 'highly inappropriate or even detrimental' (p. 105). Using self-reflexivity to address our need for the right solutions (Mason, 1993) and truths, our discomfort towards uncertainty, our response to the pressures placed upon us to 'assess, manage, monitor' (Moore, 2005, p. 105) and allocate resources can really help us to adopt a more systemic 'both/and' instead of an 'either/or' position, which 'invites us to avoid the true/false, real/not real dichotomy of choice in relation to different views (Burnham, 1992).

The importance of reflexive supervision

a) Awareness of professional self and protective connections

Given the complexities of EP practice and the context in which we operate we have argued for reflexivity and self-reflexivity being an important and necessary shift for educational psychology leadership and practice. Pressures to hold multiple narratives in mind and act in morally responsible ways can place huge amounts of emotional pressure on us as team leaders and practising EPs. Yet we often neglect the care of ourselves despite the highly emotional narratives we work with daily. Atkinson and Posada (2019) recently highlighted the importance of supervision for PEPs and in their research with a group of PEPs, found that PEPs often sought out opportunities for supervision from other psychologists. Foucault (1990) pointed out that 'the care of the self is not an act of solitude; it is a social practice' (Moffatt et al., 2016, p. 29). Wong (2013) in turn, used this principle to suggest that 'reflexive practice can develop reciprocal relations' (Moffatt et al., 2016, p. 29) and argued that the act of self-examination, in relation to trusted others, not only allows the individual to exercise autonomy and freedom 'but also leads to enlightenment and strengthened relations with others both personally and professionally' (p. 29).

---

1 Gender, gender identity, geography, race, religion, age, ability, appearance, class, culture, ethnicity, education, employment, sexuality, sexual orientation and spirituality.

This is in line with the BPS professional practice guidelines, which conceptualised supervision as 'having a space where it is possible to open up thinking to the mind of another with a view to extending knowledge about the self' (BPS, 2017, p. 12) and emphasised the place of supervision in 'addressing knowledge atrophy over time, including the stereotypes, biases and faulty reasoning present in the thinking of even the most experienced practitioners' (Kennedy, Keany, Shaldon, & Canagaratnam, 2018, p. 283). Therefore, reflexivity and self-reflexivity explicitly practised in supervision and whole team discussions can not only address our philosophical stance, ethical and moral positioning and how they shape the communities we serve but also become the exact practice that can help our team members feel connected to those around them and emotionally contained in the light of all the pressures they might face in their professional lives. If PEPs do not have psychologically safe supervision where they can explore such issues for themselves, how can they be expected to provide this for other EPs or SEPS and *contain the containers*. We recognise that in the educational psychology profession the opportunities and structures for PEPs to receive such supervision are frequently unavailable and wonder how action can be taken for this to be recognised and embedded as a matter of course.

b) Ethical awareness and continued professional development

According to Vetere and Stratton (2016) reflexivity practised in supervision and team discussions can take us beyond 'routine maintenance'. Ericsson (2006) also argued how the majority of family therapists (and we would add professionals) 'reach a stable, average level of performance, and then they maintain this pedestrian level for the rest of their careers' (p. 685). However, we believe that for EPs to continue to develop professionally, beyond the point of qualification, and therefore maintain a sense of fulfilment in their work, they need to remain curious and question the assumptions underlying dominant approaches in medical, therapeutic, educational and child development practices (Vetere & Stratton, 2016). Daniel Kahneman (2012) became very popular recently by describing how automatic and competent 'fast thinking' can be 'limiting and inimical to progress' and in the form of prejudice it 'can begin to look like unconscious incompetence all over again' (Vetere & Stratton, 2016, p. 15). Therefore, the practice of reflexivity is vital in slowing down our thinking and bringing these in-context automatic processes into light for self-examination, with a view to choosing the most ethical course of action and achieving 'higher level of understanding of our own learning processes' (p. 16).

'The modernist spell, demanding coherence and consistency' (Vetere & Stratton, 2016, p. 62) is ever present in the EP work and supervision. People usually want 'to present themselves as valid and valuable, sensible and intelligible' (p. 62), especially amongst less experienced colleagues and in a context where casework supervision is often delivered by the same person who engages in managerial performance-related tasks. However, when practitioners adopt a position of knowing how things should be (Cecchin, 1993), they can limit the creativity of their thinking, return to familiar patterns and hypotheses and potentially fall into biased thinking and ethical traps. According to Vetere and Stratton (2016), the practitioner in the supervisee position can give permission to themselves to be vulnerable and expose biases or ethical dilemmas only 'if the supervisor repeatedly insists that there is no need to be exact' (p. 62). However, for this to happen 'supervisors need to let themselves become part of this fluid and complex space' (p. 62), whereas in our work with clients they consciously let go of the need for control and certainty and become fellow travellers through their emotional availability, their belief in the effectiveness of the safe uncertainty (Mason, 1993) and their commitment in building a safe, secure base and psychological safety (Cliffe, Beinart, & Cooper, 2014; Vetere & Stratton, 2016).

As pointed out by Faris (2012), 'an understanding of the self of the practitioner is intrinsically connected to the supervisor's understanding of her/himself within the supervisory relationship' (p. 92). Kennedy et al. (2018), in explaining the value of developing a relational model to supervision, argued that 'a capacity to take up a systemic position that locates supervisory relating and reflecting in the broader organisational, societal and cultural context is essential' (p. 288). Equally, they suggested that being conscious and open about our 'differences in family systems, identities and experiences of power and oppression' (p. 289) is critical in thinking about how these differences get in the way of ethical relating both in our work with clients and with each other.

Financial accountability and the traded context

Managing budgets is not part of educational psychology training and whilst leaders of EPSs have generally been responsible for their budgets, they may not be well prepared for the financial complexity and additional responsibility associated with income generation and the trading of educational psychology services. Recognition of this complexity and the ethical dilemmas associated with selling services resulted in the publication of *Ethical Trading: Guidelines for Educational Psychology Services* (BPS, 2018). EPS leaders need to make real life financial decisions that affect their team members and members of the community, for example, the number of EPs to employ, whether to pay for staff training or expensive independent specialist placements for children, how much to charge for services and how much income to generate from publicly funded institutions. Decisions that govern the distribution of public sector services are issues of social justice (Fox, 2015).

Reflexivity and self-reflexivity can allow us to think about and understand our relationship with money and accounting, our underlying beliefs about how money should be spent and whether there are influences such as gender, politics, culture, education and parenting that might influence the financial decisions that we make. For example, female PEPs with budgetary responsibility might consider whether the women in our families have typically assumed the role of the financial decision makers and if not, how might this shape our perceptions and decisions in relation to the role? Are we trustworthy and responsible enough? What is it about our underlying beliefs that have led us to think this is the best use of public funds? To what extent have we examined and re-examined the choices that we make? Such beliefs from dominant discourses about gender may undermine practice and need to be challenged through self-reflexivity.

Conclusions

Ethical and responsible leadership is more important than ever in the current climate of public sector austerity, tough decision-making and traded EPSs. We have suggested that ethical leadership is about who and how we are as much as what we do. We have presented ideas from philosophy and systemic thinking, particularly reflexivity and self-reflexivity and suggested how they apply to aspects of leadership practice including self-care and the care of teams, supervision for all service members, developing team practice and making decisions whether they be financial or otherwise. We have focussd on understanding how these ideas can be applied to the self, as we were keen to illustrate how the ongoing nature of such processes informs our actions and interactions every day. We recognise that there are helpful tools and techniques, beyond the scope of this chapter, which can be learned by those who are interested.

References

Adriansen, H. K., & Knudsen, H. (2013). Two ways to support reflexivity: Teaching managers to fulfil an undefined role. *Teaching Public Administration, 31*(1), 108–123.

Atkinson, C., & Posada, S. (2019). Leadership supervision for managers of educational psychology services. *Educational Psychology in Practice, 35*(1), 1–16.

Archer, M. (2007). *Making our way through the world: Human reflexivity and social mobility.* Cambridge: Cambridge University Press.

Avey J. B., Wernsing, T. S., & Palanski, M. E. (2012). Exploring the process of ethical leadership: The mediating role of employee voice and psychological ownership. *Journal of Business Ethics, 107*(1), 21–34.

Beauchamp, T. L., & Childress, J. F. (2009). *Principles of biomedical ethics* (6th ed.). Oxford: Oxford University Press.

Bedell, G. (2016, February 27). Teenage mental health crisis: Rates of depression have soared in past 25 years. *The Independent.* Retrieved from https://www.independent.co.uk/life-style/ health-and-families/features/teenage-mental-health-crisis-rates-of-depression-have-soared- in-the-past-25-years-a6894676.html

British Psychological Society (BPS). (2009). *Code of ethics and conduct: Guidance published by the ethics committee of the British Psychological Society: Division of Educational and Child Psychology.* Leicester: BPS.

British Psychological Society (BPS). (2017). *Practice guidelines* (3rd ed.). Leicester; BPS.

British Psychological Society (BPS). (2018). *Ethical trading: Guidelines for practice for educational psychologists: Division of Educational and Child Psychology (DECP)* (2nd ed.). Leicester: BPS. Retrieved from https://www.bps.org.uk/member-microsites/division- educational-child-psychology/resources

Brown, B. (2018). *Dare to lead: Brave work. Tough conversations. Whole hearts.* London: Vermilion.

Brown, M. E., & Mitchell, M. S. (2010). Ethical and unethical leadership: exploring new avenues for future research. *Business Ethics Quarterly, 20*(4), 583–616.

Brown, M. E. & Trevino, L. (2006) Ethical leadership: A review and future directions. *The Leadership Quarterly, 17*(6), 595–616.

Brown, M. E., Trevino, L., & Harrison, D. A. (2005). Ethical leadership: A social learning perspective for construct development and testing. *Organizational Behaviour and Human Decision Processes, 97*(2), 117–134.

Burnham, J. (1992). Approach-method-technique: Making distinctions and creating connections. *Human Systems: The Journal of Systemic Consultation & Management, 3*, 3–26.

Cecchin, G. (1993). Workshop presentation. In B. Mason, Towards positions of safe uncertainty. *Human Systems: The Journal of Systemic Consultation & Management, 4*, 189–200.

Children and Families Act. (2014). Retrieved from http://www.legislation.gov.uk/ukpga/2014/6/contents/enacted

Cliffe, T., Beinart, H., & Cooper, M. J. (2014). Development and validation of a short version of the Supervisory Relationship Questionnaire. *Clinical Psychology and Psychotherapy, 23*(1), 77–156.

Cunliffe, A. L. (2009). The philosopher leader: On relationalism, ethics and reflexivity – A critical perspective to teaching leadership. *Management Learning, 40*(1), 87–101.

Cunliffe, A. L., & Jun, J. S. (2005). The need for reflexivity in public administration. *Administration and Society, 37*(2), 225–242.

Dallos, R., & Draper, R. (2015). *An introduction to family therapy: Systemic theory and practice.* New York: Open University Press.

Department for Education (DfE). (2010). *The importance of teaching: The Schools White Paper.* Crown copyright. Retrieved from https://www.gov.uk/government/publications/the-importance-of-teaching-the-schools-white-paper-2010

Department for Education & Department of Health (DfE & DoH). (2014). *Special educational needs and disability code of practice: 0–25 years. Statutory guidance for organisations who work with and support children and young people with special educational needs and disabilities.* Crown copyright. London: DfE & DoH. Retrieved from https://www.gov.uk/government/publications/send-code-of-practice-0-to-25

Department for Education & Department of Health & Social Care (DfE, DoH & SC). (2018). *Government response to the consultation on Transforming children and young people's mental health provision: A green paper and next steps.* Crown copyright. London: DfE & DoH & SC. Retrieved from https://assets.publishing.service.gov.uk/government/uploads/system/uploads/attachment_data/file/728892/government-response-to-consultation-on-transforming-children-and-young-peoples-mental-health.pdf

Eissenbeiss, S. A., & Brodbeck, F. (2014). Ethical and unethical leadership: A cross-cultural and cross-sectoral analysis. *Journal of Business Ethics, 122*(2), 343–359.

Ericsson, K. A. (2006). The influence of experience and deliberate practice on the development of superior expert performance. In K. A. Ericsson, N. Charness, P. J. Feltovich, & R. R. Hoffman (Eds.), *Cambridge handbook of expertise and expert performance* (pp. 685–705). Cambridge: Cambridge University Press.

Faris, J. (2012). Some reflections on process, relationship, and personal development in supervision. In D. Campbell & B. Mason (Eds.), *Perspectives on supervision* (pp. 88–109). London: Karnac.

Foucault, M. (1990). *The care of the self: The history of sexuality.* London: Penguin.

Fox, M. (2015). 'What sort of person ought I to be?' Repositioning EPs in light of the Children and Families Bill (2013). *Educational Psychology in Practice, 31*(4), 382–396.

Gillon, R. (1995). *Philosophical medical ethics.* Chichester: John Wiley & Sons.

Goldner, V. (1985). Feminism and family therapy. *Family Process, 24*(1), 31–47.

Hare-Mustin, R. T. (1984). A feminist approach to family therapy. In P. P. Rieker & E. Carmen (Eds.), *The gender gap in psychotherapy.* Boston, MA: Springer.

Health and Care Professions Council (HCPC). (2012). *Standards of conduct, performance and ethics.* London: HCPC.

Heifetz, R. (1994). *Leadership without easy answers*. Cambridge, MA: Harvard University Press.

HM Treasury. (2010). Spending review 2010. Retrieved from https://www.gov.uk/government/uploads/system/uploads/attachment_data/file/203826/Spending_review_2010.pdf

Kahneman, D. (2012). *Thinking fast and slow*. London: Penguin.

Keeney, B. P. (2002). *Aesthetics of change*. New York: Guilford Press.

Kennedy, E. K., Keany, C., Shaldon, C., & Canagaratnam, M. (2018). A relational model of supervision for applied psychology practice: professional growth through relating and reflecting. *Educational Psychology in Practice, 34*(3), 282–299.

Lamson, A., Meadors, P., & Mendenhall, T. (2014). Working with providers and healthcare systems experiencing compassion fatigue and burnout. In J. Hodgson, A. Lamson, T. Mendenhall, & D. R. Crane *(Eds.), Medical family therapy: Advanced applications* (pp. 107–123). New York: Springer.

Lang, P. W., Little, M., & Cronen, V. (1990). The systemic professional: Domains of action and the question of neutrality. *Human Systems: The Journal of Systemic Consultation & Management, 1*, 39–56.

Lepper, J. (2018, October 25). Increase in number of children at risk of abuse and neglect. *Children & Young People Now*. Retrieved from https://www.cypnow.co.uk/cyp/news/2005990/increase-in-number-of-children-at-risk-of-abuse-and-neglect

Martin, K., & Cullen, J. B. (2006). Continuities and extensions of ethical climate theory: A meta-analytic review. *Journal of Business Ethics, 69*(2),175–194.

Mason, B. (1993). Towards positions of safe uncertainty. *Human Systems: The Journal of Systemic Consultation & Management, 4*, 189–200.

Mason, B. (2012) The personal and the professional: Core beliefs and the construction of bridges across difference. In K. Ingra-Britt (Ed.), *Culture and reflexivity in systemic psychotherapy: Mutual perspectives*, London: Karnac.

Mason, B., & Sawyerr, A. (Eds.), (2002). *Exploring the unsaid: Creativity, risks and dilemmas in working cross culturally*. London: Karnac.

Moffatt, A., Ryan, M., & Barton, G. (2016). Reflexivity and self-care for creative facilitators: Stepping outside the circle. *Studies in Continuing Education, 38*, 29–46.

Moore, J. (2005). Recognising and questioning the epistemological basis of educational psychology practice. *Educational Psychology in Practice, 21*(2), 103–116.

Muturano, A. (2005). Executive education: On being a moral agent: Teaching business leaders to think ethically. *European Business Forum, 20*(Winter), 68.

Paré, D. A. (1996). *Culture and meaning: Expanding the metaphorical repertoire of family therapy*. New York: Wiley.

Pellegrini, D. W. (2009). Applied systemic theory and educational psychology: Can the twain ever meet? *Educational Psychology in Practice, 25*(3), 271–286.

Resick, C. J., Martin, G. S., Keating, M. A., Dickson, M. W., & Kwong Kwan, H. (2011).What ethical leadership means to me: Asian, American and European perspectives. *Journal of Business Ethics, 101*(3), 435–457.

Ricoeur, P. (1995). *Oneself as another*. Chicago: University of Chicago Press.

Rogers, M., & O'Bryon, E. (2008). Advocating for social justice: The context for change in school psychology. *School Psychology Review, 37*, 493–498.

Roth, S., & Weingarten, K. (1995). *Listening to, engaging, and expanding the story: Narrative couples therapy*. Presentation at Harvard Medical School Conference on Couples, Boston.

Sartre, J.-P. (1965/1993). *Essays in existentialism.* New York: Citadel Press, Kensington Publishing.

Sellick, C. (2011). Privatising foster care: The UK experience within an international context. *Social Policy & Administration, 45*(7), 788–805.

Shacklock, A., Manning, M., & Hort, L. (2011). Ethical climate type, self-efficacy, and capacity to deliver ethical outcomes in public sector human resource management. *Journal of New Business Ideas & Trends, 9*(2), 34–49.

Shotter, J., & Cunliffe, A. L. (2002). *Managers as practical authors: Everyday conversations for action.* In D. Holman & R. Thorpe (Eds.), *Management and language; The manager as practical author.* London: Sage.

Vetere, A., & Stratton, P. (2016). *Interacting selves: Systemic solutions for personal and professional development in counselling and psychotherapy.* New York: Routledge.

White, M., & Epston, D. (1990). *Narrative means to therapeutic ends.* New York: Norton & Company.

Wong, J. (2013). Self and others: The work of care in Foucault's care of the self. *Philosophy Today, 57*(1), 99–113.

4

Managing Change in an Educational Psychology Service
Janet Crawford

Introduction

In all teams, services and organisations, leaders, managers and the workforce are required to operate in a changing context. This changing context may require minor adjustments or much larger structural and operational responses. There are times when changes are imposed and on other occasions, change may be driven internally as part of the ongoing development and reflection of a learning organisation.

Educational Psychology Services (EPSs) are often situated within a larger organisation, such as a Local Authority (LA) and always work as part of a continually changing broader social, economic and political context. To survive and thrive as a healthy organisation requires EPSs to continually reflect on their practices, learning and moving forward in order to maintain relevance.

This chapter explores Theory of Change as an approach to change management that promotes positive change at strategic, operational and individual practitioner levels. It is an approach that applies psychology to understanding the process of change within the context of 'Service Leadership', identified as a key element of a quality service within the Division of Educational and Child Psychology (DECP) Quality Standards for Educational Psychology Service (British Psychological Society [BPS], 2019) strands on Leadership and Professional Practice.

Theory of Change methods are contrasted with more traditional logic models, making an argument that this approach has greater epistemological congruence with change in complex social organisations. Reference will also be made to learning from positive psychology approaches and Self-Determination Theory (SDT; Ryan & Deci, 2000), and the inclusion of a case study illustrating how this approach has been used in practice.

Why Think About Managing Change?

In accepting the dynamic nature of the world in which EPSs function service leaders are required to reflect on their approaches to managing change and developing positively. Managers of EPSs are applied psychologists, and as psychologists, reflecting on the

Leadership for Educational Psychologists: Principles & Practicalities, First Edition.
Edited by Julia Hardy, Charmian Hobbs and Mohammed Bham.
© 2020 John Wiley & Sons Ltd. Published 2020 by John Wiley & Sons Ltd.

process of change is one of our key professional skills. We should not only be interested that change happens but also in understanding the process of change and being able to explain the factors that helped or thwarted the process in order to continually move forward. A range of factors drive change for an organisation; these can be both positive and negative, top down or bottom up. However, a leader has a responsibility to move forward positively and to create the conditions that enable the organisation and all of its all members to flourish as best as possible and for all to be able to do their job well. The challenge is how to do this.

Application of Theory of Change methodologies can offer a tool for positive change management for leaders of EPSs which enables:

- All staff to have a clear and shared purpose that informs activity in the change process and beyond;
- The development of team confidence so that individuals know what they should be doing to contribute to good outcomes in sometimes challenging and turbulent times;
- Leaders to create the conditions that allows this to happen;
- The organisation to evaluate whether progress is being made towards change and development; and
- Information to be developed and used to communicate impact at all levels of the system.

Epistemological Stance

An important conceptual starting point in applying a Theory of Change approach is to recognise that services themselves are complex social organisations and that these social organisations are made up of people with differing perspectives, working within broader and complex contexts, also composed of many other people all with their own perspectives. This fluid and variable context has a bearing when selecting a valid approach for both service planning and evaluation.

A more positivist rational approach to the situation requires inputs, outputs and processes to have an immutable nature that does not match with complex social systems and their analysis. However, postpositivist, critical realist approaches argue that the theories or hypotheses generated by people in their social contexts can be seen as real tools which can aid understanding rather than somehow being used to test hypotheses in order to produce absolute objective truths. This stance recognises that social events and mechanisms are not fixed in the same way as physical events and that individual agents in the process influence both the activity and outcome in ways that cannot always be known at the outset (see, for example, Dewey, 1933 and Allen, Brown, Karanasios, & Norman, 2013). Theory of Change approaches are based on the premise that change in a social context is socially mediated, requiring an appreciation of the agency of all individuals within the system, and that the precise route and plan cannot be fully known at the start because of the complexity of unknown and uncontrollable factors. It also offers causal explorations of *why* change occurs that in turn support future planning, rather than merely describing that change has happened.

What Is Theory of Change?

In 1995 Carol Weiss (1995) began to elaborate a planning and evaluation process which recognised the complex and messy nature of change in a social context and is generally seen to be the first proponent of Theory of Change methods as a recognised approach. Over time Weiss' work has grown in influence and developed to include projects in the fields of education, social care and international development (see Stein & Valters, 2012).

In a Theory of Change process the stakeholder groups elaborate their goals and the conditions (or indicative outcomes of success) that are required for these goals to be met and then explore the interventions required to achieve these. During the process a map is developed where the likely causal connections between the different outcomes are illustrated and the assumptions of stakeholders, sometimes based on prior practice knowledge or research evidence, are explored. The resultant product is described as a 'Theory of Change' that is then subject to scrutiny and review through data collection and analysis in interim feedback loops.

The process is probably best described as a participatory collaborative method for service or project design and subsequent evaluation. The participatory element is crucial as it recognises that all stakeholders have views and perspectives of the world that will have an impact on the success of the project or service plan. It acknowledges that whilst the content of an intervention is necessary to the eventual outputs this is not sufficient. Theory of Change emphasises that the process of change is also a necessary element of achieving change in social contexts. In their application of Theory of Change, Pawson and Tilley (1997) describe how change is brought about by the interplay of the programme contents and the mechanisms that underpin it. These mechanisms crucially involve people, and it is the people and the theories that they bring that leads to sustained change.

Undertaking a Theory of Change Process

At first glance Theory of Change appears straightforward in form and is based on a five step approach beginning with the identification of long term organisational goals and backwards mapping a causal pathway to achieve those goals. It is a facilitated process and the role of the facilitator is crucial. It is also essential that all members of the organisation contribute to the process, including developing indicators that demonstrate progress and the actions that are required to bring about that change. The facilitator supports the explicit articulation of these steps and underlying assumptions enabling all stakeholders to be able to reflect on progress towards achieving goals, the mechanisms that have supported or thwarted change, which then informs next steps towards achieving the organisational goals.

Before starting all participants should have a basic overview of the principles of Theory of Change in order that they are able to participate meaningfully. From a practitioner educational psychologist's (EP's) point of view this is also a helpful step as it can offer a development opportunity to understand Theory of Change as a tool for more general EP practice. It is an excellent tool for facilitating the process of positive change for individual children and young people, school staff and families and projects where there are often complex narratives and assumptions that require exploration. Taplin and Clark (2012) describe the steps in the process:

Figure 4.1   Theory of Change process.

1) Identify the long-term goal or goals.

   The context for change may have been set for you or be driven internally by the needs of the organisation. It can often start with a question to be answered or a problem that needs to be solved and working together to understand the nature of the issue then leads to the elaboration of the goal. What is important at this stage is that all stakeholders develop a shared understanding of what the desired outcomes/goals actually mean and the assumptions underpinning them. The goal(s) needs to be positively framed, clear, concrete and understood. There is sometimes more than one goal set but general guidelines suggest no more than three.

2) Elaborate the preconditions that need to be in place to achieve this.

   This backward mapping exercise identifies the preconditions that are necessary to achieve the goal (i.e. what needs to be in place), drawing on the perspectives and narratives of the participants. This is an essential element of the process as the 'theories' of the participants are clarified, as are their assumptions and justifications that can have an impact on the success of the plan. It is important to avoid a natural rush to describe what action will be taken at this point, as what is required is to understand the intermediate steps on the way, the hypotheses and causal links in the chain that will get the organisation to its goals. There may be several pathways that lead towards the outcome. It is the facilitator's role to listen for, challenge and explore assumptions in the process.

3) Prioritise the interventions to achieve the desired change.

   At this point the participants can begin to explore the activities that will bring about change, that is, what are the various team members going to do that contributes to the desired change. Doing this at this point in the process should enable a visible and clear relationship between the activity and desired outcome, with participants able to articulate this relationship. These activities are likely to be at different points in the system, with some being dependent on others. Any hierarchical or causal relationships are also mapped which can help to inform the order in which activities are undertaken. It also enables all stakeholders to see how their actions link to the bigger picture and to others in the organisation.

4) Identify the indicators that measure progress towards the desired outcome and that will be used as part of the ongoing evaluation.

   Indicators should offer clear and measurable evidence that a goal or outcome is being met and are regularly reviewed within the organisation over time. There may be multiple indicators leading towards an outcome and indicators may be developed further later in the process of change.

5) Write up a narrative account to explain the logic.

   The process requires a facilitator/facilitators, is based on active exploration and discussion with the group, and can sometimes feel messy. Sticky notes and flipcharts are essential elements and at the end of the process the facilitator creates a record, usually in diagrammatic form, with an accompanying narrative to easily illustrate the developed 'Theory of Change'.

Taplin and Clark (2012) suggest in reviewing the logic you should be able to demonstrate that your Theory for Change is:

- Plausible – does it make sense?
- Achievable – is it realistic with the resources you have?
- Testable – can you evaluate your project?

Theory of Change and Logic Models

Logic models are also widely used as planning and monitoring tools. They are useful in that they enable a clear and logical approach to describing the steps on the way to achieve an outcome (see Clark & Anderson, 2004). They often start with a programme and describe a plan of inputs, activities and outputs leading to desired outcomes. The steps and outcomes are clearly described so it is possible to monitor whether the desired changes have occurred. However, such approaches have limitations when it comes to planning and evaluation in complex systems as their application assumes that all variables are known and can be planned for. Social contexts are much less predictable and one size does not fit all. They are inhabited by people with their own perspectives and theories, not all of which can be known at the outset, and which will almost certainly shift over time. Locally developed bespoke solutions are required.

Theory of Change methodology gathered momentum in recognition of the limitations of more traditional logic models and has gone on to offer value as a planning and evaluation tool in a range of complex national and international projects (James, 2011) as well as smaller scale projects. Theory of Change implicitly acknowledges a distributed leadership perspective (Harris, 2009), and the socially mediated nature of activity within complex social organisations. These approaches explain that human behaviour is locally contextualised and draws on the work of activity theorists (see Engeström, 2005) in terms of understanding social activity and change, describing that in the interaction of people something new, an additional element, is added which leads to a change in practice. Engeström discusses how dissonance in a system, often dissonance between the agents in the system, makes things happen. He also acknowledges the value of congruence between agents. As an evaluation framework Theory of Change can be seen as having its roots in locally based participatory action research (Dewey, 1933) where individuals work together to identify a problem, generate hypotheses that inform action, which is then subject to critical investigation in an iterative cycle. This is in contrast to traditional approaches which might draw summative conclusions against success criteria.

In describing the Theory of Change approach and its underpinning epistemological framework it is possible to see its merits as a tool for change management. However, this change management approach also offers an embedded method for service planning, evaluation and promoting staff motivation and engagement as part of the process of change, which resonates with positive psychological approaches and the principles of SDT which will be familiar to many EPs. Methods that support management practice aligned with the DECP Quality Standards strands of 'Professional Practice' and 'Leadership' (BPS, 2019).

Theory of Change as a Tool for Planning

More traditional logic models of change have been discussed as striving to define both the desired outputs and the inputs required to achieve this, assuming that all factors affecting change are known and can be controlled. Whilst this is appealing in so much as the resultant plan appears clear and logical, in complex social systems and organisations not all is known and there is seldom a linear route between input and output. Not least because of the varying narratives and assumptions of the actors and stakeholders in the process. As a planning tool traditional logic models often lack attention to the intermediate steps and causal links to the overall goal evidenced by the lack of interim feedback loops and more rigid nature.

In Theory of Change methods evaluation of progress towards the preconditions enables a greater dynamism and flexibility in planning, allowing the change theories to be revised on the basis of feedback. The explicit exploration by stakeholders of what is contributing to change is as important to next steps planning as the fact that change has happened. Whilst the intended outcomes might be driven externally, the plan to achieve them emerges as part of the participatory process and is legitimate as long as it satisfies the criteria of plausibility, achievability and testability described by Taplin and Clark (2012).

From a leadership perspective this does require comfort with a more distributed style of leadership acknowledging the interdependencies of agents in the system, again drawing on the work of activity theorists such as Engeström (see Harris, 2009). In this approach senior leaders in the organisation must enable and empower individuals in the organisation, having confidence that they understand what is required and using the feedback loop as a way of checking the integrity of the plan and contributions towards it. Whilst the approach is undoubtedly a led and managed one, this is not the same as a management-controlled system.

Theory of Change as an Evaluation Tool

One of the essential elements of Theory of Change is its inherent feedback loops. The indicators that relate to the interventions, that relate to the preconditions formed during the initial discussions, then go on to form the basis of data collection. Evaluation of this data informs whether progress is being made which then shapes what happens next as information about what is working, or not, is gathered. This is essentially practitioner action research and has merit at both an individual practitioner and organisational level.

Theory-based approaches to evaluation build on the premise that change in social contexts is underpinned by the activity undertaken by people in the system. Stame (2004) helpfully describes what she calls 'the black box' approach to evaluation suggesting that in theory-based evaluation one is not considering the input and output as you would in traditional positivist approaches to research, but rather it is the processes of change that are being explored. In exploring the links between events it is possible for managers and practitioners to understand their 'theories' and why something works or not and what was going on that supported it to happen. Stame drew on practitioner action research methodology in seeking the experiences of the stakeholders to evaluate practice. She describes how the 'black box' is full of theories (individual assumptions and understandings) that are brought to light in the process of exploration with members of a community. This also resonates with the work of psychodynamic practitioners, for example, Hanko (2002) who discuss the role of group narrative approaches in terms of informing future practice. In these approaches the nature of what is to be known is socially mediated and based on the multiple and collected constructions of activity by those in the community. The learning is ongoing and is based on the continual feedback and exploration loops.

Stame (2004) also describes how theory-based evaluation enables individuals in the process to explicitly articulate their assumptions and links between events. All in the organisation, including the individuals or smaller parts of an organisation, are clear about their role and contribution and whether they have achieved it. They are also more likely to be able to understand the barriers to lack of progress. As such this approach can lend itself to organisational evaluation and impact measures, as well as to individual practitioner supervision and development.

Theory-based evaluation approaches are continuing to grow in their reputation as a tool in the evaluation of community-based initiatives, some of which are multilayered and highly complex. For example, Dyson and Todd (2010) undertook an evaluation of the Full Service Extended Schools Initiative and Comic Relief commissioned an evaluation of their complex community initiatives (James, 2011) as they were explicitly interested both in what changes occurred and how those changes happened. In this type of evaluation a theory of change is built and is then subject to iterative systematic and critical challenge.

Theory of Change as a Tool to Support Staff Engagement and Motivation

Many change management approaches have the goals and needs of the organisation at the centre. However, Theory of Change methodology enables supporting and sustaining change and development at both the organisational and individual practitioner level. This aligns well with Self Determination Theory (SDT Ryan & Deci, 2000) and can achieve balance in meeting the needs of both the individual and the organisation.

SDT offers a broad framework for understanding human motivation and activity. As a leader in an EPS one is concerned with the motivation, well-being, commitment and reliability of individuals both for the individual's sake but also in terms of the health and productivity of the organisation. Ryan and Deci (2000), proponents of SDT, describe how individuals should be understood as active engagers within their community looking for fulfilment and self-coherence. The organisational culture that leaders create can facilitate or thwart this motivation.

The essential elements suggested in SDT for an individual to thrive are:

- Autonomy
- Competence
- Relatedness

Applying Theory of Change processes as a planning and evaluation tool has the potential to support these elements, offering an opportunity to meaningfully align individual and organisational goals in a way that enhances rather than thwarts motivation.

Autonomy is not about absolute freedom, in a work context this is more likely to relate to an endorsement of what needs to be done, an understanding of the rationale in order to work effectively.

Competence is making sure that individuals in the organisation have the knowledge and skills to succeed.

Relatedness refers to an individual feeling connected and valued and their views (or theories) respected well enough.

All of these elements are potentially supported in the steps of the Theory of Change process described previously.

In a management context this translates to an autonomy supportive environment rather than a controlling one. Development of SDT in a human resources management context (Rigby & Deci, 2018) is clear about the benefits of actively considering the *process* of engagement rather than engagement itself, resonant of the themes in Stame's (2004) developments of Theory of Change. Rigby and Deci (2018) describe a continuum of motivation (a 'Motivational Quotient') within a work context. Organisations that move away from 'thwarting' motivational elements such as external pressures in the form of rewards and threats, and internal pressures such as guilt and shame and move towards motivational enablers such as developing shared values (even though the tasks may not always be enjoyable the direction of travel is shared) are much stronger. The benefits of aligning organisational and individual motivational goals have also been shown to improve job satisfaction, task completion, worker trust and loyalty, well-being and attendance (Guntert, 2015; Williams et al., 2014)

Applying Theory of Change methodology enables a sufficient alignment of organisational and individual goals, has regard to the narratives and theories of participants in the process, supports connection with others in the organisation, and can support greater management confidence in staff acting with a degree of autonomy within the agreed framework.

EP Services: Understanding and Communicating Impact

Demonstrating impact as an EPS can be challenging but is necessary, not only to justify value in a climate of austerity but also in order to be confident that we contribute to positive change for children, young people and those who support their development. EP work rightly values the narratives, contributions and actions of all stakeholders in this process of change. However, if a more traditional product-based approach to impact evaluation is taken this can be challenging in terms of defining the particular contribution of the EP.

The Theory of Change method with its clear articulation of goals, preconditions, interventions and indicators of success offers an opportunity to illustrate the contribution of educational psychology to the process of achieving organisational outcomes. Exploring the important programme contents, causal links and processes should provide EPS leaders with the data to be able to articulate our contribution at the level of the EPS, individual practitioner and also at a wider profession level.

Case Study

The following case study illustrates how Theory of Change methods are being used in a large LA EPS. Whilst the initial impetus was to develop a new approach to service delivery as a consequence of significant structural changes within the wider organisation and service, what has developed is a Theory of Change that has informed high-level goals, planning, evaluation, as well as the leadership and management culture within the service.

Background

An earlier restructure within the LA had seen the EPS incorporated into locality teams with a matrix management model and loss of a broad, central EPS (see Chapter 2 for a discussion of matrix management approaches). Although there were merits in terms of EPs working within a broader multiagency team, further changes as a consequence of the challenging economic climate saw a reversal of earlier decisions and the reinstatement of a single, integrated EPS. This coincided with a change in the leadership and management structure and personnel within the EPS and a change in the funding arrangements including a requirement to income generate in order to maintain a broad offer for children and young people within the LA. Across the whole of the public sector, including in this LA and EPS, it was a time of significant change and turbulence.

Within the new management team of the EPS the first priority was to settle and develop the team enabling the service to respond collectively and positively to the changing context. It was essential to find a process that helped us to have a collective and coherent understanding of our role and contribution as a united LA EPS, to develop a plan to achieve this and for us as a service and as individual practitioners to be able to demonstrate our contribution and impact working towards achieving this. An approach that acknowledged the very varied experience of personnel in the service was also required.

Theory of Change offered an appropriate conceptual framework, which aligned with the needs of the service recognising that:

- Managing change requires planning.
- Activity in social contexts is socially mediated.
- Services are complex and operate within broader complex organisations requiring management tools and techniques that recognise this complexity.
- All actors in the system have agency.
- Systems should support the alignment of individual and organisational goals in order to achieve maximum service impact and individual job satisfaction and impact.
- In a dynamic and creative organisation all practitioners, at all points in the system, should routinely reflect on practice generating evidence for future action.

A service day was scheduled to develop initial planning. Of course, the process took much longer than a single day ....

Theory of Change Planning – How the Five Steps Were Followed

1) Identify the long-term goal or goals.

   The day began with a briefing session on Theory of Change methodology, and then working in groups and armed with sticky notes the groups began exploring the question 'What is the function of a LA EPS?'

   Most of the session was spent exploring this and terms such as well-being, achievement, attainment and independence emerged frequently. In addition, there was much discussion as to who were our clients and customers, topics sharpened by recent changes in funding.

   What emerged was explicit consensus that our role was to facilitate the inclusion of children and young people within their educational community. Whilst this was not an explicitly espoused goal of the LA it is a key feature of the Salamanca Statement (UNESCO, 1994) to which all directors of children and young people's services must have regard and as such was felt to be an implicit higher level goal of the LA.

   However, it was quickly apparent that the word 'inclusion' does not necessarily pass the test of being clear and concrete, and assumptions about what it meant and how we would know if we had achieved it required further interrogation.

2) Elaborate the preconditions that need to be in place to achieve this.

   A further session was spent exploring inclusion research, practice guidance and resources. Underpinning rationales and assumptions were discussed in order to achieve a working definition of the concept of inclusion that we all shared and understood. The session moved from abstract discussions about rights to a more local, operational understanding helped by referencing and modifying Booth and Ainscow's (2002) definition of inclusion.

   Booth and Ainscow (2002) described 'inclusion' as 'presence, participation, achievement and acceptance'. As a service we modified this to meet our needs and theories and established that the necessary conditions to achieve our goal were that children in their educational community should:

   • Be present
   • Participate
   • Achieve
   • Belong

   By the end of the second session there was agreement as to what the term inclusion meant for us as a group and what the essential preconditions described previously meant in terms of the inclusion of children and young people.

   What we required next was to translate this into EP activity.

3) Prioritising the interventions to achieve the desired change.

   From this all team members were able to discuss what actions they were, or would be, taking that would promote these. The Currie matrix (Scottish Executive, 2002) was used as a prompt to consider the range of activity areas that EPs were engaged in at leadership, management and operational points of the system. As a group we discussed how all activity undertaken should link causally to the preconditions. We tested out activities we were typically engaged in, making sure we were able to focus the activity directly to the preconditions. EP activity required clear prior thought about purpose. For example, no longer was it acceptable just to attend a review meeting without thinking – what is my purpose here? How does my activity actively link to and promote one or more of the preconditions? As a strategic manager hoping to attract funding from commissioners for a resilience project – ask how does my activity link to and promote the agreed preconditions? It was agreed that this test could and should be applied to all service activity including service days, various meetings and direct work with children and young people, their families and other professionals.

4) Identify the indicators that measure progress towards the desired outcome and that will be used as part of the ongoing evaluation.

This element of the process has proved to be more of a challenge as the world beyond the EPS was composed of many others, all with their theories about what inclusion is and is not. However, from an EPS perspective we have been able to use feedback loops to evaluate impact and progress towards the agreed goal at an individual EP and service organisation level.

a) Individual EPs.

When planning work individual EPs explore with schools and settings their needs and plan using a slightly adapted version of the Currie matrix (Scottish Executive, 2002) and data sets relating to the school including attendance data, special educational needs and disability rates, in-year transfers, exclusions and funding. The planning document explicitly references the four preconditions of inclusion. At the end of the school year the EP reflects with school staff about the work that has been undertaken, how this has contributed to the goal of inclusion, what processes were helpful or not and the evidence base for these considerations.

The same questions also feature regularly in each supervision as part of 'practice reflection' with the same questions being explored in relation to a piece of work brought by the supervisee. This is in line with DECP Quality Standards (BPS, 2019) with all members of the EP team encouraged to reflect on and develop their practice as part of an organisation that values high achievement and promotes an effective learning environment.

b) Service level

At a whole service level the reviews from individual EPs are collated along with results of an annual survey which asks similar questions of school leaders and special educational needs co-ordinator (SENCOs). The results are explored and themes identified which contribute to end of year service internal review and reporting to more senior leaders in the LA. Again, the headings of presence, participation, achievement and belonging offer a framework for this review and reporting. The results of the thematic analysis informs the service continuing professional development (CPD) programme, service delivery and promotional material. More recently in-year online feedback methods have been introduced to offer more responsive feedback loops relating to specific involvements.

Impact discussions remain high on the agenda and further work is underway to develop approaches that enable the views of children, young people and their families about inclusion and EP practice to be better understood.

The activity of individual EPs is increasingly forming a body of practice evidence for the service. From a management perspective these impact reflections inform next steps planning and enable the contributions of the individual and organisation to be considered alongside our Theory of Change plan and any changes and developments to the plan are informed by this feedback.

5) Write up a narrative account to explain the logic.

After the initial events, service documentation was developed to summarise and share our vision and activity. In practice, these documents have been used more often to describe to others what we are doing rather than for internal use. It has been the process of ongoing exploration and articulation of key actions rather than the product that has been more helpful to developing practice.

Summary and Discussion

Utilising the Theory of Change methodology has given a helpful, conceptually appropriate structure to the leadership and management of the service, starting with change management but also importantly including planning and evaluation in the service as part of an action research cycle. This research cycle applies to the service as a whole and to the practitioners within. It is revisited frequently as a process by individual practitioners, and as a service usually towards the end of the academic year when collating evaluation reflections, and at the beginning of the year as planning and CPD priorities are set.

It has also supported the sense of competence, autonomy and relatedness within the service, as described in SDT. The service maintains better than typical sickness absence rates when compared with other teams in the directorate, and our recruitment and retention rates are also healthy, with a typical vacancy rate of less than 5% in a service which has seen an establishment growth of approximately 40% in 4 years. These data suggest that from a management perspective paying attention to the elements of SDT may have contributed to a healthy organisation.

The question of whether we are impacting on positive inclusion beyond service activity is more challenging. Although the goal of inclusion has been explored within the EPS the participatory requirements of Theory of Change methods have not yet sufficiently involved all partners. Whilst it is increasingly part of the language of EPs in their conversations and explorations with schools, parents and young people, a broader piece of work is required across the local area. The hope is that this will help to develop shared understandings of what inclusion means to different stakeholders so that we are more able to plan together and understand how together we can work to achieve our goals.

Whilst the process has been very helpful, it is not complete and in reality may never be complete. However, what it continues to provide is coherence and clarity about our function, helps plan steps on the way to achieving our goals and a tool to reflect on how we are doing. There are likely to be many next steps and crucially these will include engaging more broadly with other stakeholders across the local area using this Theory of Change as tool for planning and evaluation.

Conclusion

The Theory of Change approach described in this chapter draws on fundamental concepts in applied psychology as they relate to complex social organisations. It recognises the dynamic and socially mediated nature of EP activity and embeds change management in the broader context of a learning organisation which has a clear purpose. This in turn informs service delivery with plans developed and refined in the light of ongoing feedback at both an individual and organisational level and can support staff well-being and motivation. Utilising these methods in EPSs has the potential to offer support to every aspect of day-to-day operations, not as an occasional occurrence, but with general application in support of achieving quality standards in EPS leadership.

References

Allen, D.K., Brown, A., Karanasios, S., & Norman, A. (2013). How should technology mediated organisational change be explained? A comparison of the contributions of critical realism and activity theory. *MIS Quarterly, 37*(3), 835–854.

Booth, T., & Ainscow, M. (2002). *Index for inclusion: Developing learning and participation in schools.* Bristol: Centre for Studies in Inclusive Education.

British Psychological Society. (2019). *Quality Standards for Educational Psychology Services. Division of Educational and Child Psychologists.* Leicester: BPS. Retrieved from https://www.bps.org.uk/member-microsites/division-educational-child-psychology/resources

Clark, H., & Anderson, A. A. (2004). Theories of change and logic models: Telling them apart. Presented at the American Evaluation Association conference, Atlanta, Georgia.

Dewey, J. (1933). *How we think: A restatement of the relation of reflective thinking to the educative process.* Boston: Houghton Mifflin.

Dyson, A., & Todd, L. (2010). Dealing with complexity: Theory of change evaluation of full service extended schools initiative. *Journal of Research and Methodology in Evaluation, 33*(2), 119–134.

Engeström, Y. (2005). *Developmental work research: expanding activity theory in practice.* Berlin: Lehmanns Media.

Guntert, W. T. (2015). The impact of work design, autonomy support and strategy on employee outcomes. A differentiated perspective on self-determination theory at work. *Motivation and Emotion, 39,* 74–87.

Hanko, G. (2002). Making psychodynamic insights accessible to teachers as an integral part of their professional task. *Psychodynamic Practice, 8*(3), 375–389.

Harris, A. (2009). *Distributed school leadership: Developing tomorrows leaders.* London: Routledge.

James, C. (2011). *Theory of change review: A report commissioned by Comic Relief.* New York: ActKnowledge.

Pawson, R., & Tilley, N. (1997). *Realistic evaluation.* London: Sage.

Rigby, C. S., & Deci, E. I. (2018). Self-determination theory in human resource development: New directions and practical considerations. *Advances in Developing Human Resources, 20*(2),133–147.

Ryan, R. M., & Deci, E. L. (2000). Self determination theory and the facilitation of intrinsic motivation, social development and well being. *American Psychologist, 55*(1), 68–78.

Scottish Executive. (2002). *Review of provision of Educational Psychology Service in Scotland.* Edinburgh: Scottish Executive.

Stame, N. (2004). Theory based evaluation and types of complexity. *Evaluation, 10*(1), 58–76.

Stein, D., & Valters, C. (2012). *Understanding theory of change in international development.* London: The Justice and Security Research Programme LSE.

Taplin, D. H., & Clark, H. (2012). *Theory of change basics: A primer on theory of change.* New York: Act Knowledge.

UNESCO. (1994). The Salamanca Statement and Framework for Action on Special Needs Education. Adopted by the World Conference on Special Needs Education: Access and Quality. Salamanca, Spain.

Weiss, C. (1995). Nothing as practical as a good theory: Exploring theory-based evaluation for comprehensive community initiatives for children and families. In J. Connell, A. Kibish, L. Schott, & C. Weiss (Eds.), *New approaches to evaluating community initiatives.* Washington DC: Aspen Institute.

Williams, G. C., Halvari, H., Niemiec, C. P., Sorebo, O., Olafsen, A. H., & Westbye, C. (2014). Management support for basic psychological needs, somatic burden and work related correlates. A self determination theory perspective. *Work &Stress, 28*, 404–419.

5

Women in Leadership

Charmian Hobbs and Mandy Owen

Research into leadership is extensive with a smaller but significant section concerned with leadership and gender. In both of these areas there is almost no research directly related to applied psychologists and what might be the most relevant approaches to examining and enhancing leadership practice among psychologists. This chapter considers the discourses around leadership and what impact, either positive or negative, these discourses have on women in leadership roles in general and as they relate to the profession of educational psychology. It considers the presence or absence of gender in leadership theories, the different ways of theorising gender within leadership, the evaluative stances that are used to assess movement towards gender equality and what may be supportive action for women leaders within the profession.

Firstly Numbers!

In 2016, women's gross hourly earnings were on average 16.2% below those of men in the European Union (EU) (Eurostat, 2018). In professional occupations in the UK, the gender pay gap was 11.7% (Office for National Statistics, 2018) with a decrease of 0.5% from the previous year. This presents strong evidence that women are less likely to be earning salaries associated with the more highly remunerated posts. Women remain heavily underrepresented at the higher levels of academia in the UK (Murphy, Bishop, & Sigala, 2014) and similarly within the United States where women outnumber men within psychology professions, they still continue to lack equity with their male colleagues when it comes to money, power and status (Fassinger, 2017). Why does this continue to be the case despite equality legislation and the rising numbers of highly qualified women psychologists? The situation in psychology is no different from that in the majority of other fields of work. Women are underrepresented in leadership roles internationally and nationally (UNESDOC, 2018). Whilst there are strong moves to address this concern, it stubbornly remains in place.

On the other hand, women practitioners outnumber men by a ratio of almost 9:1 in English Educational Psychology Services (EPSs) (Truong & Ellam, 2014). The research on the educational psychologist workforce published in March 2019 showed that in England the gender profile of educational psychologists (EPs) in 2018 was 83% female. This situation will not change in the near future as women now outnumber men on degree courses and psychology has the second largest gender divide (Universities and Colleges Admissions Service, 2016). In associated fields such as directors of Children and Adult Services (Association of Directors of Children's Services, 2019) data show a 7:8 ratio in favour of women and in educational leadership head teachers are now two thirds female (Department for Education [DfE], 2018). So is there now beginning to be a gender bias towards women in some related professional fields?

There can be no doubt that the presence of women within the workforce has changed considerably over the last decades. In most countries men tend to participate in labour markets more than women, but all over the world women of working age participating in work has increased. This perhaps surprisingly is attributable to the increased participation of married women (Ortiz-Ospina & Tzvetkova, 2017). However, within the UK, women are more likely to be in low-paid sector jobs than their male counterparts and even within 'professional occupations', where women form 45% of full-time workers, they are likely to earn 11% less than men. Meanwhile, men are more likely than women to work in highly paid occupations, like managers, directors and senior officials, where women earn 16% less per hour on average (Office for National Statistics, 2017). Women working full time as professionals in the public sector earn 5% less than men (Office for National Statistics, 2017). The changes in working patterns for women have not yet brought about greater equality in pay or greater presence in higher status jobs. In the words of Beverley Alimo-Metcalfe (2010) when reviewing the developments in women and leadership from 1995 there is little to celebrate. Jewel and Bazeley (2018) underline this view:

> 'Women are still significantly under-represented in positions of power. This picture is changing but the pace of change remains far too slow. The inequality we find in the data is stark. It suggests that women are still being systematically excluded from the institutions which govern our public and political life and from the most powerful private sector corporations. Some women, for example, Black, Asian and Minority Ethnic (BAME) women, or disabled women, are even less likely to be represented.
>
> ...the collated sum of this data makes for depressing reading. In only two areas of public life identified were women equally represented (or close to it) – appointments to public bodies, and the Shadow Cabinet. Women also make up 74% of the top 20 magazine's editors. Otherwise, women remain at less than 45% representation across the board – and substantially below that proportion in many cases'. (p. 2)

So why?

Number Crunching

Sustainable Goal 5 of the United Nations (2016) is 'Achieve gender equality and empower all women and girls'. It sets out a number of targets including *'Ensure women's full and effective participation and equal opportunities for leadership at all levels of decision-making in political, economic and public life'*. One indicator of progress towards this target is *'proportion of women in managerial positions'*. The preceding section clearly suggests that progress so far in relation to this goal has been limited. The strategy of considering the implementation of equal opportunity legislation and monitoring the presence or absence of women in certain categories has been the mainstay of practices to support changes towards gender equality, but is this approach enough? Under the Equality Act (2010) there are a number of protected characteristics that cannot affect your chance of securing a job, and one of these is gender. However, you cannot 'benefit' from one of these characteristics through positive discrimination – that is, someone gives you a job because of a protected characteristic. That is illegal. Some have suggested positive action, which would include such initiatives as mentoring of particular groups, and others have gone further to suggest that quotas rather than targets are needed (Thomson Reuters, 2018). The Labour Party in England has worked with all-women short lists since 1997 and this has significantly increased the number of female Labour MPs. However, quotas are controversial as both men and women argue they do not want to be seen as securing a position because of a gender quota.

> 'Continued research is needed to determine how exactly gender quotas impact substantive representation in different institutional environments. Existing evidence demonstrates how quotas can change attitudes through providing information to reduce statistical discrimination and increasing the confidence of female constituents or leaders. An important area of future research will be on direct empowerment effects'. (Pande & Ford, 2011, p. 28)

Many institutions now list a whole range of actions to improve gender equality such as targeted advertising, bespoke career advice, encouragement to seek promotion, mentoring, benchmarking and auditing (see for example Foreign and Commonwealth Office, 2017); however, the gender gap remains. Unconscious bias is often cited as a major influence in decision-making. Indeed this is highlighted for practitioner psychologists in the recent edition of British Psychological Society (BPS) Practice Guidelines (2017) but applies equally to recruitment and selection procedures and the accompanying organisational culture. Unconscious bias refers to views and opinions based on background, cultural environment and personal experience. We are unaware of these prejudices but apply them within our everyday activities. Research has found that bias can heavily influence recruitment and selection decisions. Moss-Racusin, Dovidio, Brescoll, Graham, & Handelsman (2012) randomly assigned candidates for a senior manager post to a male or female gender with the same application information. Male candidates were far more likely to be successful with either male or female selectors. The now famous case study of Heidi/Howard (McGinn & Tempest, 2000) emphasised the clear bias towards appointing men over women.

So a range of goals, targets, quotas and positive action have not yet enabled a significant shift in gender equality. We would argue that there are more pervasive discourses disturbing the way in which women are able to achieve leadership positions within our society. These discourses are considered in the next sections.

Absence

In Barbara Kingsolver's book *Unsheltered* (2018), she writes about Mary Treat. You are very unlikely to have heard of her and Kingsolver herself says, 'Mary Treat was a nineteenth century biologist whose work deserves to be better known' (p. 463). Mary Treat corresponded extensively with Darwin and other natural scientists about plant life. Her work was published widely. However, she is absent from the history of the biological sciences. Absence is a familiar story for women in probably all fields of work. When Donna Strickland won the Nobel Prize for physics in 2018, the first female physics winner in 55 years, you wouldn't have been able to find any reference to her in Wikipedia. The oversight has once again highlighted the marginalisation of women in science and gender bias at Wikipedia and beyond. Given this narrative, it is then perhaps not surprising that women are faring less well than men in positions of leadership.

This absence is evident in leadership theory, especially early leadership theory. Understanding leadership is a slippery process, in that there are many differing and changing definitions. Alimo-Metcalfe and Alban- Metcalfe (2001) strongly suggest that when considering any research into leadership it is as well to ask some key questions about the context, background and agenda of the researchers. This is simply to emphasise the shifting approaches to studies on leadership. Early approaches can loosely be organised into the 'trait or great man approach', the 'behavioural approach', and the 'situational approach'. The trait approach assumed that leaders are born with particular characteristics that differentiate them from nonleaders. This idea was taken from the 'great man theory' in which leaders are born not made and by definition are male and upper class. Although there is no evidence to support the relationship between particular characteristics and leadership, and empirical studies were largely abandoned in the 1950s, it is possible to see the continuation of such ideas in the search for the male and female brain and the continuing arguments for and against the biological and psychological differences between men and women (see Fine, 2018, for a discussion of this). This view of gender difference still permeates much popular discourse about women's capabilities. Behavioural approaches took a somewhat opposite view in that it championed the view that leaders are made not born. It looked to explore leaders' behaviour in relation to task ('getting things done') and relational ('getting people comfortable'). The behaviours were developed from studying current leaders' behavior and drawing together styles of leadership which were seen to be the most successful. Again the search for the universal effective set of leadership behaviours proved elusive although the approach is still evident today in, for example, 'the leadership behavioural framework' (University of Kent, 2016). This strongly suggests that leaders should demonstrate a set of particular behaviours to distinguish them from nonleaders. Although the recent frameworks are much more sophisticated, it should still be remembered that the behaviours identified were initially drawn from research into leaders of the 1950s and 1960s who were male. Situational (or contingency) leadership acknowledged a relationship between leadership style and the characteristics of those who are being managed. Simply put leaders are more effective in some situations than others but this still related to internal traits or behaviours of both leaders and followers. These leadership theories all present a transactional model in which the leader and followers operate on a reward-based model. Leaders use a range of incentives, salary, benefits, etc. to encourage employees to achieve an already ascribed outcome. They sit more easily into an understanding of management whose purpose is to maintain order, predictability and the status quo. Within these early theories it is hard to find any reference to gender.

Following the turbulence created by the oil crisis in the 1970s, there was a recognition that organisations needed to be flexible and adaptable if they were going to succeed. Previous models of leadership based on stability and consistency were replaced by ideas around the 'transforming leader'. This kind of person presented as articulating a vision, showing passion and charisma and shaping the culture of the organisation. *In Search of Excellence* by Peters and Waterman (1982) is perhaps the most well known of all approaches in driving ideas about the role of the 'transforming leader'. This inspirational approach was seen as superior to previous models of leadership because it brought about greater satisfaction and higher performance. The focus was on chief executive officers and very senior managers, almost all of whom were male and probably white. This 'heroic' model of leadership did not take account of leadership in smaller scale enterprises where leaders were in more direct contact with their workforce nor did they acknowledge the growing feminist literature being published at that time which argued that the experience of men and women in organisations was very different.

Normalising Judgments

Although leadership theory has moved on (of which more later), it is important to consider the background to the development of ideas about leadership. The research is decontextualized and depoliticized. It ignores the social and cultural expectations and stereotypes that are associated with gender and how such normative gendered assumptions shape institutional and individual practice. Foucault (1991) introduced ideas about normalising judgments. The '*normalising judgment*' involves establishing what are the 'normal' or standard behaviours and practices for an individual and those outside such norms are viewed as abnormal. These norms are then maintained and disciplined by the overall group which Foucault called 'modern power'. You do not need an external threat to maintain conformity; the group expectations maintain accepted standards. There is a strong link here to intersectionality theory where oppression succeeds in dominating by functioning at multiple and interlocking layers of society that combine to perpetuate the interests of privileged members, whether their privilege is based on race, gender, class, or other categories. It is a theory that takes into account sociological, organisational, interpersonal and intrapersonal factors (Collins, 2000).

So returning to leadership theory, the lens is male and leadership characteristics are associated with men. Conversely, characteristics associated with women are not seen as appropriate for leadership. In Charol Shakeshaft's (1987) words:

> 'We are left wondering why if gender is not the overriding explanation of a profession structured according to sex, why are men managers and women teachers? How is it that women, more than men, are in positions low on power and opportunity? Why is it that teaching is a high opportunity profession for men but not for women?' (p. 87)

Although the position of women has improved over the last 3 decades since this publication, it highlights the failure to notice gender as a key part of any theory. 'Most of the decisions affecting the largest number of people in our society are made by homogeneous groups. Even today the closer to the top you go, the whiter, more male, more heterosexual, more middle-aged and middle class the group looks' (Kline, 1999, p. 87).

Silence

> 'That's an excellent suggestion, Miss Triggs. Perhaps one of the men here would like to make it'.

Mary Beard (2017, p. 7) notes this Punch cartoon in her recent book *Women and Power*. She argues, drawing on classicist knowledge, that the silencing of women was an essential part of growing up as a man. This could be literal, as in the removal of the tongue but equally disabling by describing the female voice as high pitched and strident or women speaking out in public as 'unnatural freaks'. Does this matter? Well yes because this idiom persists today and subverts women's authority to speak and be heard. As long as voice itself is gendered then women's presence and possibility of influence are limited. Similarly Pat Barker's (2018) *Silence of the Girls*, a retelling of the Iliad through the experience of the women, highlights that although they are not entirely silent, the women speak only to lament their dead son, lost home, ruined city and own freedom. So when women contribute they are challenged both on the style of their speech and their authority to make a contribution. As much as women are silenced, women also self-silence. They do not speak out about discrimination, careful not to place themselves as challenging of more powerful superiors. Perhaps the most marked example of both silence and the strength to act is the 'MeToo' movement. It has taken years for women to speak out about the expectation and practice within the film and related industries which has prevented many from moving into this career never mind leadership roles. However, women are now 'speaking out' and some are being heard. Luo (2016) cites the assumptions that women can make about their potential career paths. She notes that women can debar themselves from seeking senior leadership positions, believing that commitments or obligations to others such as family will interrupt their career path, that senior positions will not provide for their need for a work–life balance or that their value culturally is represented in presentation rather than leadership. Such assumptions prevent women for seeking and speaking out about their potential contribution to leadership.

Ambition

It has been argued that women lack ambition (Fels, 2004). This is seen in research that suggests women apply for less jobs than men, wait longer to apply for promoted posts and are reluctant to seek leadership positions unless they feel fully equipped. Sheryl Sandberg (2013) urges women to stand against this questioning of capabilities and to *lean-in* to the corporate world. Men are more likely to reach out for opportunities/projects. Women are more cautious about role-changing and seeking challenges. The many negative feelings associated with taking on a leadership position discussed in Chapter 2 emphasise this uncertainty.

Caring responsibilities are often cited as a reason for this apparent lack of ambition. It remains the case that women continue to both see themselves and be seen as the main carers for their children and for elderly relatives. It is perhaps not remarkable that women are concerned to provide the best parental support for their children and that this can interrupt a career path. It is remarkable though that this is normalised as both expected and laden with guilt. The view that women are more 'naturally' capable of caring is widely shared and that mothers should be at home rather than at work (or at least not full time) still endures. A quick search of Google brings up numerous sites that offer advice for 'working mothers' such as 'Top ten tips for family-work balance'. There are sites considering working fathers; however, these are largely focussed on the impact of fatherhood in the workplace rather than the relationship between home and work. It is the case that traditional working patterns are changing with more flexibility for both men and women in the workplace, particularly those with professional skills. However, the different entitlements in parental leave and remuneration do contribute to the likelihood that new mothers will take more time away from work than their male partners and this creates an uneven gender balance in parental roles. Men are reluctant to take parental leave as they believe, probably rightly, that this will affect their career prospects, because it does for women. The provision of childcare within the UK is both expensive and limited which further affects the possibility of effectively managing family and work. Although working practices are changing with more part-time work, working from home and self-employment, this does not appear to be improving the family–work balance for women. Technology which might have been seen as providing support for innovative practice has instead largely invaded home with work. Women still do 60% of the housework (Office for National Statistics, 2016). 'Mental Load: A Feminist Comic' by Emma (2018) clearly highlights the gender imbalance with cartoons noting, 'You only had to ask' when women complain that 'things' haven't been done. Women continue to do the 'worry work' that is keeping track of what needs to be done and when.

As well as frequently taking the lead role in parenting women are also more likely to take on a caring role with elderly relatives (Carers UK, 2016). Caring falls particularly on women in their 40s, 50s and 60s. One in four women aged 50–64 has caring responsibilities for older or disabled loved ones. This can be a time when women are more able to move into leadership positions but can be faced with both parental and older relative responsibilities.

So then are women less ambitious? Do they choose to put more time into the home at the expense of promotional opportunities in the workplace? We would argue that the expectations of women (which have become part of the way we think about work patterns) are gendered. Women and paid work, especially mothers and paid work, are viewed in a very different way from men and paid work.

Style

Numerous researchers (see Eagly, Johannesen-Schmidt, & van Engen (2003) for meta-analysis) have looked at differences in leadership style between men and women. Women are seen as supportive, nurturing, connected and relational as opposed to the more direct and decisive style associated with men. Men focus on achieving success; women put more effort into creating a positive group effort. However, there is considerable pressure to conform to accepted feminised behavior within the workplace. If women behave competitively or forcefully they are often viewed negatively and acting 'like a man'. This persistent stereotyping demonstrates the double standards that permeate leadership for men and for women. Women are expected to show leadership styles that are associated with masculine traits but may then be penalised for doing so. Ideas around 'style' and gender have largely ignored the socially constructed views of leadership. In particular these discussions draw on leadership theory that suggests a range of skill sets can be learnt in order to become a more effective leader. However, a postmodern

> 'conceptualization defines leadership as the joint property of the group and elevates followers to the role of collaborators. Such a definition downplays the importance of leadership as a specialized activity that is separable from management and, instead, emphasizes the collaborative, relational process of leadership'. (Watson, 2016, p. 6)

Nancy Kline in *Time to Think* (1999) stresses the importance of developing a Thinking Environment and that

> 'from the beginning of their life men are taught, in the name of their manhood, to divest their behavior of all ten components of a Thinking Environment. They are not supposed to give quality attention to people. They are told to control, not to be at ease. They must criticize, not appreciate. They are not allowed to cry. Women, on the other hand, from the beginning of their life, and in the name of their womanhood, are allowed to retain Thinking Environment qualities'. (p. 187)

Programmes such as Insights (and the C-me colour profiling, https://colour-profiling.com/) are increasingly being used by businesses and public sector organisations to help individuals, teams and the wider organisation to harness natural talent and build long-term success. The focus of the Insights programme is about increasing self-awareness, making the best of the strengths we already have, and working on challenges. The focus is not on gender differences but on differences of style and the interplay of different styles. When people can take an honest look at their personal style, they can start to ask vital questions such as 'What kind of leader am I now and how can I be better'.

Power

Power is usually seen as the influence that comes with higher status or authority such that individuals or groups are able to direct others who do not share their position. Using this description, women define power differently from men in leadership positions. Women see power as getting things done through collaboration and consensus, whereas men see power as the ability to lead through having greater knowledge or information around them.

Women define power as 'power to', that is, the ability to empower others to make their own decisions collaboratively and carry them through collectively and inclusively. Men may however view power as 'power over' others such that they can command or convince others to act in the desired direction.

Power can also be viewed in a Foucauldian (Foucault, 1991) sense in which power becomes an accepted way of being within a particular society or culture. In this sense there are many accepted 'truths' that remain unchallenged because they are seen as normal. This power then monitors what is considered valuable to research and whose views should be acknowledged. Given that discourses about women are often absent and silent then the power of women is very limited in making their presence felt within leadership circles. However, because 'truths' are not facts but socially accepted ways of understanding, this also gives rise to possible action. The absence and silence of women can be challenged so that women's experience is no longer submerged, excluded, or generalised into men's experience. By making women and men aware of marginalising practices they can be challenged.

Intersectionality

Intersectionality is important here. Experiences are not homogeneous. Ethnicity, gender, age, class and disability all have an impact on lived experiences. So although we are talking about women and leadership the impact of different narratives interact and potentially oppress in different ways. Considering ethnicity, Gillborn, Rollock, Warmington and Demack (2016) argue that 'The overwhelming view among stakeholder interviewees is that race inequality is no longer taken seriously as an issue by national government' (p. 4). Similarly David Lammy (Banerjee, 2018) stated that 'For this government, race has fallen off the agenda' (para. 1). A recent report by Rollock (2019) concludes that 'Black female Professors experience a messy, convoluted and protracted path to Professorship that is characterised by a lack of transparency and fairness,' which includes 'racial stereotyping and racial microaggressions' (p. 4). Hill (2016) concludes that for women of colour leadership is particularly elusive and furthermore existing research for the most part overlooks women of colour. Hill notes that racial and gender stereotypes overlap to create powerful barriers such that the obstacles faced by white women and women of colour can differ considerably. The impact of additive and intersecting combinations of protected characteristics that result in dual/multiple discriminations are yet to be charted, though Showunmi, Atewologun and Bebbington's (2016) use of an intersectional framework demonstrates 'that socio-demographic identities should be considered simultaneously in order to challenge universalist, gender and ethnic neutral assumptions of leadership' (Fuller, 2017, p. 6). For many people with a disability, the path to leadership can be fraught with challenges. Todd (2018) notes that this was her own experience working within disabled people's organisations (DPOs). Within the gendered structures discussed in the preceding sections, women with disabilities experience these expectations along with societal views about disability. Structures and systems are often antithetical to those with a disability and practices are often seen as 'an add on' to those available to the nondisabled. It is essential to highlight the social construction of gender, ethnicity and disability such that women can examine how they are defined by the cross-cutting interests of race, class, sexual identity etc. to confront how these constructions enable or disable voice and power.

Newer Leadership Theories

The 'heroic' model, though still very much in evidence (see for example Stanley's [2017] critique of the hero model for headteachers which has been current as an answer for 'failing schools') has been challenged in the early twenty-first century, not least because of the catastrophic failure of a number of large organisations (cf Enron, The Financial Crash) but also in recognition of its limitations, which are

- The dominance of US research to the exclusion of a more global perspective
- The focus on very senior staff which did not necessarily relate to lower levels of management or leadership
- The absence of any consideration of day-to-day interaction between leaders and staff who were in regular and frequent contact
- The focus on the views of senior leaders and the absence of the views of staff
- The failure to consider gender or diversity

A more favoured model that has taken hold is that of 'employee engagement'. This is a 'relational' model that considers a two-way interaction between employee and employer.

> 'Increasing employee engagement is highly dependent on leadership and establishing two-way communication where people's work and views are valued and respected'. (Scottish Executive, 2007, p. 56)

This model recognises that effective leadership does not reside solely in an individual but in the relationship between leader and staff. The aim is to develop a more motivated and participating workforce by acknowledging and harnessing their skills, ideas and knowledge to improve outcomes. In this context a leader behaves very differently from the characteristics associated with the 'heroic model'. Alimo-Metcalfe and Alban-Metcalfe (2001) have developed and researched a model within the UK context and including the public sector which takes forward the ideas about the nature of leadership within the context of a model of 'employee engagement'. They outline the characteristics of their view of leadership as:

> 'First, the emphasis is not on heroism but on serving and enabling others to display leadership themselves. It is not about being an extraordinary person, but rather a somewhat *ordinary, vulnerable and humble* or at least a very open accessible and transparent individual.
>
> Second, it contains a persistent theme of team working, collaboration and 'connectedness', and of *removing barriers to communication and ideas* whether between individuals at different levels, or in different teams and departments, or with outside 'stakeholders' and partners. It consistently echoes the desire to see *the world through the eyes of others*, and to take on board their concerns, agenda, perspectives on issues and to work with their ideas.
>
> Another persistent theme is to *encourage questioning and challenge* of the status quo and to ensure this happens by creating an environment in which these ideas are encouraged, listened to and truly valued; and in which *innovation and entrepreneurialism is*

encouraged. A culture that supports developments is created in which the leader is a role model for learning, and in which the inevitable mistakes are exploited for their learning opportunities. Leadership acts as a 'cognitive catalyst', shocking and even iconoclastic'. (pp. 11–12)

Does such a model provide for a more inclusive and nongendered view of leadership? The discourses that surround women and leadership still remain; however, this model offers a challenge to traditional ideas about what you might look for in a leader. It rejects the view of 'a born leader' either through status or through personality. There are personal qualities and values that equate with leadership however these relate to developmental and enabling skills. In this context a leader is promoting an organisation which is learning, encouraging, supporting, questioning and challenging its entire workforce. Leadership is distributed throughout the organisation so that all talent can be nourished. Leadership is not dependent on particular styles, attributes, or skill sets; it is dependent on connectedness that is building a community of practice within the workplace. What society (and leadership within our society) needs is an environment which has the best of both women's and men's cultures and which questions and discards the conditioning of both. 'In such an environment people will be confident and humble, out-spoken and quiet, logical and spontaneous, decisive and flexible and always inclusive and respectful' (Kline 1999, p. 95).

How Can Women in Leadership Roles Within Educational Psychology Be Supported?

Rowland (2008) found the elicited attributes of Principal Educational Psychologists (PEPs) to include interpersonal skills, empathy and collaborative and democratic styles of interacting. If leadership is a process which requires nurture then PEPs may be the best people to provide this both for their peers and for aspiring leaders within their services. This may be why PEPs speak so positively of the opportunities they have to meet with their PEP colleagues across a region.

The 2019 research on the educational psychologist workforce (DfE, 2019) not only points out that 83% of the workforce in England is female but also that there are a number of 'supply and demand issues'. An important part of the demand-side issue is 'the increasing proportion of EPs who are female and relatively young and who, consequently, are more likely to take breaks from educational psychology employment for periods of maternity leave' (p. 74). Many of those who take maternity leave then also request part-time or other 'flexible working' arrangements. Whilst flexible working is increasingly supported within EPSs this not necessarily the case for PEPs, as there is an expectation that such a role requires the person to work full time. For many female EPs the barriers to leadership outlined in this chapter may be compounded by a system which does not encourage or enable flexible working in senior leadership roles. Many PEPs have indicated that whilst they have encouraged and enabled EPs to take on senior educational psychologist (SEP) roles when it comes to moving into a PEP role the Local Authority (LA) has been less flexible.

For many, leadership seems to be thrust upon them with little planning or preparation. For women, there are narratives that suggest leadership positions are less attainable than for their male counterparts. In order to challenge these narratives, there needs to be in place:

- A recognition that development is a long-term process where capacity is built over time through access to appropriate programmes and where qualities of leadership are recognized and nurtured throughout the organisation.
- Opportunities are available for learning from each other both in peer-to-peer situations and in mixed levels of experience.
- There is space to talk about individual experience and to encourage reflection.
- There is an openness to new ideas.
- There is a range of routes to leadership.
- There is an expectation of inclusion and diversity.
- There are greater opportunities for flexible working in leadership roles.

The importance of leadership supervision for managers of EPSs is recognised by Atkinson and Posada (2019) who found that PEPs are 'finding creative ways to access the supervisory experiences they feel they need, in some cases outsourcing support both formally and informally' (p. 43). They also noted that factors inhibiting leadership supervision included time, competing pressure and service capacity. It could also be argued that the lack of recognition within the literature that supervision is important for, or even essential to PEPs, means it has no clear mandate and consequently can be easily overlooked; particularly in the face of competing pressures and limited availability (Booker, 2013).

Conclusion

Unequal access is not only individually frustrating, it also limits the overall pool of talent within leadership and the diversity of views and perspectives this brings. Although there may be a belief that women no longer experience difficulties with promotion in the workplace, it is clear that women remain underrepresented in positions of leadership. It could be argued that within educational psychology, the gender bias towards women within the profession diminishes any barriers to attaining leadership positions. However, we would suggest that this is to ignore the powerful societal and cultural narratives that operate within everyday practice and have an impact on how women and in particular women in leadership continue to be viewed. New theories of leadership are providing support for more connected, distributed and collaborative ways of working which can enable more diversity and equality in the workplace. Developing training and support networks for current and future leaders in educational psychology is a priority. It is the responsibility of all current leaders to encourage and enable potential future leaders as part of succession planning in a profession which is seeing increasing challenges to recruitment and retention of staff. It may be helpful for the British Psychological Society's Division of Educational and Child Psychology (BPS, DECP) and the National Association of Principal Educational Psychologists (NAPEP) to work together to establish a framework for the leadership development of educational psychologists and the requirement for them to receive appropriate leadership supervision and mentoring.

References

Alimo-Metcalfe, B. (2010). Developments in gender and leadership: introducing a new 'inclusive' model. *Gender in Management: An International Journal, 25*(8), 630–639.

Alimo-Metcalfe, B., & Alban-Metcalfe, J. (2001). *Engaging leadership: Creating organisations to maximise the potential of people.* London: CIPD.

Association of Directors of Children's Services. (2019). Directors of Children's Services. Retrieved from http://adcs.org.uk/contacts/directors-of-childrens-services#view1

Atkinson, C., & Posada, S. (2019). Leadership supervision for managers of educational psychology services. *Educational Psychology in Practice, 35*(1), 35–49.

Banerjee, R. (2018). 'For this government, race has fallen off the agenda'. David Lammy on bias in Britain's housing sector. *New Statesman.* https://www.newstatesman.com/spotlight/housing/2018/08/government-race-has-fallen-agenda-david-lammy-bias-britain-s-housing

Barker, P. (2018). *The silence of the girls.* London: Hamish Hamilton.

Beard, M. (2017). *Women and power: A manifesto.* London: Profile Books.

British Psychological Society (BPS). (2017). *Practice guidelines.* Leicester: BPS.

Booker, R. (2013). Leadership of education psychology services: Fit for purpose? *Educational Psychology in Practice, 29*(2) 197–208.

Carers UK. (2016). 10 facts about women and caring on International Women's Day. Retrieved from https://www.carersuk.org/news-and-campaigns/features/10-facts-about-women-and-caring-in-the-uk-on-international-women-s-day

Collins, P. H. (2000). *Black feminist thought: Knowledge, consciousness, and the politics of empowerment.* New York: Routledge.

Department for Education (DfE). (2018). School workforce in England: November 2017. Retrieved from https://assets.publishing.service.gov.uk/government/uploads/system/uploads/attachment_data/file/719772/SWFC_MainText.pdf

Department for Education (DfE). (2019). Research on the educational psychologist workforce; research report. Retrieved from https://www.gov.uk/government/publications/educational-psychologist-workforce-research

Eagly, A. H., Johannesen-Schmidt, M. C., & van Engen, M. (2003). Transformational, transactional, and laissez-faire leadership styles: A meta-analysis comparing women and men. *Psychological Bulletin, 95*, 569–591.

Emma. (2018). *Mental load: A feminist comic.* New York: Seven Stories Press.

Equality Act. (2010). Retrieved from https://www.legislation.gov.uk/ukpga/2010/15/contents

Eurostat. (2018). Gender pay gap statistics. Retrieved from https://ec.europa.eu/eurostat/statistics-explained/index.php/Gender_pay_gap_statistics#Gender_pay_gap_levels_vary_significantly_across_EU

Fassinger, R. (2017). *The changing gender composition of psychology: Update and expansion of the 1995 Task Force Report.* Washington, DC: American Psychological Association. Retrieved from http://www.apa.org/pi/women/programs/gender-composition/index.aspx

Fels, A. (2004). *Necessary dreams: Ambition in women's changing lives.* New York: Pantheon Books.

Fine, C. (2018). *Testosterone rex: Unmaking the myths of our gendered minds.* London: Icon Books.

Foreign and Commonwealth Office (FCO). (2017). *Pay gap report 2016–2017*. London: FCO.

Foucault, M. (1991). *Discipline and punish: The birth of a prison*. London, Penguin.

Fuller, K. (2017). Women secondary headteachers in England: Where are they now? *Management in Education*, 1–15.

Gillborn, D., Rollock, N., Warmington, P., & Demack, S. (2016). Race, racism and education: Inequality, resilience and reform in policy & practice. Retrieved from https://www.researchgate.net/publication/325011060_Race_Racism_and_Education_inequality_resilience_and_reform_in_policy_practice_A_Two-Year_Research_Project_Funded_by_the_Society_for_Educational_Studies_SES_National_Award_2013

Hill, C. (2016). *The color of leadership: Barriers, bias, and race*. Washington, DC: American Association of University Women.

Jewel, H., & Bazeley, A. (2018) *Sex and power 2018*. London: Fawcett Society.

Kingsolver, B. (2018). *Unsheltered*. London: Faber and Faber.

Kline, N. (1999). *Time to think*. London: Cassell.

Luo, X. R. (2016). Women's biggest obstacles are their own assumptions. Retrieved from https://www.thenational.ae/business/women-s-biggest-obstacles-are-their-own-assumptions-1.138249?videoId=5770738884001

McGinn, K. L., & Tempest, N. (2000: revised April 2010). *Heidi Roizen*. Harvard Business School Case 800–228. Cambridge, MA: Harvard Business School.

Moss-Racusin, C., Dovidio, J. F., Brescoll, V. L., Graham, M. J., & Handelsman, J. (2012). Science faculty's subtle gender biases favour male students. Retrieved from http://www.wiset.soton.ac.uk/files/2013/04/MossRascussin2012Science.pdf

Murphy, F. C., Bishop, D. V. M., & Sigala, N. (2014) Women scientists in psychology – time for action. *Psychologist*, *27*(12), 918–922.

Office for National Statistics. (2016). Women shoulder the responsibility of 'unpaid work'. Retrieved from https://www.ons.gov.uk/employmentandlabourmarket/peopleinwork/earningsandworkinghours/articles/womenshouldertheresponsibilityofunpaidwork/2016-11-10

Office for National Statistics. (2017). How do the jobs men and women do affect the gender pay gap? Retrieved from https://www.ons.gov.uk/employmentandlabourmarket/peopleinwork/earningsandworkinghours/articles/howdothejobsmenandwomendoaffectthegenderpaygap/2017-10-06

Office for National Statistics. (2018). Gender pay gap in the UK: 2018. Retrieved from https://www.ons.gov.uk/employmentandlabourmarket/peopleinwork/earningsandworkinghours/bulletins/genderpaygapintheuk/2018

Ortiz-Ospina, E., & Tzvetkova, S. (2017). Working women: Key facts and trends in female labor force participation. Accessed from https://ourworldindata.org/female-labor-force-participation-key-facts

Pande, R., & Ford, D. (2011). *Gender quotas and female leadership: A Review. Background paper for the World Development Report on Gender*. Washington, DC: World Bank.

Peters, T., & Waterman, R. H. (1982). *In search of excellence*. New York: Harper Collins.

Rollock, N. (2019). *Staying power: The career experiences and strategies of UK Black female professors*. London: University and College Union.

Rowland, K. (2008). *A study investigating the role of the principal educational psychologist and associated theories of leadership*. Birmingham: University of Birmingham.

Sandberg, S. (2013). *Lean-in: Women, work and the will to lead.* New York: Random House.

Scottish Executive. (2007). Employee engagement in the public sector: A review of literature. Retrieved from https://www2.gov.scot/Publications/2007/05/09111348/0

Shakeshaft, C. (1987). *Women in educational administration.* Newbury Park, CA: Sage.

Showunmi, V., Atewologun, D., & Bebbington, D. (2016). Ethnic, gender and class intersections in British women's leadership experiences. *Educational Management Administration & Leadership, 44*(6), 917–935.

Stanley, J. (2017). *No more hero heads.* Retrieved from http://www.headteacher-update.com/editorial-comment/no-more-hero-heads/164563

Thomson Reuters Legal Insights Europe. (2018). Tackling gender equality. Are quotas the answer? Retrieved from https://blogs.thomsonreuters.com/legal-uk/2018/09/21/tackling-gender-inequality-are-quotas-the-answer/

Todd, Z. (2018). Developing inclusive leadership in the disability movement: lessons and learning from Australia and New Zealand. Retrieved from https://www.wcmt.org.uk/sites/default/files/report-documents/Todd%20Z%20Report%202016%20Final_0.pdf

Truong, Y., & Ellam, H. (2014). Educational psychology workforce survey 2013. Retrieved from https://www.gov.uk/government/publications/educational-psychology-workforce-survey-results-2013

Universities and Colleges Admissions Service. (2016). Data on admissions to full-time undergraduate higher education in the UK 2015. Retrieved from https://www.ucas.com/corporate/news-and-key-documents/news/ucas-data-reveals-numbers-men-and-women-placed-over-150-higher

UNESDOC. (2018). Gender review: meeting our commitments to gender equality in education. Retrieved from https://unesdoc.unesco.org/ark:/48223/pf0000261593

United Nations Sustainable Development Goals. (2016). Sustainable Development Goal 5. Retrieved from https://sustainabledevelopment.un.org/sdg5

University of Kent (2016). Leadership behavior framework. Retrieved from https://www.kent.ac.uk/hr-learninganddevelopment/documents/leadership%20Behaviour/leadershipbehaviourdoc.pdf

Watson, C. (2016). A critical feminist perspective on leadership excellence and gender. Conference paper. Retrieved from https://www.researchgate.net/publication/306280878_A_Critical_Feminist_Perspective_on_Leadership_Excellence_and_Gender

6

Inspiring Leadership and Outward-Facing Leadership for Community Educational Psychology Services

Kevin Rowland and Poppy Chandler

'Leaner', 'meaner', 'fitter', 'better': are just some of the words which can now be overheard in even the deepest recesses of county and city hall throughout the country. They are the stringent qualities by which today's managers are asked to judge themselves in an increasingly competitive marketplace where providing more for less has become the major driving force'. (Cameron, 1995, p. 44)

Twenty-five years ago Sean Cameron (1995) contributed to the 'Silver Edition' of Educational Psychology in Practice titled, 'Special Issue: Management'. The articles focussed on 'leadership' but used the words 'management and administration'. In 1973, 47 years ago, Jack Wright, Principal Educational Psychologist (PEP), Hampshire, presented the profession's first paper on management and leadership: 'The Psychologist as Administrator' (Wright, 1973) at the Association of Educational Psychologists (AEP) training course to fellow PEPs. In 1978 Wright said

'Management is not something that just concerns area leaders or leaders of whole authority teams, it concerns every psychologist. I hope indeed that similar courses will be arranged, and that area and principal psychologists will encourage staff to attend. They can usefully discuss management even if they are at the beginning of their careers'. (Wright, 1978, pp. 24–25)

We believe that Wright (1978) captures our thinking and approach to leaders and leadership and, indeed, to a large extent determines it. We also feel that Cameron (1995) reflects our early experiences as fledgling educational psychologists (EPs) coping with the marketisation of education. Importantly, Cameron (1995) also drew upon his understanding of Abraham Maslow to inform his explorations of management and leadership; again, we believe this inspired us to use our understanding and application of psychology to develop our theories of leadership in relation to educational psychology.

The Emergence of Leadership in Educational Psychology Services (EPSs)

In this chapter we have endeavoured to contextualise the development and thinking about leadership by highlighting our shared experiences as we joined the professional of educational psychology in 1990, especially our application of personal construct psychology (PCP) as PEPs. We then go on to explore the key issues and differences regarding leadership, management and change (Kotter, 1996). From that point we consider leadership as it relates to EPSs (inspiring leadership) and leadership for service delivery (outward-facing leadership) where we have endeavoured to consider the emergence and development of leadership within educational psychology and to highlight our use of psychology. We have become increasingly aware that our early exposure to PCP (1995) via The University of Birmingham's professional training course (1989–1990) has informed and shaped our understanding of leadership and that PCP underpins our personal theories about leadership and continues to do so.

At the time of our training in educational psychology, via the 'Reconstructing Movement' (Gilham, 1978; McPherson & Sutton, 1981), EPs were arguing for a greater community focus, the use of consultancy, linking EPSs with other organisations, including health and social care, adopting the principles of organisational psychology and 'giving psychology away' based on notions of social justice (Gilham, 1978; McPherson & Sutton, 1989; Orford, 1992; Rhodes, 2017). At this time EPs drew upon their knowledge of psychology to inform their thinking about management and leadership, for example, 'Management by Objectives' (Trafford, 1978) and McGregor's Theory X and Theory Y (cited in Smith, 1978) which was based on Maslow's hierarchy of needs.

Thus, our practices as maingrade, senior and Principal EPs are rooted in the foundations of social justice (Gilham, 1978; McPherson & Sutton, 1981), systemic approaches, thinking reflectively rather than 'robotically' (Burnham, 1986; Hanson, 1995; Harri-Augstein & Webb, 1995; Schon, 1987) using psychology to inform our thinking. Harri-Augstein and Thomas (1991) propose that

> 'Learning is the construction of meaning. Self-Organised Learning is the conversational construction, reconstruction and exchange of personally significant relevant and viable meanings with awareness and controlled purposiveness. This process forms the personal experience which is the basis of all our anticipations'. (p. 27)

This definition of learning owes much to Kelly's (1955) PCP and underpins our understanding of leadership, both outward-facing and inspiring leadership, especially in co-constructing a shared narrative around future (anticipative) actions that embrace social meanings with a 'controlled purposefulness' (Harri-Augstein & Thomas 1991, p. 27). These considerations also embrace the concept of power within collaborative contexts (Himmelman, 1996) and we argue strongly that our models of leadership challenge inequalities (interpersonal and structural) and promote democratic communication and empowerment (Argyris & Schon, 1974) within the EPS via considering leadership to be a 'distributed property' (Gronn, 2000). A key factor for us in construing services and organisations as 'complex living systems' was the emphasis on the Birmingham training course (1989-1990) on understanding family systems (Burnham, 1986; Hanson, 1995) and perceiving the actions of people as intricate parts of those systems, including 'symptom formulation' (Burnham, 1986, p. 35) and analysing the balance between 'stability and change' (p. 35) at key points of transition.

Personal Construct Psychology and Leadership

This section specifically highlights our thinking about PCP (Kelly, 1955) and leadership. We propose that the 'fundamental postulate' is at the very heart of our constructions surrounding leadership. It is generally accepted that leadership is a forward-looking process that relates to a vision of a future that anticipates change (Kotter, 1996) based on the range of shared values.

> 'The fundamental postulate:
> A person's processes are psychologically channelized by the ways in which he anticipates events'. (Kelly, 1955, p. 46)

Table 6.1 provides examples of the relationship between PCP and Leadership that informs our thinking, reflections. and learning. We would emphasise that this is a summary of our understanding; however, we believe it provides a starting point in understanding the relationship between PCP and leadership.

The profession of educational psychology has always sought to use psychology reflexively (Budgell & Gallivan, 1981). By using PCP as the base psychology upon which to integrate Maslow's ideas it allows for the simultaneous development of theory and action in relation to leadership for EPs within the scientist-practitioner paradigm (Hagstrom, Fry, Cramblet, & Tanner, 2007).

Whilst we draw on PCP as a foundation for our thinking, actions and learning we also see it as necessary to integrate other psychologies and associated approaches (Argyris & Schon, 1974; Argyris, 1990) within our theoretical paradigm and indeed this is a feature of community educational psychology (Rowland, Traxson, & Roberts, 2010). Before discussing inspiring leadership and outward-facing leadership we think it is helpful to share our understanding about the differences between leadership and management as this will help define our constructs in relation to leadership.

Thinking about Leadership and Management

Whilst leadership and management are interlinked we recognise the need to state some key differences that we identify. We view leadership as being linked to the 'big picture' and the forces acting upon the profession including; the Division of Educational and Child Psychology (DECP), the special educational needs and disability (SEND) code of practice, the AEP, schools and academies, the Local Area, the communities we work in etc. This is a complex range of influences that we need to integrate, look ahead and work with others to form a vision. These actions create a forward-looking service that works across a number of

Table 6.1   Examples of personal construct psychology in relation to leadership

Personal Construct Psychology	Considerations for Leadership
Philosophy: Constructive Alternativism verses Accumulative Fragmentism. The person endeavours to understand themselves in relation to their world and there are multiple ways to construe the same event.	There are multiple realities when construing events and it grounds leadership within a philosophy which embraces multiple realities and experiences. Perceptions are open to question and reconsideration.
The fundamental postulate: A person's processes are psychologically channelised by the ways in which he anticipates events.	This is future orientated thus the future can change. Experience is psychologically channelised and coherence can be built upon. This invites critical thinking.
Constructs are bipolar discriminations and construing is a process of predicting. Constructs are organised hierarchically – core to peripheral constructs. Important constructs provide a greater degree of successful anticipations and certainty.	In leadership people make predictions about the future (vision) and act on those hypotheses and are open to change and help develop the construct system. Core constructs are similar to 'values' which are intrinsic to operationalising effective leadership.
Propositional construing. The idea that constructs are hypotheses and are there to be tested. Propositional communication promotes team working by enabling democratic theories of action via the Sociality Corollary.	This allows leadership to be considered within the 'invitational' mode rather than imposition. You cannot force someone to perceive you as a leader. This provides a democratic mode for leadership interaction.
Emotion is an actual or impending change: anxiety, threat, hostility, guilt, fear, aggressiveness. These emotions relate to a person's construct system and how that interrelates to other construct systems.	This informs leadership about considering the emotional aspect of change. Leadership is predominantly about change and PCP relates this to emotions associated with change.
The 11 corollaries process construing in 'motion' and invite a consideration of how a person's constructs are formed and developed. Five of the 11 corollaries have been chosen to exemplify the relationship between PCP and leadership.	**Individuality corollary**: people differ and we need to seek to understand the construing (anticipations) of people as we lead or distribute leadership. **Organisation corollary**: leadership would recognise the ordinal structure of the construct system, for example, people are stuck due to a belief. **Choice corollary**: a person can choose to lead or follow. It is an elaboration of the constructs. **Commonality corollary**: in leadership terms this helps to understand the degree that construing is similar between persons, thus, building a group versus a team. **Sociality corollary**: people try to make sense of one another's constructs, constructions and construing and they play roles in relation to each other, for example, leader, team, service and there is a process of everyone trying to build meaning through interactions

Extracts from Bannister & Fransella (1989) and Bannister & Mair (1968)

agencies ages 0–25 where all EPs act as leaders and contribute to delivering the service vision. Figure 6.1 shows our conceptualisation of the interrelationship between leadership and management and Table 6.2 exemplifies the differences illustrating leadership focusses on people and management on tasks and procedures.

In Figure 6.1 we consider that management focuses on the implementation of policies, procedures and practices which ensure the realisation of the agreed vision related to the service's values. It also incorporates policies that ensure that roles and responsibilities are discharged appropriately including workforce development, recruitment, quality assurance procedures, disciplinary and conduct issues as well as promotions, financial management and accountability etc. EPs have been engaged in considerations in relation to management since the 1970s (Stratford & Ward, 1978; Stratford, 1995). Our experiences of educational psychology includes using managerial programmes and approaches such as Business Excellence Model (BEM), 1998; British Standards Institute (BSI), 2015; and Investors in People (IiP), 2000. In the EPSs that we have worked in we have both been part of working parties or groups that have developed and reviewed management policies. In Table 6.2 we have summarised examples of key differences between leadership and management.

Whilst Table 6.2 isn't exhaustive it provides an overview of some of the key characteristics we use when differentiating between leadership and management. We note that our continuing professional development (CPD) activities in finance, management and leadership have enabled us to apply our psychology (as described previously) to develop business models as PEPs maintaining successful service outcomes within Local Authority (LA) landscapes which have become much more focussed on trading. Sharp, Frederickson and Laws (2000) captured the changing context for EPs; trading, competition, shrinking finances, privatisation and the growth of academies (Rowland, 2002).

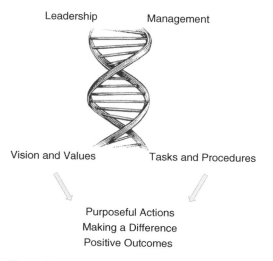

Figure 6.1 Conceptualising leadership and management as interrelated.

Table 6.2   Examples of differences between leadership and management

Leadership (where are we going?)	Management (how do we get there?)
Do the right things, values, ethics, perceptions.	Do things right, implement policies correctly.
Asking 'why', 'what'?	Asking 'how'?
About trust, people, self-actualisation, integrity, honesty, relationships, emotional intelligence.	About systems, procedures, controls, administration, protocols.
Innovation, creativity, new initiatives, curiosity, personal growth.	Tasks, repetition, routines.
Empowering people, taking risks, freedom to act within the vision and challenge the vision.	Ensuring conformity, consistency, controlling actions and monitoring adherence for accountability.
Development, coaching, distributing leadership, independent decision-making within the vision.	Controlling behaviours, dealing with policy breaches.

Change and Leadership

Considerations in understanding change (Kotter, 1996) have been synonymous with the emergence of leadership within the profession of educational psychology since 1913 (the appointment of Sir Cyril Burt) where every generation refers to the challenge of 'unprecedented change',

> 'Educational psychology services are entering a period of unprecedented change'. (Sharp et al., 2000, p. 98)

Leadership is about change (Kotter, 1996) that's linked to values, a collective vision and a set of professional principles, ethics and practices (British Psychological Society [BPS], DECP, 2015) that we aspire to adhere to. It is about the psychology of everyone in an organisation and we would contend that everyone has leadership responsibilities within an EPS. Our understanding of change is fundamental to the practice of educational psychology and drawing upon evidence-based models of change. Stoll and Fink (1995) link their theory of change to Kelly (1955):

> 'Since change in organizations is about change in people, attention to their perceptions of reality and particularly their sense of self is a key to successful 'change agentry' ... Leadership is about communicating invitational messages to individuals and groups with whom leaders interact in order to build and act on a shared and evolving vision of enhanced educational experiences for pupils'. (Stoll & Fink, 1995, p. 109)

Bartram and Wolfendale (1999) argued that a business culture is required and, as such, this requires PEPs to change in order to fulfil that role.

'Recent legislation has produced a climate in which EPSs are having to face the challenges presented by a market-led, consumer-orientated culture and the current practice of extending inspections to LEAs ... It is clear that as a business-orientated approach to service delivery strengthens and with it the primacy of customer satisfaction, EPSs are no longer able to exist in a climate of operating as they wish and providing services they see fit to deliver'. (Bartram & Wolfendale, 1999, pp. 55–56)

Here we see that by establishing a business-like approach (e.g. Business Excellence Model, British Quality Foundation, 1998; BSI, 2015; IiP, 2000) to service polices with a 'customer' focus, in line with commerce and industry, EPSs were to be able to adapt and compete within a market framework. In the 1990s we were aware that some EPSs were engaged in producing 'portfolios' for traded service delivery and auditing what practices were central to achieving good outcomes. We have both worked in EPSs which have responded to the marketisation in education, including successfully introducing traded services and 'full cost recovery' models.

Thus, we were thrust into a change model whose values included the promotion of ethical practices, challenged social injustice and structural inequality to promote an inclusive society free of discrimination (Gillham, 1978) but engaged with the relentless drive towards embracing market forces and establishing managerialist business models. We both recall working alongside EPs who rejected the introduction of business models within educational psychology due to the clash of the need for 'trading' and 'giving psychology away'.

Inspiring Leadership in Others

Within our services we promote the idea of matching colleagues to roles and duties that they are most curious about, interested in and excited by. This theory was first espoused by Maslow (1962 and republished 1998). In relation to PCP, a person achieves 'optimal functioning' whereby a human being is in the right place at the right time to be actively enquiring, discovering and experimenting and finding validation of their whole construct system in their meaningful interaction with their chosen context (Fransella & Dalton, 1990) and contend that this is commensurate with Maslow's 'self-actualisation'. Maslow responded to McGregor's (1960) theories about leadership, which were based on Maslow's own hierarchy of needs.

McGregor (1960), a social psychologist, initially proposed that managers had two theories of motivation of employees: Theory X – 'you can't trust them' and Theory Y – 'you can trust them'. Thus, establishing trust became an important construct with regard to leadership.

In response to McGregor, who had cited Abraham Maslow's hierarchy of needs as the underpinning model of Theory X and Theory Y, Maslow (1962 and 1998), proposed Theory Z. He contended that if you match a person's values and interests to the position they hold within an organisation they will seek to 'self-actualise' in that role and motivation will be optimal as they seek to 'be all that they can'. Maslow (1998) applies this thesis to the field of leadership:

'... one who has all his basic needs gratified, that is, the needs for safety, for belong-ingness, for loving and for being loved, for prestige and respect and finally for self-confidence and self-esteem. This is the same as saying that the closer a person approaches toward self-actualising, the better leader or boss he is apt to be in the general sense of the largest number of situations'. (Maslow, 1998, p. 164)

Maslow (1998) argued that a synergistic relationship can be cultivated which simultaneously benefits the person, the organisation and those associated with the organisation. He predicated this on the principle that if a person is placed in circumstances which foster personal growth the sense of achievement and fulfilment will lead to higher levels of motivation. Thus, an effective leader understands where a person can find this role within an organisation. Maslow (1998) proposed that it is the genuine validation of the self which leads to a positive self-concept and high self-esteem. Thus, it is possible to conceptualise an EPS where people's construct systems are validated through effective organisational change (i.e. leading and psychologically complementing each other) rather than invalidated and causing negative emotions as identified by Kelly (1955).

Leadership, learning and personal and collective psychology are intrinsically interconnected and can be considered in the form of agency and structure (Gronn, 2000: Gunter, 2001). By creating an organisational culture based on Theory Z, colleagues inspire each other and seek new knowledge to share, and ideally, create an excitement/energy about the activities and progression of the service: 'a buzz' (joint experimentation and discovery in a mutually beneficial social context). This leads to a service where people strive to 'lead', for example, they desire to elaborate their construct systems (Kelly, 1955) and share new knowledge and practices in staff development meetings. Thus the concepts of 'distributed leadership' and a 'learning organisation' become real within a mutually supportive context. However, Argyris (1990) states that organisations can create a culture of defensiveness and proposes the use of a democratic communication style, 'Model 2' (pp. 106–107) to create greater openness and challenge controlling toxic micro-management. By overcoming organisation defensiveness, which inhibits learning, we propose that people can lead and experience a feeling of empowerment creating a culture whereby people are more likely to self-actualise (Maslow, 1998) and experience optimal functioning (Fransella & Dalton, 1990) even when an EPS might be embedded in a wider defensive culture.

Argyris (1990) argues that within a healthy organisational culture there are open feedback loops incorporating 'double loop learning' where everything is discussable (pp. 93–94) and leads to greater involvement and commitment and ultimately improved outcomes. Maslow's Theory Z further reinforces Argyris' (1990) assertions, in that, people in roles that allow them to engage and express their values become increasingly more motivated to achieve all that they can. Figure 6.2 demonstrates a virtuous cycle of organisational growth that creates a culture of learning, increased motivation, cycles of continuous improvement and good outcomes. The relative successes, failures and improvements of the eight services that we have worked in leads us to believe that Figure 6.2 provides a useful template for considering holistic approach to thinking about leadership, change and continuous improvement.

We would argue that the model of leadership adopted by the service lead (Rowland, 2002) can create an organisational culture whereby everyone is a leader and leads by

Figure 6.2 Contemporary leadership model based on Maslow's Theory Z.

example (Roffey, 2000), 'culture is determined by ... the participants within the organisation at the time, their cohesion and flexibility' (p. 13). We argue strongly that all EPs should be leaders within the EPS – for example, working a patch of schools and providing the lead for initiatives, meeting with children, parents and others – and must pull together to create the necessary culture. Gronn (2000) uses sociocultural theory to provide an understanding of distributed leadership, power, agency and structure; he proposed that the division of labour is central to the idea of activity theory (Engestrom, 1999). This creates a context for groups of EPs to engage, discover and experiment and consequently elaborate their personal construing but in connection with others. Here leadership is considered to be a distributed property supporting conjoint activity between purposeful actors who share common cognitive properties (Kelly's commonality and sociality corollaries, 1955), language, and learning (Vygotsky, 1962). Within this, Gronn (2000) highlighted the need to reflect on the distribution of power where some groups or individuals express and exert more influence than others in particular organisational cultures. Gronn, using activity theory, emphasised a democratic value base when accounting for the division of labour where power is a distributed phenomenon.

> 'Activity is the bridge between agency and structure ... The key component in the activity system which accounts for organizational leadership taking a distributed form, as I have been arguing, is the division of labour'. (Gronn, 2000, pp. 318–333)

Through activities, each individual (agency) has the opportunity to bridge the socially defined gap between themselves and the organisational structures (structure) which distribute power evenly (or not). In our model, building relationships and creating trust are vital. Eco systemic and interactionist frameworks (Cooper, Smith, & Upton, 1994; Dowling & Osbourne, 1995) again strengthen the view that leadership is the 'glue' that binds and holds people together, especially in a crisis.

If Maslow's (1998) Theory Z is actioned within Kelly's (1955) 'invitational mode' and everyone, as far as possible, occupies a role that they are passionate about, they become highly motivated and inspire others within the EPS. Importantly, we see that by managing EPS culture, via a myriad of interactions, colleagues are inspired to lead and educate their colleagues. Senge (1990) makes the link between an effective learning organisation and leadership.

> 'The new view of leadership ...are responsible for building organisations where people continually expand their capacities to understand complexity, clarify vision and improve shared mental models'. (Senge, 1990, pp. 340–360)

The modelling of continuous learning by PEPs is crucial in fostering learning within EPSs (Rowland et al., 2010). Senge (1990) made the connection between a learning organisation and developing a shared vision, where all people are part of the visioning process and whereby their own personal visions become integrated into the process for realising an organisational vision, securing an emotional commitment rather than behavioural compliance.

Forty-one years ago Wright and Payne (1978) drew attention to the importance of EPs participating in decision-making processes.

> 'We aim to involve all psychologists in decision-making activities that concern our development'. (Wright & Payne, 1978, pp. 24–28)

This work led to services developing as learning organisations (Senge, 1990). Harrison, Mulrooney, Stratford and Walker, (1996) reported that 84% of EPSs had an established CPD co-ordinator's post facilitating personal and professional development within educational psychology. With EPSs evolving as learning organisations the profession engaged more systematically in challenging and changing multiagency contexts (AEP, 2008, 2009).

Inspiring leadership creates a context whereby colleagues inspire each other through the creation and sharing of new knowledge through creating an organisation where everyone leads. Such an organisation then reaches out to work collaboratively with other organisations.

Outward-Facing Leadership with Others

The link between inspiring leadership (in others) and outward-facing leadership is strategic thinking (refer to Figure 6.3), the link between the organisation and external organisations. In order to collaborate (Huxham, 1996) and develop partnerships that will make service delivery more efficient and achieve better outcomes for children there needs to be an understanding of the commonalities between the EPS and other agencies as well as differences; therefore, a strategic analysis is required and it is this that helps a EPS decide in which partnerships to invest time and energy in for the benefit of children.

We consider a strategic approach to be predicated upon three components: firstly, a long-term view (what's on the horizon, e.g. new legislation, changes in initial training in the next 3 years); second, a view across the bandwidth of potential change, e.g. Children's Social Care, Adult Social Care, Department for Education (DfE), Clinical Commissioning Groups (CCG), schools and lastly, infrastructure change, e.g. LA structures, policies, funding, policies etc.

EPS Leadership ⟷	Strategic Leadership ⟷	Outward Facing Leadership
Inspiring Leadership All staff within the psychology service are leaders	**Long-Term View** This relates to the vision, values and external drivers for change	**Community Partnerships** The Local Area and Working Across Boundaries and Networks
Within the Service	**Connection with the World**	**Partnerships**

Figure 6.3   Showing the strategic linkage between an EPS and partnership working.

Proactive and strategic leadership (Figure 6.3) has been required potentially placing the PEP in a new strategic role within a LA (Courtney, 2002; Preedy, Glatter, & Wise, 2003). Courtney (2002) uses the term strategic management to reflect a composite of activities.

> '... strategic management to denote the whole process of innovation, strategic analysis, formulation and implementation emphasizes the continuous nature of the process and makes it much more likely that any strategies which are decided on will be implemented'. (Courtney, 2002, p. 8)

Strategic activity embodies collaboration across many areas and arguably the long-established practice of multiagency working within educational psychology provides PEPs with an embedded historical knowledge base to support such strategic activity. Chazan, Moore, Williams and Wright, (1974) noted that 'The Chief Educational Psychologist attends meetings of the Schools' Sub-committee' (p. 348) and further described a wide range of representation which suggested that perhaps the strategic aspects of the PEP role have been around for quite some time.

The child guidance movement (Chazan et al., 1974), and the tradition of multiagency working in the school psychological services has arguably placed co-operation and collaboration at the core of the profession for some years.

The introduction of Every Child Matters (DfES, 2004) in the early 2000s through to 2010 emphasised multiagency working, network leadership and working across boundaries (Sullivan & Skelcher, 2002) and establishing educational partnerships and collaborative practices (Huxham, 1996; Huxham & Vangen, 2005). In contemporary EPSs all EPs can be involved in representing the profession by working with Public Health, Adult Social Care and third sector organisations, whereas originally this was conceived as a role for the PEP. This reinforces the argument that all EPs are leaders. Thus, LA EPs can significantly influence policy development, CCGs and Academy Chains by acting outside of the EPS.

Over the last 30 years we have experienced a significant increase in working strategically with head teacher groups, third sector organisations and public services (Public Health, CCG, Social Care, DfE). We consider this a vital role for the future development of educational psychology. Stratford and Ward (1978) argued that EPS links with other organisations should be prioritised to maintain involvement with policy development.

> 'The promotion of community based services ... the adoption of a consultancy model ... links with other organisations ... It will also be important to keep in touch with the

needs of other services, and the 'network' principle of the means of doing this ... extends the sphere of influence'. (Stratford & Ward, 1978, pp. 30–31)

Earlier than this, Chazan (1972) highlighted the needs for EPs to work across outside agencies within a LA, especially in the area of mental health. The following extract highlights our positive experiences of ensuring that all EPs within an EPS engage with systems and hierarchies of systems in order to extend the influence of educational psychology.

'There are a number of reasons why there should be a close association between school psychological services and community mental health programmes: an active preventative policy means that the focus of attention must be on the emotional and social adjustment of children; socio-economic factors within the community affect; emotional disturbance in any individual often affects the family as a whole ... a great need for co-operation between the social service departments, the health services if the aims of a community mental health approach are to be realised'. (Chazan, 1972, pp. 10–15)

The role of the EP working across systems, services and agencies (AEP, 2008, 2009) has been a central consideration for nearly 50 years (Jones, 2006). Our view is that this should be reflected in the EPS vision and the role of the PEP in accordance with the DfEE Research Report (2000), Current Role, Good Practice and Future Directions of Educational Psychology Services which stated:

'Leadership of the education psychology service is also a key factor ... Where the Principal Educational Psychologist provides strong leadership and a clear agenda for the work of the service this helps to build understanding of and respect for the service. However, where only the Principal Educational Psychologist is involved in working with the LEA directorate, other members of the service do not feel part of it and the team may feel ... distanced from the decisions that they are taking on their behalf'. (pp. 79–80)

The DfEE consulted with Health Services and Social Care in researching the role extending across systems. Since the 1970s the shift has been from locating leadership and change to solely the Chief Educational Psychologists, to involving all staff, hence our contention that *all* EPs are leaders, including local, regional and national developments. Currently, a maingrade EP in Shropshire is involved in national developments about mental health and a senior educational psychologist (SEP) in local and regional policy developments. Jones (2006) provides an account of a contemporary community EPS in Plymouth with a clear description of its development and work, especially applying a systems model of psychology with parents.

Fullan (2005) provided a research-base for leadership across systems, leadership which we refer to as 'outward-facing leadership'. We believe that EPs are system thinkers in action and work across systems using a theoretical understanding of systemic processes and structural processes, including power differentials related to structural inequality and social justice (Rhodes, 2017). Fullan's (2005) research suggested the 10 following guidelines for developing network leadership:

1) The reality test
2) Moral purpose
3) Get the basics right
4) Communicate the big picture
5) Provide opportunities for people to interact with the big picture
6) Intelligent accountability
7) Incentivise collaboration and lateral capacity building
8) The long lever of leadership
9) Design every policy, whatever the purpose, to build capacity,
10) Grow the financial investment

(Fullan, 2005, pp. 84–85)

These guidelines underpinned the Business Transformation Plan (2010–2018) in Sandwell's Inclusion Support Service that led to the emergence of a number of initiatives working across systems, including: public health, children's social care, health visitors, school nurses, CCG, early years' multiagency services and schools. This meant that the EPS was able to shape public policy in relation to community psychology, early identification, assessment practices, collaborative working, whole school initiatives and direct work with parents and children, reducing exclusion rates (especially for children with an education and health care plan [EHCP]).

We have drawn upon research from the National College for School Leadership (NCSL, 2006): System Leadership in Action: Leading Networks Leading the System and adapted this to outward-facing leadership. In 2006 it was proposed that:

> 'Evidence suggests that effective networks establish collective vision and values early. In many cases the role of leaders in articulating this vision has appeared to be crucial in building relationships and fostering common purpose. One of the indicators of growing network maturity may be the movement from minority leadership visions, however flexible, towards dynamic, mutual, enacted values'. (NCSL, 2006, p. 3)

Thus, it is vital that an EPS has very clearly articulated vision and values that are indicative of the organisational culture. The evidence further suggests that they require leadership models that create collaborative enquiry, build trusting relationships and break down traditional command and control/leader follower dynamics. In turn this can improve the credibility and standing with other organisations leading to more effective joint working and better outcomes.

We have related the foregoing to PCP and we would argue that the principles of 'propositional thinking' – the 'individuality, commonality and sociality corollaries' (Kelly, 1955) – help us to understand and put into practice approaches to leadership across systems and links directly with good communication and collaboration (Argyris & Schon, 1974).

The PEP in Portsmouth LA led the EPS to become the highest rated service in England 1997–2000. This built upon Jack Wright's (1978) foundations and the work of the reconstructing movement and illustrated the power of outward-facing leadership across agencies including, the police, youth offending teams, the third sector, social care and health. The PEP always maintained that the future of educational psychology lay in working across systems and that it was vital that EPs had a visible presence at all levels (Bronfenbrenner, 1979) influencing policy, commissioning, multiagency structures, collaboration and practice. With the advent of the Children and Families Act (2014) his predictions became enshrined in law.

We would both implore PEPs and the whole team to write an 'outward-facing development plan' and establish a strategy for making presentations and representations to other organisations on regular basis, including parent groups and forums.

Final Reflections

The reconstructing movement of the 1970s and 1980s moved from a clinical, pathologised view of children towards a community understanding where social justice and structural inequality, including poverty, greatly determined the psychological development of children. In order to deliver services that embrace this understanding and challenge discrimination and inequality we need EPSs located with local government that can help determine policy and impact on practices related to *all* children. To this end we have argued we need a psychology for leaders and leadership that is focussed on creating the best communities for children to grow-up in. In the 1960s Abraham Maslow (1998) stated

> '... the closer a person approaches self-actualising, the better leader ... apt to be in the general sense of the largest number of situations ... must have as a psychological prerequisite, 'the ability to take pleasure in the growth and self-actualisation of other people' (Maslow, 1998, pp. 165–166).

We consider that 'inspiring leadership (in others within the EPS) and outward-facing leadership (partnership working outside the EPS) creates an organisational culture which maximises self-actualisation (Maslow, 1998) and optimal functioning (Fransella & Dalton, 1990) and achieves better outcomes for children, young people and their families. It has the added benefit in that the well-being of staff is enhanced and has been considered to be successful in traded and nontraded EPSs.

References

Argyris, C. (1990). *Overcoming organisational defenses: Facilitating organisational learning.* Upper Saddle River, NJ: Prentice Hall.

Argyris, C., & Schon, D. (1974). *Theory in practice: Increasing professional effectiveness.* San Francisco: Jossey-Bass.

Association of Educational Psychologists (AEP). (2008). *Psychologists in multi-disciplinary settings. Investigations into the work of educational psychologists in Children's Services Authorities.* Durham: AEP.

Association of Educational Psychologists (AEP). (2009). *The role of educational psychology in safeguarding and child protection in the UK.* Durham: AEP.

Bannister, D., & Fransella, F. (1989). *Inquiring man: The psychology of personal constructs* (3rd ed). London and New York: Routledge.

Bannister, D., & Mair, J. M. M. (1968). *The evaluation of personal constructs.* London and New York: Academic Press.

Bartram, P., & Wolfendale, S. (1999). Educational Psychology Services: The pursuit of quality assurance. The role of service level agreements. *Educational Psychology in Practice, 15*(1), 51–56.

British Psychological Society (BPS). (2015). *Guidance for Educational Psychologists (EPs) when preparing reports for children and young people following the implementation of the Children and Families Act 2014.* Leicester: BPS, Division of Educational and Child and Child Psychology.

British Quality Foundation. (1998). *Guide to the Business Excellence Model.* London: British Quality Foundation.

British Standards Institute. (2015). *Quality management systems requirements: BS EN ISO 9001 2015* (6th ed.). London: BSI.

Bronfenbrenner, U. (1979). *The ecology of human development: Experiments by nature and design.* London: Harvard University Press.

Budgell, P., & Gallivan, M. (1981). A reflexive educational psychology. *Association of Educational Psychologists Journal, 5*(5), 13–21.

Burnham, J. (1986). *Family therapy.* London: Routledge.

Cameron, R. J. (1995, April). Management in educational psychology: The people factor. Special Issue: Management. *Educational Psychology in Practice,* 44–52.

Chazan, M. (1972). The role of the educational psychologist in the promotion of community mental health. *Association of Educational Psychologists (AEP) Journal and Newsletter, 3*(1), 9–16.

Chazan, M., Moore, T., Williams, P., & Wright, H. J. (1974). *The practice of educational psychology.* London: Longman.

Children and Families Act. (2014). Retrieved from http://www.legislation.gov.uk/ukpga/2014/6/contents/enacted

Cooper, P., Smith, C., & Upton, G. (1994). *Emotional and behavioural difficulties.* London: Routledge.

Courtney, R. (2002). *Strategic management for voluntary non profit organisations.* London: Routledge.

Department for Education and Employment (DfEE). (2000). *Educational Psychology Services (England): Current role, good practice and future directions.* Research report. Nottingham: DfEE Publications.

Department for Education and Science (DfES). (2004). *Every child matters: Change for children.* Nottingham: DfES Publications.

Dowling, E., & Osborne, E. (1995) *The Family and The School: A Joint Systems Approach to Problems with Children.* London: Routledge.

Engestrom, Y. (1999). Activity theory and individual and social transformation. In Y. Engestrom, R. Meittinen, & R. L. Punamaki (Eds.), *Perspectives on activity theory* (pp. 19–38). Cambridge: Cambridge University Press.

Fransella, F., & Dalton, P. (1990). *Personal construct counselling in action*. London: Sage Publications.

Fullan, M. (2005). *Leadership and sustainability: System thinkers in action*. London: Sage Publications.

Gillham, B. (1978). *Reconstructing educational psychology*. London: Croom Helm.

Gronn, P. (2000). Distributed properties: A new architecture for leadership. *Educational Management and Administration, 28*(3), 317–338.

Gunter, H. (2001). *Leaders and leadership in education*. London: Paul Chapman Publishing.

Hagstrom, R. P., Fry, M. K., Cramblet, L. D., & Tanner, K. (2007). Educational psychologists as scientist-practitioners: An expansion of the meaning of a scientist-practitioner. *American Behavioral Scientist* [online] https://doi.org/10.1177/0002764206296458. ISSN: 1552-3381.

Hanson, B. G. (1995). *General systems theory: Beginning with wholes*. Toronto: Taylor and Francis.

Harri-Augstein, S., & Thomas, L. (1991). *Learning conversations: The self-organised learning way to personal and organisational growth*. London and New York: Routledge.

Harri-Augstein, S., & Webb, I. M. (1995). *Learning to change: A resource for trainers, managers and learners based on self-organised learning*. London: McGraw-Hill.

Harrison, J., Mulrooney, C., Stratford, R., & Walker, C. (1996). Can a Psychological Service be a learning organisation? *Educational Psychology in Practice, 13*(3), 50–58.

Himmelman, A. T. (1996). On theory and practice of transformational collaboration: From social service to social justice. In C. Huxham (Ed.), *Creating the Collaborative Advantage* (pp. 19–43). London: Sage Publications.

Huxham, C. (1996). *Creating collaborative advantage*. London: Sage Publications.

Huxham, C., & Vangen, S. (2005). *Managing to collaborate. The theory and practice of collaborative advantage*. London: Routledge.

Investors in People. (2000). *Overview of the Investors in People Standard*. London. Investors in People.

Jones, P. (2006). Every child's parent matters: Community educational psychology and the Plymouth Parent Partnership Service. *Educational and Child Psychology, 23*(1), 15–26.

Kelly, G. (1955). *The psychology of personal constructs*. New York: Norton.

Kotter, J.P. (1996). *Leading change*. Boston: Harvard Business School Press.

McGregor, D. (1960). *The human side of enterprise*. New York: McGraw-Hill.

McPherson, I., & Sutton, A. (1981). *Reconstructing psychological practice*. London: Croom Helm.

Maslow, A. H.(1998). *Maslow on management*. New York: Wiley.

National College for School Leadership. (2006). *System leadership in action: Leading networks leading the system*. Nottingham: National College for School Leadership.

Orford, J. (1992). *Community psychology: Theory and practice*. Chichester: Wiley.

Preedy, M., Glatter, R. and Wise, C. (2003) *Strategic leadership and educational improvement*. London: The Open University.

Rhodes, E. (2017). 'Clear basis for change' on social justice. *The Psychologist, 30*, 15. Retrieved from https://thepsychologist.bps.org.uk/volume-30/april-2017/clear-basis-change-social-justice

Roffey, S. (2000). Addressing bullying in schools: Organisational factors from policy to practice. *Educational and Child Psychology*, *17*(1), 6–19.

Rowland, K. (2002). Effective leadership and service improvement in contemporary Educational Psychology Services: Modernize, demonstrate quality of be privatized. *Educational Management and Administration*, *30*(3), 275–291.

Rowland, K., Traxson, D., & Roberts, W. (2010, December). Community educational psychology and ethical leadership. *Debate*, no. 137, 4–12. Leicester: BPS.

Schon, D. A. (1987). *Educating the reflective practitioner*. San Francisco: Jossey-Bass.

Senge, P. M. (1990). *The fifth discipline: The art and practice of the learning organisation*. London: Random House.

Sharp, S., Frederickson, N., & Laws, K. (2000). Changing the profile of an Educational Psychology Service. *Educational and Child Psychology*, *17*(1), 98–109.

Smith, J. (1978). Contemporary management principles. In R. Stratford & J. Ward (Eds.), *Occasional Publication* (pp. 4–9). Southampton: University of Southampton.

Stoll, L., & Fink, D. (1995). *Changing our schools*. Buckingham: Open University Press.

Stratford, R. J. (1995, April). Managing Educational Psychology Services. Special Issue: Management. Educational Psychology in Practice, 2–5.

Stratford, R., & Ward, J. (1978). Overview: Management principles for Senior Educational Psychologists. In R. Stratford & J. Ward (Eds.). *Occasional Publication* (pp. 30–32). Southampton: University of Southampton.

Sullivan, H., & Skelcher, C. (2002). *Working across boundaries: Collaboration in public services. Government beyond the centre*. Houndmills: Palgrave MacMillan.

Trafford, V. (1978). Management by objectives in local government. In R. Stratford & J. Ward (Eds.), *Occasional Publication* (pp. 9–15). Southampton: University of Southampton.

Vygotsky, L. S. (1962). *Thought and language*. Cambridge, MA: MIT Press.

Wright, H. J. (1973). The psychologist as administrator. *Association of Educational Psychology Journal*, 3(5).

Wright, H. J. (1978). Management and the SPS in the new County of Hampshire. In R. Stratford & J. Ward (Eds.), *Occasional Publication* (pp. 24–29). Southampton: University of Southampton.

Wright, H. J., & Payne, T. A. N. (1978). *An evaluation of a school psychological service: The Portsmouth pattern*. Winchester: Hampshire County Council.

Section 2

Practical Themes

7

Understanding Your Organisation: Where to Start as a Leader

Julia Hardy and Mohammed Bham

Principal Educational Psychologists (PEPs) and Senior Educational Psychologists (SEPs) work within Local Authorities (LAs) of varying sizes and as these are public sector organisations which include education and social care services, EPSs are either placed within special educational needs and disability (SEND) services, under social care or education and skills departments. The overall reduction in funding of LAs and focus on outsourcing of services have significantly altered the way in which many EPSs now work. However, understanding your organisation remains a central concern. This is also the case for leaders of EPs who may be responsible for teams who work in the private sector. Typically, LAs are hierarchical organisations and are directed by national and local policy which frames priorities and directs decision-making. Within this context EPS leaders need to consider how they can act effectively within their organisation.

Introduction

When we both reflected on our experiences of becoming an EPS 'leader', both in the posts as a SEP and when new to PEP posts, we were aware that we were on a journey of developing our understanding of and familiarity with the organisation, the colleagues we were getting to know and build collaborative alliances with, and, most important, building initiatives within our EPS. This chapter will cover the different starting points, including having a framework to structure one's thinking about the organisation, as well as determining the priorities, such as having an agreed vision and values. There is a tension between getting to grips with the operational, here and now daily demands and having a focus on the future strategic developments.

There is no right, logical way to go about the process of understanding your organisation. For some leaders working in a large organisation, it is difficult initially to make sense of how things function. Your priorities in developing your understanding will vary hugely, depending on the context. Your EPS may have a history and hidden agendas that you need to uncover both with regard to the perspective of the EPs and also how the service is understood by others, whether they are parents, young people, schools, or colleagues within the organisation. The organisation may also be new, such as a community interest company,

Leadership for Educational Psychologists: Principles & Practicalities, First Edition.
Edited by Julia Hardy, Charmian Hobbs and Mohammed Bham.
© 2020 John Wiley & Sons Ltd. Published 2020 by John Wiley & Sons Ltd.

where the top tiers (from director to the second and third tiers of line management) are actively working together to agree upon the organisation's values, strategic plan and initial priorities. Alternatively, it may be a well-established organisation, where you might have been promoted from a maingrade post or have previously worked as a trainee; here the task is to shift your perspective to understand your new role and the developing different relationships and alliances.

This chapter will also provide a range of 'tools' that we have both found useful in helping us to understand what is going on within the organisation; this ranges from the specifics of influencing change and thinking about work with stakeholders to the more general perspective on the whole organisation's culture. The chapter will end with a discussion of the importance of relationships and how leaders need to be self-reflective on the dynamic nature of relationships, especially within the challenging context of dealing with austerity measures within LAs.

Where to Start as a New EPS Leader?

For a new PEP/SEP, where they start in coming to understand the EPS and the organisation within which it is embedded depends on their values. Quinn, Faerman, Thompson, McCrath and St. Clair (2003) described the values falling within two continua: (a) how controlling/flexible you are, and (b) how much the focus is on internal or external matters. When the first author of this chapter started as a PEP, her focus was on getting to know the people, whereas the director was keen (in a newly formed leadership team) to focus on strategy. Certainly, new PEPs need to discover how the organisation functions, the norms for behaviour and any current tasks (either written into the strategic plan or directed by the PEP's director and line managers). Often, if the organisation is undergoing change, there is a reconsideration of the structure, and as Hardy, Braithwaite and Hobson emphasise in Chapter 12, in this age of austerity the PEP has to be mindful of available resources and any pressures to generate income.

As new PEPs both authors found it was necessary to deal with many factors within the organisation (see Figure 7.1). Figure 7.1 covers all the elements within the organisation, but one other way of understanding the organisation is to look at the external environment too. A range of structures have been used to analyse the macro-environmental and the simplest current one is the STEEPLE: the Social, Technological, Economic, Environmental, Political, Legal and Ethical factors (Carr & Nanni, 2009). This was previously called PESTLE, before the ethical element was added (Aguilar, 1967).

One of the tools that is easy to use for analysis is a 'force-field' analysis, described initially by Lewin (1948) where he wrote about a culture being dynamic, with driving forces (positive influences) and restraining forces (obstacles) in the leader's task to move from the present state to the desired state. This tool enables you to map the desired state at the centre with the counterbalancing forces one on each side. It is simple and yet brings clarity to dilemmas many EPS leaders may be facing in implementing changes.

Another tool is to undertake a SWOT analysis (Strengths, Weaknesses, Opportunities and Threats), which has been used for decades in leadership practice (Johnson & Scholes, 2002; Johnson, Scholes, & Whittington, 2005), in EP evaluative practice (Atkinson, Corban,

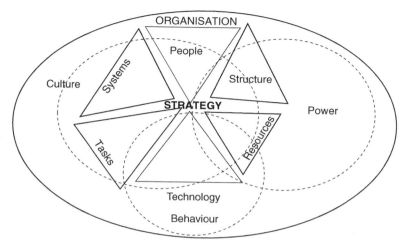

Figure 7.1 Factors that a new EPS leader has to understand.

& Templeton, 2011) and in coaching (Bond & Naughton, 2011). This is especially useful when working with your team/service to plan future strategies as it helps EPs to start with their focus on the current strengths and weaknesses and then as a part of envisioning the future, to plan and discuss the opportunities and threats in the future.

Figure 7.2 is an example of using SWOT when preparing an EPS to incorporate a Mental Health Support Team for Schools within the service, under the line management of PEP/SEPs:

Annual Cycles

If you have moved into a service with little fixed in terms of its systems, processes and procedures, it is helpful to map these out. Both authors found it useful to look at the annual cycle of events that the EPS leadership had to attend to, some of which occur at a predictable time of year (such as indicating to the universities that you wish to have a trainee EP, or the appraisal/team planning timescales required by the LA), whereas others may be dependent on unpredictable changes (such as recruitment – see Chapter 9) or they need to be scheduled into your planning cycle at a time that you choose (such as agreeing the continuing professional development [CPD] plan, which may be negotiated at the time of appraisals for the service). The leadership team need to agree their vision, values and underpinning principles; one key principle for the two authors is to reflect on how much do you wish/are you able to apply a positive psychological stance rather than a reactive/defensive one, both in devising and agreeing upon a service strategy and in your daily actions as a leadership team (see Figure 7.3).

What is important in this endeavour is to agree upon the underlying principles, to allow time to communicate and come to agreement in practice, as well as to apply your equalities principles in reflecting on the impact and ways in which the policy in practice will be evaluated to ensure consistency and fairness.

Strengths	Weakness
EPs capable of line managing the Mental Health Support Practitioners (MHSPs)

EPs to co-ordinate MHSPs work in schools, therefore avoid duplication or competition

Additional capacity in the EPS delivery of service

When EPs identify needs, MHSPs can provide time-limited evidence-based interventions

MHSPs will hold postgraduate mental health qualifications | Takes up EP capacity fulfilling HR requirements

Reduces profile of EPs as providers of mental health support

Reduced opportunities for EPs to deliver therapeutic interventions with children with lower level needs, leaving EPs to work at more complex high need level

Sharing office and resources |
| Opportunities | Threats |
| For EPs to develop skills, experience and materials for psychological assessment and psychological interventions

CPD possibilities increasing through skill-sharing and learning on the job

More scope for involvement with psychological interventions | Can be seen by schools or LA as a cheaper option paid for by Health

Labelling kids with mental health needs and expecting 1-1 therapy

Could reduce resources for investing in TEPs or assistant EPs |

Figure 7.2   An example of a SWOT analysis for incorporating a Mental Health Support Team for Schools within an EPS.

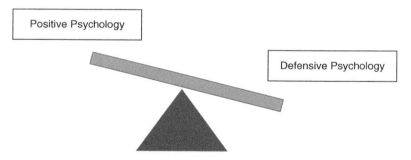

Figure 7.3   What stance do we take in talking about EPS processes and procedures?

Fairness in the workplace is not a 'nice to have', it is the law. In order to safeguard the welfare of all practitioners in the EPS, the decision-making and behaviour of all practitioner psychologists will need to be governed by the council's staff handbook (or similar document including the council's policy documents relating to employees) which will provide guidance to help employers and employees to understand the basics of supporting equality and preventing discrimination; the Health and Care Professions Council's (HCPC's) Standards of Conduct, Performance and Ethics (2016); the British Psychological

Society (BPS) (2018) Code of Ethics and Conduct and the BPS (2017) Professional Practice Guidelines. All practitioners in the service should have copies of these documents and opportunities to explore and clarify issues.

To help EPS staff deal confidently with equality matters, the following four principles need to be applied in the workplace (Advisory, Conciliation and Arbitration Service, 2015)

1) Equality must be embedded in the values and professional purpose of the organisation.
2) Explain to staff why it is important to treat people fairly and lawfully to avoid discrimination.
3) Set achievable equality aims in the team plan.
4) Monitor progress towards these aims, reporting honestly about successes and challenges.

Strategic Elements

Early on in the PEP's work within a LA it is imperative that they work with leaders and the whole EPS to communicate and develop a shared vision (see Chapters 1 and 2). As Senge (1990) observed 'where there is a shared vision ... people excel and learn, not because they are told to, but because they want to' (p. 9). A 'shared vision involves the skills of unearthing shared 'pictures of the future' that foster genuine commitment and enrolment rather than compliance' (p. 9). Pendleton and Furnham (2016) define vision as 'a compelling view of the future and the place the organisation wants to occupy in that future' (p. 50). They contrast the day-to-day 'present and specific domains' with the 'future and generic' ones (p. 53).

The literature on leadership uses many metaphors. Morgan (1986) wrote about how the images or metaphors through which we read organisational situations help us to describe the way organisations are and offer clear ideas and options as to how they could be. He suggested that using the metaphors as organisations as organisms and organisations as brains helps our understanding. One metaphorical concept often mentioned in the leadership literature is that of *helicopter vision*, in which one needs to keep in mind the overall current context, as well as possible futures, when trying to get a realistic picture of where your EPS is and where you all want to get to in developing your strategy. The 'organisational culture' is described metaphorically by Van den Berg and Wilderom (2004) as forming 'the glue that holds the organisation together and stimulates employees to commit to the organisation and to perform' (p. 571). They define organisational culture as shared perceptions of organisational work practices within organisational units that may differ from other organisational units; stressing that organisational work practices are the central part of this definition. The definition is a shortened version of Kostova's (1999) definition: 'particular ways of conducting organizational functions that have evolved over time ... [These] practices reflect the shared knowledge and competence of the organization' (p. 309).

So culture can be defined as 'the way things are done here'. Culture can be defined by the staff in the organisation. However, staff may differ in the ways they define the culture which can then lead to confusion. There are differences in definitions about organisational culture which focus on different aspects of the organisation: if simply considered to be one facet of an organisation then that might be considered easy to change, such as changing the service plan or team structure.

Operational Elements

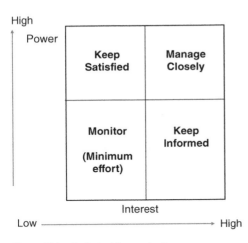

Figure 7.4 Stakeholder analysis.

PEPs, SEPs and others leading EPS developments need to continually fluctuate between the operational, day-to-day demands and having a coherent plan for the future. When focusing on the present, the EPS leadership team can map out the recurring tasks (in the planning cycle mentioned previously) and agree what are the priority tasks and who should lead on them. The WWWWH (What, Where, Why, When and How) questioning framework is helpful in agreeing this (which is known as the the 5Ws and How and is attributed to Aristotle; Sloan, 2010).

Another aspect that leaders need to attend to is the influence of stakeholders. There is extensive work on the importance of stakeholders, particularly in the leadership literature focusing on industry (deriving from Porter, 1980) or the differentials in organisational structures (such as Mintzberg, 1983) but also including working with those who are proactive (Ali, 2018). Work within complex systems needs to consider the different levels of stakeholders, such as client, provider, organisation and the wider service system (Rodríguez, Southam-Gerow, O'Connor, & Allin, 2014). A simple stakeholder analysis (see Figure 7.4) helps us to decide how to focus our time in influencing others, by asking who has more power and influence amongst the stakeholders with whom you wish to work?

This is also important when planning and deciding: Which strategic or operational meetings to attend? Which boards or working groups to participate in? Where to prioritise your service/council resources to address particular development priorities? Which partners are provided access to the highly specialist knowledge and skills EPs offer with systemic work, including training, staff coaching, or supervision, whole school or Local Authority level research and development in organisations?

Understanding Your Organisational Culture

As mentioned in Chapter 2, the organisational web explores six interrelated elements to reflect upon in attempting to understand your organisational culture (Johnson & Scholes, 2002), see Figure 7.5.

- **Stories**: the past and present events and people talked about inside and outside the company.
- **Rituals and routines**: the daily behaviour and actions of people that signal acceptable behaviour.

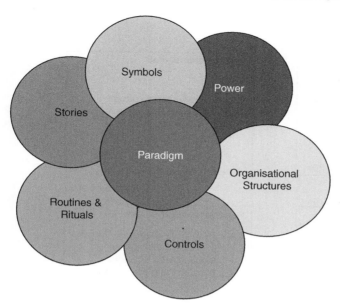

Figure 7.5   The Organisational Web (Johnson & Scholes, 1988).

- **Symbols**: the visual representations of the company including logos, office decor and formal or informal dress codes.
- **Organisational structure**: structures defined by the organisation chart and the unwritten lines of power and influence that indicate whose contributions are most valued.
- **Control systems**: the ways that the organisation is controlled including financial systems, quality systems and rewards.
- **Power structures**: in this element the power in the company/organisation may lie with one or two executives, a group of executives, or a department. These people have the greatest amount of influence over decisions, operations and strategic direction.

We are well aware that organisations are complex structures and consequently there are many and diverse ways of illustrating the varying emphases placed by leaders and managers on their tasks. Quinn et al. (2003) acknowledge that there are competing values in deciding what to focus on when implementing change (refer to Chapter 4), with two dimensions in which their focus can vary: (a) that of flexibility versus control as well as (b) how much leaders place an emphasis on their own aspect of the organisation or that of the wider external elements, as illustrated in Figure 7.6 (adapted from Quinn et al., 2003).

As well as using the aforementioned frameworks to understand the organisation and its culture, there are also aspects of size and stage of development to be considered. Most local authorities within which we work have been in place for a substantial length of time; nevertheless there are sometimes new developments (such as moving from a traditional LA to a community interest company which provides the service previously under LA management, such as Achieving for Children) which is a legal form of social enterprise (Defourny, 2001; Deforny & Nyssens, 2006).

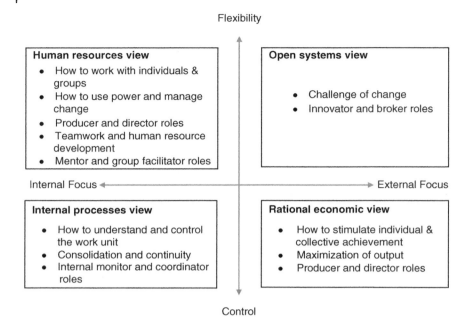

Figure 7.6 Quinn et al.'s (2003) competing values model and change.

It could be that with a new director and organisational structure, the mission of the organisation, together with its remit and size, may need to change. Greiner (1972) wrote about the five stages of organisational growth. He argued that gradual evolution is not inevitable but that some organisations go through turbulent times of revolution. As organisations grow the leadership style adapts; with the small, possibly young organisation, there is scope for growth through creativity. As time passes there may be the first crisis, that of leadership. Once this has stabilised and the leader has adjusted and is accepted, there is a phase when the organisation grows with a clear (and, it is hoped, shared) direction. The next crisis is that of autonomy, when the more experienced staff want freedom to choose and act with some independence. Once this change is stabilised then there is more clarity about delegation in line with the need for autonomy. The next two phases are relevant only if the organisation is much larger; with a crisis of control (who is in charge of what and how) which leads to the need to grow through better co-ordination between colleagues. Greiner (1972) suggested that there may then be too much bureaucracy, and the next crisis might be that of red tape. Although this is a somewhat simple model, it is of use when EPSs are within a growing organisation, or indeed when an EPS leader moves from one service to another that is a very different size (see Figure 7.7).

When working within a changing organisation the parable of the boiled frog (Senge, 1990) comes to mind. If you are in a slowly changing organisation, especially where the changes are maladaptive, it is useful to be reminded that as with the frog in a gradually warming pan, you may not notice these changes occurring and this prevents you from jumping out of the organisation (or saucepan) before damage is done.

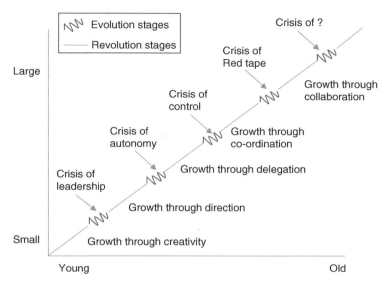

Figure 7.7 Understanding your organisation (Greiner, 1972).

Over the many years that the authors have been delivering leadership courses, one of the key influences on discussions about communicating with and engaging members of the team has been Nancy Kline (1999, 2009) in her thought-provoking descriptions of how she has worked with others to create 'Time to Think'. One concept that she describes is 'limiting assumptions', which 'seem like the truth' and yet make it impossible for the thinker's ideas to flow further. Apart from asking directly 'what might we be assuming here that is limiting our thinking on this issue?'(1999, p. 57), Kline suggests that you can use incisive questioning in order to lift the limiting assumption. You do this by hypothesising, attaching a freeing assumption and associating this with a new goal. For instance, 'If you knew that your EPS was the most creative service to work in within your region, how would you feel about going to work?' Kline also emphasises providing valued time in which you plan for times when all colleagues have opportunities to express their individual views, with space built in to listen to each other with appreciation and without interruption (for full details see Kline's (2009) 10 components of the thinking environment).

Building Working Relationships

You may hear PEP and SEP colleagues talk about 'life being all about relationships' and some may even go as far as saying 'your effectiveness in life depends on your ability to create relationships with others – family, friends and work colleagues'.

It is crucial for the EPS leader to consider and explore some of the components of relationships in general and focus on the realism in our expectations of working relationships. The authors have included this area within this chapter as this has been a key aspect of the EPS leadership development programme for new and existing leaders to develop some of the component areas in detail.

The maturity continuum refers to where individuals go from developing from the paradigm of 'I' (independence) with self-interest to the paradigm of 'You' (dependence) with interest in others and the paradigm of 'We' (Interdependence) balancing between interest in self with interest in others.

The work of Myron Rush (1983) on relationships is of relevance here as he gives attention to the following areas:

Relationships evolve around personal needs. People need each other; and no one is self-sufficient. We all have needs that can be met only through relationships with others.

Met needs → RELATIONSHIP IS STRENGTHENED

For relationships to be mutually rewarding, the needs of all the individuals involved must be met. So our goal in any relationship must be to meet the needs within the relationship.

At work, relationships can develop into friendships; however friendships are not a requirement in the workplace. Certainly, if a working relationship is also a friendship, leaders in any organisation need to reflect on how this may have an impact on their working relationships with those who they also see as friends and for the other colleagues who they only see at work. Is this dual relationship impinging on how others see the leader(s)? Does this have any impact and hidden bias on their decision-making?

Rush (1983) goes on to describe the nature of relationships and the importance of 'building bridges': through being respected, trusted and understood at work; as well as communication and commitment at work. He emphasises the importance of building relationships strong enough to carry the weight of all we want to transport across them.

When establishing a team or joining a service in a leadership role as PEP or SEP being **respected at work** is a professional requirement. This involves the following key components:

- Setting a good example of hard work
- Behaving well and appropriately
- Showing emotional stability
- Applying fairness and consistency in dealings
- 'Delivering' the work and achieving results
- Holding to values and beliefs

Being **trusted at work** is another professional requirement. This involves the following key components *to achieve integrity*:

- Openness and honesty in communication
- Keeping one's word or promises
- Affirming good behaviour and confronting poor behaviour
- Honouring confidences
- Making decisions with people's best interests in mind
- Consistency in public and private

Being **understanding at work** is a third professional requirement. This involves the following key components *to achieve acceptance*:

- Consider everyone as unique individuals
- Individuals have different drives and preferences

- Individual backgrounds and circumstances affect us
- Adapting to individual differences is essential in relationships
- Understanding leads to unity not uniformity
- Understanding leads to complementarity not competition

Leaders need to work towards ***achieving meaning in the workplace*** and reduce vulnerability over time.

To progress in leadership involves staff experiencing and noticing your communication at work, with you as leader increasingly moving through the following levels:

- Making small talk
- Sharing facts: data and information
- Sharing thoughts and ideas
- Sharing feelings and emotions
- Sharing hopes and fears

To progress in leadership involves staff experiencing and noticing your commitment at work, key components include:

- Show interest and keep finding out new things
- Give people time with your full attention
- Take initiative so staff see you being thoughtful about others
- Help and support people in their work and concerns
- Speak positively about others wherever possible
- Learn to apologise and to forgive

Investing in Relationships

Covey's (2004) metaphor of the 'emotional bank account' (pp. 188–190) needs to be mentioned here when a leader is establishing a team and joining a new service, as this helps to inform the sophisticated and changing nature of relationships, involving making 'investments' and managing situations carefully when 'withdrawals' are made.

We all know how our bank account works. We make deposits, save money and if we need that money later, we withdraw it. An emotional bank account is an account of trust instead of money. It is an account based on how safe you feel with another person.

This is not about and not promoting 'transactional' relations; instead it is about developing 'transformational' leadership.

Covey (2004) identified the six major 'deposits' a leader should make in the 'emotional bank account of staff':

1) Understanding the person: it's important to care for others and act with kindness towards them.
2) Keeping commitments: You build up an emotional reserve by keeping your commitments.
3) Clarifying expectations: Communicating our expectations can help create a higher level of trust.
4) Paying attention to the little things: Doing something you did not have to do can help build trust.

5) Living with personal integrity: When we operate with sound moral character, it makes it easy to be trusted.

6) Apologising sincerely when we make a withdrawal: as a leader when you realise you have violated a trust, sincerely apologising is how we make a deposit to counteract the damage we have done.

Based on the content discussed here concerning building relational bridges, the authors recommend new and established leaders regularly build in time to carry out a 'working relationships audit':

Consider your six or seven most important relationships at work, choosing a mix of line manager(s), peer(s) and direct report(s).

Assess your relationship in the five areas, for each person using a rating of high, medium, or low.

In the 'level of the emotional bank account' describe its current state.

Finally, write any initiatives you might take at this time to improve each relationship.

In this tough financial climate for leaders of public services, we have to be wise about how we spend our emotions.

Froman (2010) wrote about the concept of a *virtuous organisation*. These organisations have cultures infused with a strong ethical–moral foundation and leaders who bring out the best of their employees. As Froman (2010) comments:

> 'Driven in part by the turmoil in the current economy, organizational responses often lead to job loss and other cost-cutting measures.... Organizations need to develop cultures built around principles of integrity, ethics, trust and respect. Organizations bring out the best in their members [staff] by focusing on such positive psychologic concepts as strengths, hope, optimism, self-confidence, self-motivation, resilience, joy and gratitude. Organizations of virtue strive to do well by doing good, and strive to do good by doing well. They create conditions for their members [staff] to thrive and flourish in ways that bridge economic and human development'. (p. 67)

Throughout this chapter we have shared learning from our collective leadership experience of understanding key features within organisations through internal and external models of working, as well as the interpersonal and intrapersonal factors that make organisations work effectively, in particular the importance of relationships and emotional investments.

We hope that colleagues joining the EPS leadership endeavour work towards achieving positive, ethical organisations within which applied educational psychology may flourish and through your leadership you infuse an ethical perspective into your organisational culture. Through your supportive leadership may you empower your team to succeed and do good.

References

Advisory, Conciliation and Arbitration Service (ACAS). (2015). *Steve Williams: The four principles of equality in workplaces.* Retrieved from http://www.acas.org.uk/index. aspx?articleid=5406

Aguilar, F. (1967). *Scanning the business environment.* New York: Macmillan.

Ali, M. A. (2018). Proactive stakeholder practices: A modified Reactive, Defensive, Accommodative, and Proactive (RDAP) Scale. *Journal of Managerial Issues, 30* (4), 405–421.

Atkinson, C., Corban, I., & Templeton, J. (2011). Educational psychologists' use of therapeutic interventions: Issues arising from two exploratory case studies. *Support for Learning, NASEN, 26*(4), 160–167.

Bond, A. S., & Naughton, N. (2011). The role of coaching in managing leadership transitions. *International Coaching Psychology Review, 6*(2), 165–179.

British Psychological Society (BPS). (2017). *Professional practice guidelines.* Retrieved from https://www.bps.org.uk/news-and-policy/practice-guidelines

British Psychological Society (BPS). (2018). *Code of ethics and conduct.* Retrieved from https:// www.bps.org.uk/news-and-policy/bps-code-ethics-and-conduct

Carr, L. P., & Nanni, A. J., Jr. (2009). *Delivering results: Managing what matters.* New York: Springer Science & Business Media.

Covey, S. R. (2004). *The 7 habits of highly effective people: Powerful lessons in personal change; restoring the character ethic.* New York: Free Press.

Defourny, J. (2001). *From third sector to social enterprise.* In C. Borzaga & J. Defourny (Eds.), *The emergence of social enterprise* (pp. 1–28). London & New York: Routledge.

Defourny, J. & Nyssens, M. (2006). Defining social enterprise. In M. Nyssens with the assistance of S. Adam & T. Johnson (Eds.), *Social enterprise at the crossroads of market, public policies and civil society* (pp. 3–26). London: Routledge,.

Froman, L. (2010). Positive psychology in the workplace. *Journal of Adult Development, 17*(2), 59–69.

Greiner, L. E. (1972, July-August). Evolution and revolution as organizations grow. *Harvard Business Review, 50*(4).

Health & Care Professions Council (HCPC). (2016). *Standards of conduct, performance and ethics.* Retrieved from https://www.hcpc-uk.org/standards/standards-of-conduct-performance-and-ethics/

Johnson, G., & Scholes, K. (1988). *Exploring corporate strategy* (2nd ed.). London: Prentice-Hall.

Johnson, G., & Scholes, K. (2002). *Exploring corporate strategy* (6th ed.). London: Pitman Publishing.

Johnson, G., Scholes, K., & Whttington, R. (2005). *Exploring corporate strategy: Text and cases.* Harlow: Prentice Hall.

Kline, N. (1999). *Time to think.* New York: Hachette.

Kline, N. (2009). *More time to think.* Retrieved from https://www.timetothink.com/thinking-environment/the-ten-components/

Kostova, T. (1999). Transnational transfer of strategic organizational practices: A contextual perspective. *Academy of Management Review, 24*, 308–324.

Lewin, K. (1948). *Resolving social conflicts, selected papers on group dynamics [1935–1946]* (G. W. Lewin, Ed.). New York: Harper & Brothers.

Mintzberg, H. (1983). *Power in and around organizations.* Englewood Cliffs, NJ: Prentice-Hall.

Morgan, G. (1986). *Images of organization.* London: Sage.

Pendleton, D., & Furnham, A. (2016). *Leadership: All you need to know* (2nd ed.). London: Palgrave Macmillan.

Porter, M. (1980). *Competitive strategy: Techniques for analyzing industries and competitors.* New York: Free Press.

Quinn, R. E. Faerman, S. R., Thompson, M. P., McCrath, M., & St. Clair, L. S. (2003). *Becoming a master manager.* New York: John Wiley & Sons.

Rodríguez, A., Southam-Gerow, M. A., O'Connor, M.K., & Allin, R. B. (2014). An analysis of stakeholder views on children's mental health services. *Journal of Clinical Child & Adolescent Psychology, 43*(6), 862–876.

Rush, M. D. (1983*). Richer relationships.* Wheaton, IL: Victor Books.

Senge, P. M. (1990). *The fifth discipline. The art and practice of the learning organisation.* London: Random House.

Sloan, M. C. (2010). Aristotle's Nicomachean ethics as the original locus for the Septem Circumstantiae. *Classical Philology, 105,* 236–251.

Van Den Berg, P. T., & Wilderom, C. P. M. (2004). Defining, measuring, and comparing organisational cultures. *Applied Psychology: An International Review, 53*(4), 570–582.

8

Using Appreciative Inquiry (AI) as a Solution-Focussed Approach to Organisational Change in Two Educational Psychology Services

Anna Lewis

Introduction

Appreciative Inquiry (AI) offers a solution-focused approach to organisational change that is empowering, motivating and inclusive. This chapter provides a critical account of the AI philosophy and process, exemplified by case studies where AI has facilitated positive change within two large Educational Psychology Services (EPSs) in England.

The structure of an AI fits within a model of distributed leadership (see Chapter 2) and requires the members of the Senior Leadership Team (SLT) to participate equally alongside maingrade and Trainee Educational Psychologists (TEPs). Leaders need to trust in the process and to have the strength and humility to share power and decision-making with all service members.

> 'The AI model is based on the assumptions that organizations are socially constructed phenomena, which have no tangible reality, and that ways of organizing are limited only by human imagination and the agreements people make with each other'. (Bushe, 2013, p. 1)

Critics of AI have questioned how the process can solve problems within an organisation when it only focusses on the positive. Problems are addressed in two ways: (a) by selecting the topic for the AI as a specific area for service development (e.g. communication with service users); and (b) by understanding how well educational psychologists (EPs) know their own service's strengths and difficulties. Weaknesses and negative experiences are addressed when participants 'dream' of a preferred future for their organisation (Bellinger & Elliott, 2011). It is this 'bottom-up' approach that generates change. The power of AI lies more in its generative capacity than its positivity (Bushe, 2010b).

In both of the case studies, the AIs were implemented at times of organisational stress and anxiety within the EPS. One Local Authority (LA) was about to go through a restructuring process with associated EP job insecurity and the other was experiencing an unprecedented increase in statutory assessments at a time when the LA was proposing to move the EPS into a traded company. In both of these contexts, the AI enabled EPs to feel more control

Leadership for Educational Psychologists: Principles & Practicalities, First Edition.
Edited by Julia Hardy, Charmian Hobbs and Mohammed Bham.
© 2020 John Wiley & Sons Ltd. Published 2020 by John Wiley & Sons Ltd.

over the work they engaged in, leading to a range of activities that were planned with enthusiasm and energy rather than resisted as extra work imposed by senior managers.

What is AI?

'Appreciative inquiry is...based on the premise that knowledge can enlighten and empower those who strive to change the environment in which they work and live... Appreciative inquiry is purposely not value free. As human inquiry with transformative and emancipatory intent...it joins others in their visions of world betterment'. (Zandee & Cooperrider, 2008, p. 192)

Definitions

To *appreciate* means to value; recognise the best in people or the world around us; affirm past and present strengths, successes, and potentials; to perceive those things that give life (health, vitality, excellence) to living systems. Appreciate is synonymous with value, prize, esteem, and honour.

To *inquire* means to explore and discover; to ask questions; to be open to seeing new potentials and possibilities. Inquire is synonymous with discover, search, systematically explore, and study.

(Adapted from Cooperrider, Whitney, & Stavros, 2008, p. 1)

AI has variously been defined as a philosophy and/or a process:

'Appreciative Inquiry is a philosophy that incorporates an approach, a process (4-D Cycle of *Discovery, Dream, Design, and Destiny*) for engaging people at any or all levels to produce effective, positive change'. (Cooperrider et al., 2008, p. xv)

'Appreciative Inquiry is a group process that inquires into, identifies, and further develops the best of 'what is' in organisations in order to create a better future'. (Preskill & Catsambas, 2006, p. 1)

Origins

AI began in the 1980s when David Cooperrider and Suresh Srivastva were using a problem-focussed approach to organisational change at a clinic in Ohio and noticed how discouraged everyone became. Instead, they turned the process into a shared *inquiry* into what was working well. 'The results were immediate and dramatic. Relationships improved, cooperation increased and visible commitments by the physicians to change initiatives ensued' (Ludema & Fry, 2008, p. 281). In 1987, their classic article 'Appreciative Inquiry into Organizational Life' was published (Cooperrider & Srivastva, 1987, cited in Ludema and

Fry, 2008). Cooperrider resisted creating a specific method for AI for many years, preferring to articulate a set of principles to guide attempts to inquire appreciatively (Bushe & Kassam, 2005). This led many researchers to remain unclear about how AI might be applied within their organisations (Carter, 2006; Robinson, Priede, Farrell, Shapland, & McNeil, 2012; Trajkovski, Schmied, Vickers, & Jackson, 2013).

Principles and assumptions

In developing AI, Cooperrider was strongly influenced by research studies that demonstrated the power of positive images (Coghlan, Preskill, & Catsambas, 2003). Cooperrider and Whitney (2001, cited in Bushe & Kassam, 2005, p. 166), summarise the following set of principles for AI:

1) the constructionist principle
2) the principle of simultaneity
3) the poetic principle
4) the anticipatory principle
5) the positive principle

The *constructionist principle* relates to organisations being socially constructed, so that AI should involve as many members of the system as possible. The *principle of simultaneity* refers to inquiry and intervention occurring simultaneously in AI, so that as we inquire into human systems we change them. The *poetic principle* relates to the belief that the language of the inquiry will have an impact of its own and needs to be inspirational. The *anticipatory principle* indicates that we are guided by our visualisation of the future. The *positive principle* states that momentum and sustainable change require positive affect and social bonding. Based on these principles, eight assumptions form the foundation of AI philosophy and process:

1) In every society, organization, or group, something works.
2) What we focus on becomes our reality.
3) Reality is created in the moment, and there are multiple realities.
4) The act of asking questions of an organisation or group influences the group.
5) People have more confidence and comfort to journey to the future (the unknown) when they carry forward parts of the past (the known).
6) If we carry parts of the past forward, they should be what is best about the past.
7) It is important to value differences.
8) The language we use creates our reality (Coghlan et al., 2003, p. 10).

The appreciative inquiry process

The four 'Ds' model of appreciative inquiry

The most commonly used model for AI is the 4-D cycle depicted in Figure 8.1 (Ludema & Fry, 2008). AI is a dynamic process and the 'Ds' simply represent different, intentional sets of activities and conversations, all linked to an affirmative inquiry topic.

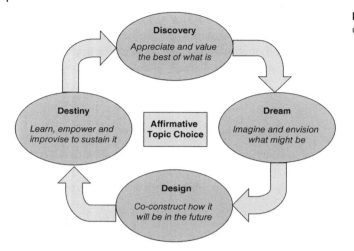

Figure 8.1 The four-D cycle of AI.

Topic choice

AI begins with carefully worded topics that focus attention on the desired outcomes of working together. This often involves rewording until the inquiry attracts genuine curiosity and interest. At this stage, a negative topic choice will be turned into what everyone wants to see instead.

Discovery

All participants are paired with people they know least well, mixing levels and areas of work. They have a set of questions to focus their conversations, sharing personal stories about times when they have experienced the best of the organisation and their contribution to it. Ludema and Fry (2008) argue that it is important to begin with these paired interviews because they '(1) give everyone equal voice; (2) establish a model of both sharing and listening in a deeply focused way; (3) offer every participant a chance to explore their own thinking in the relative safety of a one-on-one dialogue; (4) quickly generate a deep sense of connection among participants: and (5) draw out the appreciative foundations of the work to be done' (p. 286). The AI usually starts with four simple, powerful questions (Cooperrider et al., 2008, p. xix):

1) What would you describe as being the high-point experience in your organization, a time when you were most alive and engaged?
2) Without being modest, what is it that you most value about yourself, your work, and your organization?
3) What are the core factors that give life to your organization, without which the organization would cease to exist?
4) Imagine your organization five…years from now, when everything is just as you always imagined it would be. What has happened? What is different? How have you contributed to this future? (Cooperrider et al., 2008, p. 36)

The pairs then form small groups, share stories, look for themes and decide on the most powerful ones to report back to the whole group.

Dream

The same small groups share their greatest hopes and wishes, referring to the common themes from the stories and creatively developing some images of the future (e.g. in the form of art, song, role-play, poems, newscasts etc). The ideas are presented to the whole group, who then vote (if necessary) for a small number of the most powerful and attractive of the ideas. These form the focus of the next two stages.

Design

The participants choose which of the selected ideas they feel most interested in, passionate, or knowledgeable about and form new groups, each dedicated to a particular area for development. The new teams create 'provocative propositions' that describe what the dreams look like, as if they are already operating successfully. These are shared with the whole group and revised and improved so that all are involved.

> 'It is the stories of the future that create the present more than the stories of the past'. (McAdam & Mirza, 2009, p. 180)

Destiny

The groups create short-term targets and key actions for implementation based on the provocative propositions. Volunteers from each group are often asked to form a steering group that will monitor the implementation of the ideas over the next 6 months. Sometimes the event ends with participants giving feedback on what it has meant for them to be part of the whole process.

Theoretical influences

AI emerged from theoretical shifts within organisational psychology, where the idea of organisations as machines with problems to be fixed by managers started to give way to the idea of organisations as living human systems (Checkland, 2000; Lewis, Passmore, & Cantore, 2008). Seligman's work on positive psychology shifted the focus of organisational psychology towards what is right (rather than wrong) with people, and solution-focussed or strengths-based approaches to consultation have since gained in popularity (Wilding & Griffey, 2015).

Bushe's (2010c) meta-analysis of eight AIs into school learning (involving 21 schools in a large urban district in Canada) found that 'there was no relationship between how 'positive' the participants rated their experience of AI...nor how positively they felt afterwards, with the degree of change...whilst generativity does significantly differentiate degree of change' (Bushe, 2010b, p. 5). This suggests that the generative component of AI may be far more important than positivity, although the initial focus on strengths is still a necessary part of the process.

> 'Theoretical accounts are no longer judged in terms of their predictive capacity, but instead are judged in terms of their generative capacity...Instead of asking, 'Does this theory correspond with the observable facts?' the emphasis for evaluating good

theory becomes 'To what extent does this theory present provocative new possibilities for social action?' (Cooperrider & Srivastva, 1999, cited in Cooperrider et al., 2008, p. 359)

Burke (2011) argues that organisational development attempted to 'loosen up' tightly hierarchical systems (with overcontrolling leadership) and introduce models of 'bottom-up' management that are about 'humanizing the workplace' (p. 145). The leadership of EPSs is typically hierarchical, often with limited scope for distributing leadership across the service and allowing individual EPs to have genuine voice, influence and agency in creating and sustaining organisational change.

'A crucial aspect of AI is that it tries to get as much of the system working together as possible; aiming to be both 'top-down and bottom-up'...In AI the 'right people' are a group that can critically reflect on practice together, consider new solutions, *and* initiate change'. (Fieldhouse & Onyett, 2012, p. 364)

AI therefore needs particularly careful facilitation in order to manage the equal contribution of all participants working in authentic collaboration (Fieldhouse & Onyett, 2012, p. 368), simultaneously conveying confidence in a collaborative process whilst holding back from controlling the outcome (Bellinger & Elliott, 2011, p. 719).

'Its unique significance has been in bringing social constructionist theory into widespread consideration in managerial practice, identifying the power of possibility centric versus problem centric change strategies, forcing an examination of the impact of positive emotions on change processes and offering generativity, instead of problem-solving, as a way to address social and organizational issues'. (Bushe, 2013, p. 5)

What Organisational Contexts and Issues Are Most Appropriate for AI?

Curato, Niemeyer and Dryzek (2013) suggest that AI is particularly useful in creating meaningful discussions between people who are often antagonistic, requiring them to 'forge a new social relationship built on a shared vision for the future' (p. 4). This implies that AI might be especially good for building good working relationships and inventing new ways to work together, but less effective in organisations that already have a positive ethos and culture. Bellinger and Elliott (2011) suggest that AI can have a 'strengthening effect...on networks that are fragile and where there is a high risk of conflict, blame and mistrust' such as within 'state-regulated social work and education in the UK currently' (p. 722).

'In a system where there has been little appreciation, an AI process may be transformational, but over time as the system becomes appreciative, AI becomes less useful as a change process'. (Bushe, 2010a, p. 236)

Both of the EPS case studies in this chapter are focussed on using AI in challenging contexts, which may therefore have contributed to their effectiveness.

Bushe (2010a) claims that 'virtually none of the published cases examining AI take contextual variables into account' which are 'critical in untangling what kinds of changes can be attributed to the elements that are unique to AI...and what is more likely the result of effective (or ineffective) facilitation' (p. 236). Van der Haar and Hosking (2004) studied the extensive literature on AI and found very few evaluation studies or critical reflections on AI, calling for 'more narratives of AI that are written in ways that open up the multiple realities of participants and give readers greater space to form their own judgements' (p. 1032). The case studies presented next are offered as narratives of AI in practice, with the aspiration that these accounts illuminate the AI process and give the reader an opportunity to judge the potential of AI for generating positive change within their own EPS and wider organisational structures.

Case Studies

AI WITH AN EPS IN THE MIDLANDS

Background and Context

At the time of the AI, the Midlands EPS was a large service of approximately 40 EPs organised into three geographical teams. The 4-D AI cycle (Discovery, Dream, Design and Destiny) was conducted amidst considerable uncertainty about potential job losses due to the restructuring of services and significant cuts to the LA budget. Whilst the AI was implemented primarily as a solution-focussed approach to organisational change in order to develop professional practice, a TEP also investigated whether participation in the AI would have a positive impact on EPs' sense of control during such uncertain times.

Topic Selection

The Principal Educational Psychologist (PEP) initially suggested that it would be helpful to focus the AI on written communication, which was an area for service improvement (e.g. written objectives and strategies were considered not specific enough and there were inconsistencies in report writing). In order for the topic to attract genuine curiosity and interest in taking part, the planning group (including the PEP) decided instead to focus on communication more generally, titling the AI 'Communication for Change' and including the following subthemes:

- Empowering consultations
- Written communication as a catalyst for innovation and change
- Informal communication: integrity in action

The planning group then created an Appreciative Interview Guide (see Figure 8.2) based around these themes and began to collate resources for the 4-D cycle.

Communication for Change

- Empowering consultations
- Written communication as a catalyst for innovation and change
- Informal communication: integrity in action

Introduction

Thank you for taking part in this inquiry. We are interviewing each other in order to collect information about when we are all at our best as EPs so we can use this to genuinely create some new ways of working within our service in the future.

The focus of this inquiry is how we can best communicate with others so that real positive change happens as a result of our work.

Please interview each other using these thought-provoking questions to support your discussions and make a note of the most powerful stories and themes that seem to be emerging as you actively listen and learn from each other. Look out for any 'quotable quotes' and jot them down.

Getting to know you

Let's start with something about you and what most attracted you to being an EP. What is it about being an EP that is most valuable, meaningful, challenging or exciting? Why is it important to you?

Think back over important times in your life. Can you think of a story to share about when you became aware of what really matters in your life or what your purposes in life might be? What defines you as a person that you bring to being an EP?

What personal or philosophical beliefs/maxims drive your practice? How are these communicated to others to effect change?

Topic 1: Empowering consultations

- Spend a few moments reflecting on a time when your consultation with another professional was particularly successful and led to real and possibly lasting changes. Please describe this situation and tell me how it made you feel and why it was successful

  If I had been able to watch what happened during this successful consultation what would I have noticed?

Figure 8.2   Midlands EPS appreciative inquiry interview guide.

What kind of things made this consultation possible?

- When have you felt that a consultee has really understood the nature of EP consultation and that it has been an empowering experience?

- Imagine we had a conversation with SENCos/teachers/parents with whom you regularly interact and asked them to share the three best qualities they experience in consultation/conversation with you. What would they say?

Topic 2: Written communication (e.g. School Visit Summary, psychological report or profile, consultation notes, leaflet, document etc) as a catalyst for innovation and change

- Think of something you have written that has been referred back to, reflected on and acted as the *start* of something (instead of an end-point or something read and put in a file)

- Imagine I had a conversation with SENCos/teachers/parents with whom you regularly interact and I asked them to share the 3 best qualities or useful aspects of your written reports or written feedback? What would they say?

- What other written work have you been particularly pleased with? Why? How has it been effective in changing practices?

Topic 3: Informal communication (e.g. incidental talk, an email or phone call) with integrity

- Reflect back on any informal communication that had a real effect on you and led you forward. What was it? Why was it effective?

- Think of any communication as a psychologist that has taken a unique or new angle. What was it? What happened?

Future visions

Imagine you go into a deep sleep tonight, one that lasts for at least 5 years. When you wake up and go to work, everything has changed in our EP Service and it is exactly like you always wanted it to be. What's happened? What's different? What does your job look like now?

Imagine the EPS has just been awarded the new AEP/HCPC top prize for outstanding communication with its clients or stakeholders. What is said about us at the award ceremony? What are the schools, parents, other professionals, children and young people saying? What are we doing that is so highly valued?

> *Thank you so much for participating in this inquiry. Please be ready to share your partner's most powerful or compelling story and any key theme(s) with your group...*

Figure 8.2 *(Continued)*

Discovery

Using the interview guide, pairs of EPs asked each other questions designed to discover their best experiences of effective communication that had led to positive change. Pairs then formed groups of 6 to 10 EPs and shared the highlights of their stories, looking for common themes emerging. Feedback from participants afterwards suggested that this stage of the AI felt refreshing and highly affirming for the majority of EPs. They were enthusiastic about focussing on authentic positive experiences. However, they thought this stage could be even better if more time had been available for the interviews and they had been made aware of the questions beforehand so that they could reflect on them in the days leading up to the AI. The planning groups' reflections were that there were far too many questions! One EP reported that she felt a little uncomfortable at first being paired with a senior manager, but that she had enjoyed the interview experience nevertheless.

Dream

The same small groups were asked to decide on one idea that they all believed would make a real difference to the service and could realistically be implemented. It is important to remember that each group always has a mixture of senior, main-grade, and newly qualified EPs or TEPs, so the ideas can be shaped by knowledge of what is realistic within current resources and factors that are in the EPS's control. Then the groups were asked to decide how to present their idea or vision creatively to the whole service *as if it is already happening.* Group 1 focussed on an improved process for statutory assessments and created a sketch based on a popular television show where traditional vs. innovative ways of writing and acting on psychological advice competed against each other. Group 2 focussed on a new system for individual peer supervision designed to support EPs in challenging themselves and taking risks when developing their practice, designing a huge 3D tabletop board game representing the process and benefits of peer supervision. Group 3 focussed on communicating the benefits of consultation and choreographed a 'conga' to music, with labels on each person relating to different elements of effective consultation. Group 4 created a large picture collage reflecting an ideal future for service delivery to secondary schools. Each group performed or presented their ideas to the whole service.

Design

Prior to the Design stage, EPs were asked to select which of the four ideas they would most like to work on (e.g. the idea they were most interested in or knowledgeable about): more satisfying statutory work (written communication), more formalised peer supervision (communication between ourselves), schools understanding how consultation works (communication with schools), or more confidence in our work in secondary schools (communicating our expectations). There were one or two changes but the majority of people stayed within their original group. The new groups were asked to create 'provocative propositions', that is, a couple of sentences or short paragraphs that describe their dreams/ideas as if they were already happening. Drafts were shared and improved, ensuring that they captured what everyone would like to see happening in the EPS.

Destiny

The same four groups used the 'provocative propositions' to create short-term targets and innovative key actions for implementation, with individual members of the group taking responsibility for specific actions. The action plans were shared with the whole service and refined.

Implementation Stage

Over the following months, time was allocated at whole service meetings for individual groups to convene and update on their progress, whilst also providing an opportunity to present to and consult with the whole service as necessary.

Evaluation

The AI was evaluated using a simple questionnaire, completed anonymously. Questions were either open ended or made use of a simple Likert-style scale. Completed questionnaires were received from 21 out of a possible 29 EPs (72%). All (100%) of the EP respondents either agreed or strongly agreed that the AI enabled them to recognise and build upon their strengths; take ownership of change in their practice, improve the effectiveness of the service's collective practice, improve and/or 'action' the things they care about, have a 'voice' that resulted in action and communicate ideas and values to managers. However, only 38% agreed or strongly agreed that the AI had reduced their feelings of stress amidst wider LA restructuring. EP comments suggested that this was partly due to the increased pressures on their time when completing the AI activities in the implementation stage but also because their jobs remained highly insecure.

The themes in the qualitative feedback suggested that EPs particularly valued working with colleagues, the positivity and optimism generated by the AI and the opportunity to work according to their beliefs and values as psychologists. Their ideas about how the AI could be improved included:

- Allowing more time for each of the AI stages. Some EPs felt that every stage was rushed (especially towards the end of that activity) and they would have valued more time to understand and develop the ideas they had been discussing. In the literature, AIs are often scheduled for three to four days of activities for the four stages of Discovery, Dream, Design and Destiny, whereas these stages had been allocated only two afternoons.
- The implementation stage also needed to have more time allocated to the activities so that they were not competing with routine job requirements and deadlines.

- Participant grouping needs to be more consistent and the liaison between the groups facilitated so that everyone felt comfortable and could always be fully included.
- The topic choice of Communication for Change became lost at times in the excitement of sharing stories and creating new ways of working that were important to the EPs. Bushe and Kassam (2005) suggest that in order for AI to be transformational, managers need "to let go of control in planned change efforts and nurture a more improvisational approach to the action phase...a great deal of change leading to increased organizational performance can occur if people are allowed and encouraged to take initiative and make it happen" (pp. 176–177). On reflection, the wider EPS could have been involved in the selection of the topic(s) for the AI. Several suggestions for future AI topics were made by the service afterwards, including working with other agencies (e.g. child and adolescent mental health services (CAMHS), special educational needs and disability [SEND] services etc.), project work, specialisms, preschool work and focussing on the child's voice in casework.

Other benefits to the EPS were identified:

- Several EPs felt inspired to use AI to support organisational change in their schools, having experienced the process themselves.
- The AI challenged and changed the hierarchical 'top-down' management style within the EPS and facilitated 'bottom-up' communication from EPs to managers about how the service could be improved.
- EPs felt empowered to take on leadership roles in service development and motivated to make changes, despite heavy workloads.
- The AI facilitated communication between peers/colleagues across the service and provided an opportunity to share and improve their individual and collective practice.
- EPs enjoyed having a 'voice' at a time when they felt relatively powerless.

AI WITH AN EPS IN THE SOUTH OF ENGLAND

Background and Context

At the time of the AI, the South of England EPS was a large service of approximately 50 EPs and administrative support staff organised into four geographical teams. In common with many other EPSs, the number of requests for statutory assessment was rising significantly following the implementation of the Children and Families Act (2014) and the Special Educational Needs and Disability (SEND) Code of Practice (Department for Education, 2015), seriously jeopardising the amount of core and traded work that the EPS could engage in. The LA was also proposing to move all traded services (including the EPS) into an LA-owned company, which was creating huge anxiety and resistance from several EPs. The senior leadership team considered carefully whether it was the right time to hold an AI and decided to proceed, hoping that the process would allow the EPs to become actively involved in creating the type of service that mattered to them in these challenging circumstances.

Topic Selection

A planning group (representative of the whole service, including trainees and administration staff as well as EPs, senior educational psychologists [SEPs] and the assistant PEP) met to learn about AI, decide on the title of the AI and design the questions for the appreciative interviews. It was decided that the topic would be more open than it was in the AI in the Midlands EPS and focus on creating the service we aspired to be as we moved into the traded company. The title of the AI was crafted as: 'How can we realise our best hopes for creating the EPS we'd like to be?'

Discovery

EPs were placed in groups of three. One EP interviewed another using the interview questions, whilst a third person observed and recorded key stories and themes. All members of the triad took turns to be the interviewer, interviewee and observer. Following the experience of using AI with an EPS in the Midlands, it was decided that there would be far fewer questions, used flexibly in order to elicit the most meaningful or powerful stories from each EP in the time allocated (see Figure 8.3).

Dream

Groups of nine EPs (three triads) shared their stories and themes before discussing and creating a vision for the future and deciding how they would creatively present that vision to the whole service as if it was already happening. Then each group prepared, practiced and finally presented their ideas to the whole service.

Creative styles of presentation included a highly entertaining mime with huge building blocks stacking up to represent the features of an effective statutory assessment; a role play with a box of psychological approaches (represented by creative objects) being offered to a range of service users; an excellent rap and dance performed admirably and hilariously by two EPs; a Brexit-style referendum with the whole service invited to vote for one of two options; a dramatised court case with judgements made about various types of psychological approaches; and a consultation role play with key stakeholders telephoning the EPS with requests and queries.

	South of England EPS Appreciative Inquiry Interview Questions **(each printed on separate cards)**
Q1	Can you think of some work you have done that really illustrates what **matters** to you most? What was it? Why did it matter so much?
Q2	When have you felt really effective in your job? What helped this to happen? What did you do and what qualities (skills and talents) did you draw upon?
Q3	Tell me about a time when you went home and told your family about a **brilliant day** at work. What did you tell them about? Why was it so good?
Q4	Tell me about a specific time that stands out as a **high point** in your career, one of the best times you can remember (when you felt for example; motivated, engaged, inspired, innovative, valued, energised, excited). What enabled that to happen? What made it so good?
Q5	What are your **best hopes** for the EPS and your role within the EPS? Identify three things that you'd notice if your best hopes for the EPS were realised?
Q6	If you could have **three wishes** to enhance the work of the EPS in the new company, what would they be? Or Imagine you go into a deep sleep tonight, one that lasts for at least five years. When you wake up and go to work, everything has changed in our EPS and it is exactly like you always wanted it to be. What's happened? What's different? What does your job look like now?

Figure 8.3   South of England EPS appreciative inquiry interview questions.

Design

All EPs were offered the opportunity to change groups if they had more expertise or interest in the vision presented by a different group to their own. As for the Midlands EPS case study, only a small number of EPs changed groups. All of the groups then created and refined their provocative propositions, for example:

- EPs complete a statutory assessment, summarise their findings and attend a Team Around the Child meeting to coproduce the outcomes and provision parts of the education and health care plan.
- In our EPS, we write reports of only up to two pages. A longer report can be negotiated in exceptional circumstances.
- The EPS offers an entry-level package of system-level work to schools and other agencies of 1.5 days (forming the first day and a half of any school traded package).
- All EP work follows a process of collaborative consultation. School-focussed consultation is described effectively to schools and other partners.

- Space for Change: We have protected space twice a year as a whole service to explore and develop new ways of working (Development Days). Ideas developed on these days are supported by protected implementation time and inform the EPS Business Plan.
- Every EP has a specialism and time protected to offer support to other EPs. This can change every 2 years and is built into performance management and structured professional assessment (SPA) points.
- We are committed to actively promoting a breadth of psychological approaches and interventions in our work and contact with others (e.g. special educational needs coordinators [SENCos]) to have the work commissioned that we'd like to do that works. We hold an annual SENCo conference with workshops to explore and show-case effective EP approaches. The EPS has a cartoon video that shows what EPs do.

Destiny

The groups decided what actions were needed to transform their vision into a reality and who would do what. These actions were only at a very early stage by the end of the day and it was decided that a further whole service meeting would be needed.

Implementation Stage

The AI planning group met to discuss the activities arising from the AI, which were organised into four overarching themes:
- Developing the EP role in statutory assessment processes (including coproduction and writing shorter reports)
- Thinking about how we work with schools (including a new 1.5-day systems-level traded package, a collaborative consultation policy and much shorter traded reports/feedback)
- Developing what we do (including creating income-generating products that will fund development time and pro-bono work with vulnerable groups and other agencies, a process for conducting a needs analysis leading to an annual development day and proposals for specialist EP roles linked to SPA points and performance management)
- Showcasing what we do (including identifying what to promote, ensuring EPs are all aware of the evidence base for what we offer as a service and then creating a 'cartoon' video of EP practice and an annual 'expo-style' SENCo conference)

Evaluation

The AI itself was firstly evaluated according to the three objectives of the day. The results suggested that EPs would now be able to use AI in their own practice, that they had increased their participation in creating change for the future of the EPS based on past experiences of success, and that they were motivated to contribute to the implementation of the AI outcomes. This motivation is significant in the author's view when so many EPs in the service were feeling overwhelmed with negative feelings and anxiety about the future of the EPS prior to the AI. EPs also responded in writing to three qualitative open questions:

- What have you most appreciated or enjoyed about using AI with the EPS?
- How might this event have been improved?
- How might your experiences of AI today influence your work and/or practice?

The emergent themes in their responses suggest that an AI with an EPS provides much-valued nonhierarchical collaboration between colleagues, opportunities for creativity and the development of positivity and optimism amongst the team even in challenging circumstances. EPs felt that they had a genuine voice and could influence decision-making that affects their work. However, the process could have been improved by making the stages clearer and allocating more time to each activity so that the work was not rushed. After experiencing the AI themselves, EPs generally felt more confident to use AI in their work with schools and other services, adding this organisational intervention to their 'toolkit'. But they also grew in confidence as EPs, looking forward to taking an active part in implementing the activities they had created and feeling more able to take risks in future. The SEP who has been leading AI implementation activities since the author left the service in July 2018 has recently given the following reflections on the process:

> 'The AI work has led to real changes. It was through the AI that we have imagined how we would rather be working and had investigated the possibilities for this. This meant that when the opportunity presented for suggesting a new way of working to SEN and the LA we were ready to seize this opportunity and so get them on board with trying something different.
>
> My reflection would be that the crucial factor for AI being successful was that there was real commitment from the (Senior Leadership Team) to the AI process. There was an understanding that there needed to be more than just lip service paid to the AI process but that we needed to be fully committed to following up on the work and implementing new ideas and changes.
>
> We are still developing our vision of how we will work in the future and how to articulate the benefits of this to and for others'.

Learning from the AI Case Studies for Future Implementation of an AI Within an EPS

The experience of facilitating and evaluating these two AIs with EPSs has led to the following key aspects of learning:

- AI requires sufficient time for each of the four D stages. This should be not less than one full day for the 4-Ds and ideally more. The appreciative interviews in the Discovery stage could be conducted prior to the AI event with pairs of EPs interviewing each other at different times and in different places, so that EPs arrive ready to discuss and share the highlights from their interviews in small groups.

- The implementation phase needs some EP time to be protected for the work streams that follow the 4-Ds. There will be a range of projects and activities created that will need to be acted upon in small groups. The amount of time required is likely to be approximately three days per EP during the year following the AI event.
- An AI requires all members of the EPS, including all leaders and managers as well as TEPs, assistant EPs and administration staff to be present and participating fully. Attendance at an AI event needs to have high status so that there is consistency in group membership throughout the AI and its implementation.
- The planning group needs to be created with representatives from all roles and levels within the EPS as well as representation from any geographical team bases.
- Some services may like to present the theory of AI to the EPS prior to facilitating an AI, especially if EPs would like to learn more about the approach in order to facilitate AIs within their work in schools and with other services. However, Cooperrider et al. (2008) argues that knowledge of the theory is not at all necessary for participating in a successful AI.
- The topic choice can be chosen to address a known problem within the EPS but an AI can be equally effective by maintaining an open inquiry as the participants will be aware of factors that require improvement and a topic may risk limiting potential beneficial outcomes for the service.
- The interview guide should be much shorter than the one used in the Midlands EPS but could perhaps be elaborated further than the few questions forming the South of England interview guide (15 minutes per EP is insufficient time to explore individual positive experiences, in the author's view). It is helpful if participants know the questions in advance of the interview so that they can reflect back on their experiences before the AI event;
- Clear instructions and objectives should be shared with participants at each stage of the AI.

Conclusion

Both case studies have demonstrated that AI can be a positive motivating experience for EPs and generate a range of new work streams that are led by the EPs themselves, even in contexts where there is a high level of negativity and anxiety. In both of these EPS contexts, the author does not believe that there would have been such enthusiasm for participating in new work if it had been devised and directed by senior managers. Both AIs addressed problems within the EPSs, either by the choice of topic (e.g. Communication for Change) or by the EPs' knowledge and experience of the strengths and weaknesses within their EPS. The Midlands EPS created work streams that improved statutory assessment processes, provided increased peer supervision, created a better system for information-gathering for EP work in secondary schools and helped explain to schools the effectiveness of consultation. The South of England EPS also created improved processes for statutory assessment and consultation, built systems for the EPS to improve professional development; and created service development time and core work for vulnerable groups by first developing a sustainable traded income that is less reliant on EP time (e.g. centralised courses, webinars). These capacity-building ideas were inspirational for EPs in challenging the prevalent view that an impending move into a traded company could compromise their ethical stance as LA EPs. An AI can have a strengthening effect on a service in challenging times (Bellinger & Elliott, 2011). The AI allowed the EPs to take some control over the type of work they developed, even though it could not reduce the stress within the Midlands EPS caused by job insecurity.

The principles underpinning AI were exemplified by the EPs in both LAs placing a high value on working collaboratively with others in their organisation (constructionist principle) to generate ideas and visions for a better future (anticipatory principle) based on their own positive experiences of working as an EP (positive principle) and thereby creating the momentum for sustainable change. The questions for the appreciative interviews focussed the language of both inquiries on strengths and became inspirational (poetic principle). The very act of asking these questions created a shift from a previously held negative stance within a challenging EPS context (principle of simultaneity). The AIs were both transformational in achieving positive changes to systems within their EPS that were led by the EPs themselves (Bushe, 2010a); possibly *because* the AI activities were led by all members of the service with equal voice and genuine influence (Fieldhouse & Onyett, 2012). This 'flatter' hierarchy enabled a distributed leadership to emerge within the services and a new role to be formed for the senior leadership team. Managers were positioned as equal participants but were able to use their knowledge and expertise in shaping the ideas generated in order to ensure that work streams were realistic and could genuinely happen, whilst holding back from controlling the specific outcomes (Bellinger & Elliott, 2011). It is imperative that leaders and managers participate fully in AI so that they are able to fulfil this role and prevent newly generated ideas from becoming blocked during the implementation stage. It is the author's belief that an AI has the potential to shift the culture within an EPS towards one of authentic appreciation and empowerment of all staff to work in genuine collaboration to generate and sustain positive change.

References

Bellinger, A., & Elliott, T. (2011). What are you looking at? The potential of appreciative inquiry as a research approach for social work. *British Journal of Social Work, 41*, 708–725.

Burke, W. W. (2011). A perspective on the field of organizational development and change: The Zeigarnik effect. *Journal of Applied Behavioral Science, 47*(2), 143–167.

Bushe, G. R. (2010a). Commentary on 'Appreciative Inquiry as a Shadow process'. *Journal of Management Inquiry, 19*(3), 234–237.

Bushe, G. R. (2010b). Generativity and the transformational potential of appreciative inquiry. In D. Zandee, D. L. Cooperrider, & M. Avital (Eds.), *Organizational generativity: Advances in appreciative inquiry*, Vol. *3* (pp. 89–113). Bingley, UK: Emerald Publishing.

Bushe, G. R. (2010c). A comparative case study of appreciative inquiries in one organization: implications for practice. *Review of Research and Social Intervention, 29*, 7–24.

Bushe, G. R. (2013). The appreciative inquiry model. In E. H. Kessler (Ed.), *Encyclopaedia of management theory* (pp. 41–43). London: Sage Publications.

Bushe, G. R., & Kassam, A. (2005). When is appreciative inquiry transformational? A meta-case analysis. *Journal of Applied Behavioral Science*, *41*(2), 161–181.

Carter, B. (2006). 'One expertise among many' – working appreciatively to make miracles instead of finding problems: Using appreciative inquiry as a way of reframing research. *Journal of Research in Nursing*, *11*(1), 48–63.

Checkland, P. (2000). Soft systems methodology: A thirty year retrospective. *Systems Research and Behavioral Science*, *17*, 11–58.

Children and Families Act. (2014). Retrieved from http://www.legislation.gov.uk/ukpga/2014/6/contents/enacted

Coghlan, A. T., Preskill, H., & Catsambas, T. T. (2003). An overview of appreciative inquiry in evaluation. *New Directions for Evaluation*, 100, 5–22.

Cooperrider, D., Whitney, D., & Stavros, J. (2008). *Appreciative inquiry handbook: For leaders of change* (2nd ed.). Brunswick, OH: Crown Custom Publishing Inc.

Curato, N., Niemeyer, S., & Dryzek, J. S. (2013). Appreciative and contestatory inquiry in deliberative forums: can group hugs be dangerous? *Critical Policy Studies*, *7*(1), 1–17.

Department for Education (DfE). (2015). Special educational needs and disability code of practice: 0 to 25 years. Statutory guidance for organisations which work with and support children and young people who have special educational needs or disabilities. Retrieved from https://assets.publishing.service.gov.uk/government/uploads/system/uploads/attachment_data/file/398815/SEND_Code_of_Practice_January_2015.pdf

Fieldhouse, J., & Onyett, S. (2012). Community mental health and social exclusion: Working appreciatively towards inclusion. *Action Research*, *10*(4), 356–372.

Lewis, S., Passmore, J., & Cantore, S. (2008). *Appreciative inquiry for change management: Using AI to facilitate organizational development*. London and Philadelphia: Kogan Page.

Ludema, J., & Fry, R. (2008). The practice of appreciative inquiry. In P. Reason & H. Bradbury (Eds.), *The SAGE handbook of action research: Participative inquiry and practice* (2nd ed., pp. 280–296). Los Angeles, London, New Delhi & Singapore: SAGE Publications.

McAdam, E., & Mirza, K. (2009). Drugs, hopes and dreams: appreciative inquiry with marginalized young people using drugs and alcohol. *Journal of Family Therapy*, *31*, 175–193.

Preskill, H., & Catsambas, T. (2006). *Reframing evaluation through appreciative inquiry*. Thousand Oaks, London, New Delhi: SAGE Publications.

Robinson, G., Priede, C., Farrell, S., Shapland, J., & McNeil, F. (2012). Doing 'strengths-based' research: Appreciative inquiry in a probation setting. *Criminology and Criminal Justice*, *13*(1) 3–20.

Trajkovski, S., Schmied, V., Vickers, M., & Jackson, D. (2013). Implementing the 4D cycle of appreciative inquiry in health care: a methodological review. *Journal of Advanced Nursing*, *69*(6), 1224–1234.

Van der Haar, D., & Hosking, D. (2004). Evaluating appreciative inquiry: A relational constructivist perspective. *Human Relations*, *57*(8), 1017–1036.

Wilding, L., & Griffey, S. (2015). The strength–based approach to educational psychology practice: a critique from social constructionist and systemic perspectives. *Educational Psychology in Practice*, *31*(1), 43–55.

Zandee, D., & Cooperrider, D. (2008). Appreciable worlds, inspired inquiry. In P. Reason & H. Bradbury (Eds.), *The SAGE handbook of action research: Participative inquiry and practice* (2nd ed., pp. 190–198). Los Angeles, London, New Delhi & Singapore: SAGE Publications.

9

Recruitment and Retention: Building a Team and Services

Mohammed Bham and Mandy Owen

'*Great leaders do not create followers, they create more leaders*'. *Tom Peters*[1]

When embarking on the recruitment and selection of an educational psychologist for your service or when forming a team, it is important to keep in mind the efficient ways of promoting the service.

This chapter provides some insight into the different aspects of recruitment to think about when considering advertisement, attracting potential applicants, appealing to the new generations of leaders and keeping 'fit for purpose'.

The EPS Leader and the Team Are Your Best Advert!

We often hear professional colleagues refer to our educational psychology profession as being a 'small world'. Therefore it can be easy for information to get around the profession, especially in relation to the reputation of an Educational Psychology Service (EPS).

This information can be shared through a number of channels, including the following:

Trainee educational psychologists (TEPs) will have plenty of opportunities throughout their three years of doctoral training to discuss with their peers their experiences on placement within your service or sharing learning with fellow trainees at the university training programme from the experiences gained from being with your service. There will be awareness amongst professional tutors and fieldwork supervisors who may comment about the type of placement that might be experienced, via information that is gathered through three-way meetings when reviewing TEP placements. There may also be opportunities for EPS leaders to talk to their local training programme about leadership issues and EPS models of service delivery; educational psychologists (EPs) from your service may deliver aspects of specialist professional areas of practice or contribute to TEP academic requirements on the course. In addition TEPs may receive information through professional email groups, such as EPNET. All this may inform a TEP about the type of organisation your service may be to work in.

---

1 Tom Peters Quotes. (n.d.). BrainyQuote.com. Retrieved from https://www.brainyquote.com/quotes/tom_peters_382508

Leadership for Educational Psychologists: Principles & Practicalities, First Edition.
Edited by Julia Hardy, Charmian Hobbs and Mohammed Bham.
© 2020 John Wiley & Sons Ltd. Published 2020 by John Wiley & Sons Ltd.

...or experienced EPs seeking career development opportunities which may not be currently available in their current service or looking to relocate; EPs will inevitably learn about or hear about the service through networking at continuing professional development (CPD) events, information submitted by staff in professional publications, including journal articles or resource reviews, information exchange at regional networks, or professional social networking sites. Some EPs may take up fixed term positions or locum cover arrangements or commissioned through their private practice initially before considering a more permanent move into your organisation, so your investment as leader and your staff contribution to this range of activities will ensure you are exhausting all possible avenues to ensure the information that is shared about your service reflects reality as experienced by the staff in the current organisation.

As a leader, you have to remind yourself that you are also the best advert. The concept of charismatic leadership is explored by Haslam and Reicher (2012). They emphasise the importance of followers who distinguish the leader from others and confer charisma on her/him. Conferring of charisma is contingent on the leader articulating and supporting their values and goals. A non-prototypical leader can generate charisma through the use of 'us' and 'we' rather than 'I' and 'me'. The charismatic leader is one who is seen as clarifying what 'we' believe rather than telling people what 'they' believe or should believe.

We also need to consider the implications for leaders when charisma is bestowed upon them. Goffee and Jones (2006) highlighted four implications: the first is to carefully judge self-exposure that identifies your difference. This is achieved through knowing and showing yourself enough. The second is to show passion for the organisation's purpose by making use of 'tough empathy' – give people what they need rather than what they want. Thirdly, manage social distance and finally, communicate with care.

Charisma: Implications for me

Creating a Positively Productive Working Environment

It is important for the organisation to be continuously improving and in particular paying attention to the quality of the work environment. It is not solely the EPS leadership role to create such an environment but to involve all that are part of the service to inform improvements required to address the current needs. Utilising solution-focussed questioning in teams can provide some key insights in what staff value in the work context. This can then provide opportunity to further discuss and clarify what can be addressed and opportunity to discuss coping strategies for situations that may need to be tolerated. An example of a question to present to staff is provided here.

Team discussion:

If you knew you were going to have the best quality work environment, what would it look/feel like?

What would be the first step your team could take from your current work environment towards that outlined previously?

How can a leader create a positive work environment to improve employee behaviour? The following activity may help engage staff in a conversation to inform your service action plan.

Dream day: In 3 minutes write down some key details about your dream day at work

---

Dream thieves: Now write a list of all things that prevent the dream day.

Which of these are within your control and which might need to have a team or service response?

This list will provide you with a lot of leadership issues that require your attention!

When preparing for the different needs of staff and considering opportunities to fill vacant positions, a useful framework to utilise with the team was developed by Herzberg, Mausner and Snyderman (1959) which can be used to help inform service or team leaders of motivational and maintenance factors important to staff in their work context. The following example has been completed, following a team discussion and review:

What are the motivational factors important in your work context?

- Sense of achievement
- Fulfil ambition
- Promotion
- Personal development
- Belonging to group
- Pursue personal professional interests
- Money/ salary

What are the maintenance factors important in your work context?

- Service location
- Job security
- Type/variety of work
- Flexible working
- Good working environment
- Getting on with people
- Hours, holidays, pension
- Income/salary

Some of this information may help inform whether it may be worth considering a secondment opportunity for a member of the team to experience, for example, a leadership role. Some of the information may be considered suitable to include in the job advert, about 'what staff working in our team say about working with us?'

Attracting Potential Applicants

When considering the recruitment and retention of EPs, the recent findings from the South of England Principal Educational Psychologists' (PEPs) group in 2018 identified the following as important factors for attracting potential applicants to EP Services:

- Positive presence on Local Authority (LA) website and social media
- A loyal group of locum EPs
- Maintaining a variety of work
- Competitive pay range
- Programme of CPD
- Flexible working
- Good administration and technical support
- Induction process
- Peer supervision
- Autonomy

- Regular team and service meetings
- Specialisms
- Interesting work, early intervention
- Use of assistant EPs and TEPs to provide opportunity for supervision and bringing research into a learning organisation
- Clear professional career development routes
- Equitable, transparent and fair work allocation system

RACE, ETHNICITY & CULTURAL DIVERSITY in EPSs

With reference to Her Majesty's Racial Disparity Audit (Cabinet Office, 2017), information relating to the public sector workforce highlights the following:

- 43% of Black people work in the public sector (30% White peers).
- 1 in 7 teachers are Black, Asian, or minority ethnic (BAME).
- 1 in 10 head teachers are BAME.
- 1 in 1,000 head teachers are from Bangladeshi, Chinese, or other Black background.
- Less than 10 of 178 directors of Children's Services are BAME.

So what proportion of EPs is BAME? Does the EP workforce represent and reflect the diversity within any of our local communities in which they work? How many PEPs and senior educational psychologists (SEPs) are BAME? Does the leadership in our profession represent and reflect the diversity within the local community in which they lead services?

What positive steps are being taken to promote the cultural competence and the ethnic and cultural diversity in the educational psychology profession? This is an area that requires further research.

Consideration for the Generational Differences

As a leader it is important to be mindful of the developmental and generational differences between the staff in the service and in the profession of educational psychology. It is therefore useful, for example, to consider appealing in a different way to TEPs and to be mindful of the generalised findings from research on 'Millennials':

- Upbringing that has made them very self-confident, empowered, optimistic to undertake major personal projects
- Immersed in technology without authority figures controlling access to information
- Career is not the principal motivation: job flexibility, work–life balance, relationship development are more important
- Not intimidated by age or status: respect must be earned
- Expect bidirectional communication regardless of position
- Expert in multitasking
- Prefer nonhierarchical structures
- Have a strong desire to make a difference
- Expect autonomy in their responsibilities

The key findings from recent research carried out by Dr Roger Booker, who gathered the views of students on Initial EP training programmes on areas for EPS leadership improvement (Booker, 2014), included:

1) A need for closer engagement from the service leader, through visibility and contact; understand the pressures on TEPs; and be approachable.
2) A style of communication which demonstrates, listening to staff; communicating a vision; and transparency about change.
3) Model entrepreneurship: through promotion of service in LA and to schools; and demonstrate strategic skills.

With the changing work and workforce in educational psychology, consideration also needs to be given to the more experienced EPs. What similarities or differences are there between experienced EPs and millennial TEPs? What may be key drivers for experienced EPs seeking to move service, apply for a promoted post, or return to a LA EPS following a period of time in private practice? What can a leader of an EPS do to appeal to experienced EPs?

Shortage of Qualified EPs

The largest and most valuable resource within an EPS is, without question, the staff. Therefore, the quality of the staff recruited by the service and the development and retention of those staff is a key role for the leaders within the service. The Department for Education (DfE) research into the educational psychology workforce (DfE, 2019) identifies that 66% of EPSs have vacant posts. The research also identifies the range of factors behind the growing demand for qualified EPs including factors such as the rising demand for statutory special educational needs and disability (SEND) work, increase in 'traded' or 'commissioned' work and a move, by some EPs, to work in the private sector. This combined with (until recently) a static number of EPs being trained each year has increased the pressure on services to recruit and retain the best. Many EPSs place a high value on 'growing their own' through offering posts to psychology assistants (who aim to go on to train as EPs and who may then come back to that authority to work) and through offering high-quality TEP placements which may result in recruitment if a vacant post becomes available during the latter part of the placement. As a result of the current shortage of qualified EPs there has been some initial work carried out by PEPs to explore the possibility of an apprenticeship route into the profession. This could mirror some of the developments which are currently taking place within Clinical Psychology (CP) with the Clinical Associate Psychologist (CAP) route into either a career grade post as a CAP or lead on to further training as a CP.

Leaders within EPSs need to create the culture and service identity which makes their service a positive choice for those who are seeking their first job, looking to move to a service which can offer them a broader range of opportunities, or looking for career progression opportunities. The importance of a clearly articulated vision, mission and statement of core values which have been developed by the service for the service cannot be underestimated. One of the leadership standards within the Quality Standards for Educational Psychology Services (British Psychological Society [BPS], 2019) is 'Aims, values and policies influence the work of all staff and form the basis of shared values'. An EPS with a clear identity and clear values will assist in the recruitment of EPs who share these values and can contribute to the vision. The recruitment and selection processes then can focus on whether there is a good fit between the service and candidate.

Following recruitment a key aspect of development and retention is the induction given to staff. A clearly described induction process, which is relevant to the role and to the previous experience of the EP and which can be flexible according to needs of the individual and the needs of the service, is one of the best ways of nurturing new talent.

Once a new member of the EPS has completed their induction, a key part of the system to keep them engaged and supported within the service (and to aid retention) is regular supervision. EPSs need a clearly articulated and agreed supervision framework with time-scales and agreements about who will do what. As well as management supervision and reflective practice supervision there should be opportunities to share achievements and 'positive gossip'. This, along with appraisals and feedback from colleagues and service users will help provide leaders and managers with the information they need to enable them to 'talent spot' within the organisation.

Balanced Workload

One of the biggest challenges facing EPSs at the current time is that the rise in statutory SEND work which can result in a narrowing of the role for EPs as they spend more time carrying out individual assessments and writing reports as part of the statutory process. A 'balanced workload' which provides EPs with the opportunity to carry out a range of work which could include early intervention and prevention, consultation and formulation, direct work with individuals or groups and systemic or strategic work will not only enable EPs to use their skills to improve outcomes for children but it is also likely to support the recruitment and retention of staff. Given the funding restrictions on EPSs providing opportunities for EPs to carry out a range of work is only likely to happen if the service is able to engage in 'trading' or 'commissioned' work with a range of partners. Where this is happening successfully some EPSs are finding that demand for their work is outstripping supply (which may result in the EP service having to recruit more staff or employing associate psychologists or locum psychologists as a way of ensuring service capacity can meet demand). Increasing the range and diversity of the work carried out by EPSs is also providing increased opportunities for EPs to develop their own 'leadership' skills as they lead and manage projects and developments within the service.

Leadership – Staying 'Fit for Purpose'

The question of whether leadership within EPSs is fit for purpose is explored by Booker (2013) and in conclusion there is an emphasis on the need to explore the leadership capacity of teams and the training and development implications of this for an EPS. Booker notes that one of the recent developments is a move to focus on leadership at all levels of the organisation. Thus the increasing importance of recruiting and retaining staff at all levels within an EPS who themselves are able to demonstrate leadership qualities. A hierarchical model of leadership is no longer applicable in the complex world in which EPs work where individual EPs have the opportunity to shape and lead the work of the service. A model of dispersed leadership is made possible if the organisation has a clearly articulated 'common purpose' (Kurtzman, 2010) as this can empower and enable leaders as all levels. If the EPS has a 'common purpose' and a clear framework setting out its core values and vision and mission, individuals at all levels of the organisation, can be empowered and given the opportunity to innovate and to lead. The model of distributed leadership suggested by Gronn (2015) is relevant to EPSs as it considers leadership to be an activity between those with common purpose. This is also reflected in the Division of Educational and Child Psychology quality standard 'Leadership is developed and encouraged at all levels, with shared decision making and collaborative planning' (BPS, 2019).

EPSs with a service development plan which is regularly updated and reviewed provide an opportunity for staff at all levels of the service to influence and shape the future of the service. These plans can provide the 'golden thread' between national and local priorities and the individual within the service. It can also provide a framework in which each individual in the service can review their own performance, set goals for the coming year as part of their appraisal and review their progress.

Human resources teams and departments within LAs play a key role in promoting staff self-awareness regarding the leadership skills and development required to ensure promoted post-holders – PEPs and SEPs are up to date and engaged in implementing the latest knowledge and understanding of leadership competencies. Workforce development should include opportunities for leaders to engage with their CPD, through work-based opportunities with reflective practice: provided by an assigned or self-chosen coach or supervisor; frequently revisiting your values base; receiving structured feedback on demonstrating leadership competencies, for example, 360 feedback appraisals; encouragement and an expectation on leaders to link with professional and specialist peer support networks, either at regional or national levels, for example, annual courses organised by National Association of PEPs (NAPEP); British Psychological Society (BPS) Division of Educational and Child Psychology (DECP), Association of Educational Psychologists (AEP), etc.

Employers alone are not responsible for making these opportunities available; it is an expectation that PEPs and SEPs ensure that leadership is a key aspect of their CPD and being able to demonstrate how they have kept informed and practiced the skills in the domains of strategic and professional practice.

References

Booker, R. (2013). Leadership of education psychology services: Fit for purpose? *Educational Psychology in Practice, 29*(2), 197–208.

Booker, R. (2014, March). *Trainee educational psychologists views of psychological service leadership. British Psychological Society: Division of Educational & Child Psychology; Debate,* no. 154.

British Psychological Society (BPS). (2019). *Quality Standards for Educational Psychology Services: Division of Education and Child Psychology.* Leicester: BPS. Retrieved from https://www.bps.org.uk/member-microsites/division-educational-child-psychology/resources

Cabinet Office. (2017). *Race disparity audit*. Retrieved from https://assets.publishing.service. gov.uk/government/uploads/system/uploads/attachment_data/file/686071/Revised_RDA_ report_March_2018.pdf

Department for Education (DfE). (2019). *Research on the educational psychologist workforce*; *Research report*. Retrieved from https://www.gov.uk/government/publications/ educational-psychologist-workforce-research

Goffee, R., & Jones, G. (2006). *Why should anyone be led by YOU?* Boston: Harvard Business Review Press.

Gronn, P. (2015). The view from inside leadership configurations. *Human Relations, 68*(4), 545–560.

Haslam, S. A., & Reicher, S. D. (2012, July-August). In search of charisma. *Scientific American Mind, 23*, 42–49.

Herzberg, F., Mausner, B., & Snyderman, B. B. (1959). *The motivation to work*. New Brunswick [NJ]: Transaction Publishers.

Kurtzman, J. (2010). *Common purpose: How great leaders get organizations to achieve the extraordinary*. San Francisco: Jossey-Bass.

10

Educational Psychology Leadership Within a Welsh Context

Joy Mitchell and Ffion Edwards Ellis

The Welsh Legislative and Curriculum Context

Described as a 'once in a generation' reform, the landscape of Welsh Education is changing significantly over the next few years. Alongside significant curriculum reforms, there are major changes to the legislation around special educational needs (SEN), or additional learning needs (ALN) as it will be known. The ALN Bill became an act in 2017, to come into force in September 2020, with the accompanying code currently under consultation.

In 2015 Professor Donaldson's independent report Successful Futures paved the way towards the development of a new Curriculum for Wales for 3- to 16-year-olds, which removes 'Key Stages' and instead has 'Progressing Stages' at certain ages (Figure 10.1). Outcomes are personalised and future planning emerges from these (Donaldson, 2015).

Mind over Matter (Children, Young People and Education Committee, 2018) has been a contributing document to the reform agenda. The discussion within Welsh Government, Local Authority (LA), School Improvement and School Inspectorate around learner and staff well-being, as an integral part of educational experience, is refreshing and inspiring. The role of educational psychology within this is clear, but we will need to ensure that there is the right understanding about capabilities and roles at a LA strategic level.

Four curriculum outcomes are outlined:

- Ambitious and Capable Learners
- Ethical, Informed Citizens
- Healthy and Confident Individuals
- Enterprising and Creative Contributors

With six areas of Learning Experience:

- Expressive Arts
- Health and Well-Being
- Humanities
- Languages, Literacy and Communication

Leadership for Educational Psychologists: Principles & Practicalities, First Edition.
Edited by Julia Hardy, Charmian Hobbs and Mohammed Bham.
© 2020 John Wiley & Sons Ltd. Published 2020 by John Wiley & Sons Ltd.

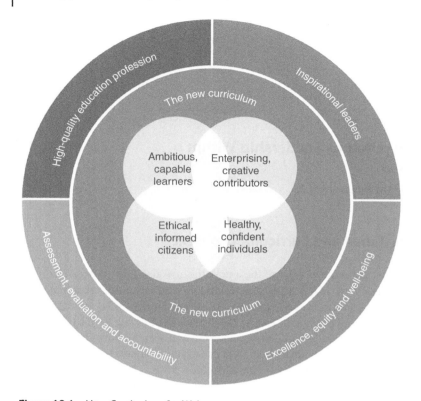

Figure 10.1   New Curriculum for Wales.

- Maths and Numeracy
- Science and Technology

Cross-curricular aspects are Literacy, Numeracy and Digital Competency.

The curriculum is part of a wider, long-term Welsh agenda outlined within the Well-Being of Future Generations Act (2015) and is also a driver behind the changes around ALN.

The initial implementation stages are underway in preparation for the first milestone of the transformation process, with schools deep in preparation for this, in the midst of shrinking budgets and Brexit.

Then along comes an additional major transformation process – the Additional Learning Needs and Education Tribunal Act (2018). This act has been in the making for a number of years, following on from Statements or Something Better in 2008 (Additional Needs and Inclusion Division, 2008). Pipped to the post by the Social Services and Well-Being Act (2014) which came into force in 2016, the ALN and Education Tribunal Act promises huge improvement to the current system, as part of the 'once in a generation' reform in Wales.

How the ALN and Tribunal Act Changes Things

Statements and Individual Education Plans will be abolished and will be replaced by Individual Development Plans (IDPs) – one document for all, a tool for person-centred practice, with emphasis on the provision required to meet needs. Most IDPs will be maintained by schools and further education institutions, with more complex IDPs maintained by the LA, and the ALN must be linked to education or training provision.

The act covers the age span of 0 to 25 years. Tribunal rights will extend to all IDPs (albeit with a requirement that processes for resolving disagreements occur with the LA first and will be robust, with independent advocacy services available). Additional learning provision must be offered in Welsh should the learner choose or require this – a challenge for out of county placements, border authorities, and some authorities where this is not required as often.

The voice of the child and family should be central in creating the plan for the individual and person-centred planning processes recommended. The UNCRC Rights of the Child (Office of the High Commissioner on Human Rights, 1989) are also at the heart of the act.

The role of the ALN Co-ordinator (ALNCo) role strengthens significantly under the new act in terms of strategic roles and responsibilities. This is of concern to smaller schools where the ALNCo role is often carried out by the headteacher or tagged on to other responsibilities.

The act places a duty to provide health provision which is held within the IDP for Health Services. This is an area of general concern for a number of reasons. It is necessary for the Health Board to appoint a Designated Education Clinical Lead Officer (DECLO) to hold strategic responsibilities in ensuring that processes are in keeping with the act and code.

Currently, we are within a consultation period for the code, the Regulations for Tribunal for Wales, and Regulations for ALNCo. The day-to-day implementation of the act is largely reliant on what emerges from this consultation. The implementation of the act will also hinge upon this. The role of the LA is quite clear in terms of responsibility and also the strategic direction of travel in ensuring good quality provision for all individuals with ALN.

There are interesting discussions around the role of educational psychology as a result of the frequent mentioning of educational psychologists (EPs) throughout the code. There are justifiable concerns regarding capacity, availability and training pathways, especially with additional requirements in working with the 0–3 and 16–25 age groups.

Welcomed are the numerous mentions of EPs as confirmation of an understanding of the importance of the profession. However, it is felt that this is open to interpretation, and this will be part of the professional associations' response to the code. The code states that consultation should occur at stages such as making decisions about whether a child has ALN, and there is not enough mention of the key responsibilities in universal and targeted training, as well as being part of the provision in terms of interpretation. Care needs to be taken around restricting the work of EPs back to a gatekeeping role.

Preparations for these changes in Gwynedd and Anglesey LAs have been in place for about 5 years. Schools are very familiar with person-centred practice and the use of local IDPs in capturing need and provision.

Croeso i Gymru (Welcome to Wales) - Whilst services across North Wales have their unique developmental history and current identity, the following offers a contrasting picture of an urban, border LA Educational Psychology Service (EPS) with a predominantly Welsh speaking and rural LA EPS.

Leadership Within a Welsh/English Border Local Authority in Wales

Croeso i Wrecsam or Welcome to Wrexham is the signpost which will meet you whether you are heading into Wales from Cheshire, Shropshire, or South and West Wales.

Wrexham is the largest conurbation in North Wales (see Figure 10.2). It is an area of social deprivation with some areas of prosperity and wealth arising in places nearest to the English border. Its numbers of homelessness now rank second to Cardiff and there are now over 50 languages spoken in Wrexham, with increasing numbers of Syrian relocated and refugee families (97). Alongside this multilingual thread, there also runs that of traditional but changing Welsh communities – historically close knit communities such as Rhosllanerchrugog and the Ceiriog Valley.

Working within Wales and being subject to Welsh Government legislation inevitably guides some of EPS priorities. Responsiveness to the wider context then has to be a key element of EPS' Service Development Plan and Principal Educational Psychologists (PEPs) as managers of the service, regularly need to reflect and plan on operational and strategic response.

For English colleagues, the ALN and Tribunal Act (2017) is the equivalent of the special educational needs and disability (SEND) legislation representing a change from the 30-year statutory system and the current statements of special educational needs. So long in the

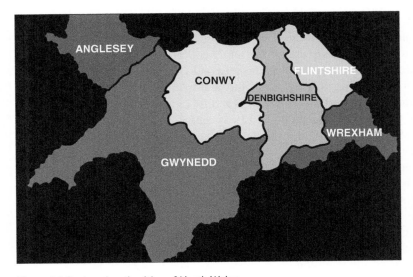

Figure 10.2 Local authorities of North Wales.

making, the new code of practice goes live in September 2020 and offers an opportunity to embed person-centredness and to ensure that person-centredness weaves through educational psychology practice through its report writing, casework practice, systemic work and strategic planning. Training staff in person-centred thinking has inevitably been a key priority for Wrexham's EPS and since 2015, all schools across Wrexham and Flintshire have received the 2-day basic training, followed by input on doing person-centred reviews.

The current multiplicity of legislative change including the New Curriculum, the Welsh Language Strategy, the Well-being of Future Generations Act as well as the new Autism Spectrum Disorder (ASD) Code of Practice and the updated national Anti-Bullying Guidance are some of the other challenges demanding an educational psychology response and involvement. For leaders of EPSs, the balance between macro, meso and micro demands is indeed a balancing act.

It is Wrexham's geographical position, as with other distant parts of the UK, which gives rise to some of the challenges and opportunities facing the management of Wrexham's EPS (see Figure 10.3). Transport from North to South, whilst very scenic, is neither easy nor accessible as the roads wind through rural mid Wales. To attend the essential National Association of PEPs (NAPEP) WALES meetings can take over a 2-hour, one-way journey to reach the midpoint meeting place of Llandrindod Wells. Cardiff as the hub of Welsh government and the home of Cardiff University (where the only doctoral educational psychology course is based) is often the venue for national meetings and conferences – for EPs in North Wales, this will require a 4-hour one-way journey. What this means is that if one thinks about opportunities and threats for the service, we are at risk of being the forgotten North and in order to develop as an outward- and forward-facing service, there needs to be a prioritisation of participation and a determination to be involved, to represent the views and ideas of the Wrexham team and to gather fresh knowledge to move forward. Skyping and live streaming as evidenced by the recent University College London (UCL) conference on dyslexia, certainly helps with the process of communication, but from the perspective of the authors, the essential networking and informal professional discussions and spontaneous meetings cannot be wholly replaced by technology. (Skype consultations, however, are something that we will be piloting in the summer term.)

Border positioning, however, provides opportunities for leadership. It is proximity to

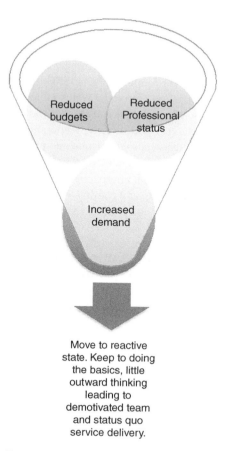

Figure 10.3   Reactive service.

England which allows for easier free flow of ideas and the development of relationships with nearby services. As part of our 'looking out' extroversion, we are open to liaising with neighbouring authorities. This has been particularly useful as we explore and investigate the potential benefits and ethical challenges involved in a traded model, which is something under consideration as we face a time of change and huge increase in workload, with the advent of the new ALN Act. As well as nurturing an outward-looking service, open to influence and self-reflection, the border position requires of EPs a necessary flexibility. There is a need to understand the English SEND system as many of the children and young people with additional learning needs, although they live in Wrexham, go to school in England.

Proximity to England, however, can pose a threat to us in some areas, notably within the area of recruitment which has been a burning issue for many of the LA services of Wales. It currently remains the case that trainees on the Welsh educational psychology training course are still under no obligation to work in Wales as their initial posting when qualified, and thus, each year Welsh trainees are lost to English authorities thereby reducing the available number of newly qualified EPs. Another challenge for recruitment in Wrexham has been the issue of the Welsh Language. Whilst Welsh Government has the admirable aspiration to have one million Welsh speakers in Wales by the year 2050, in Wrexham there is a struggle to fulfil the requirements of providing a Welsh language service to our Welsh medium schools and clients. The language of North East Wales is predominantly English. There has also been a struggle to recruit Welsh-speaking EPs to the service, in spite of the 'highly desirable' person specification in advertisements. This is partly due to the fact that the training course in Wales is not turning out many Welsh-speaking EPs and many of those who do speak Welsh, are tending to work in the western, more predominantly Welsh-speaking areas. Proactive leadership in the face of recruitment difficulties needs to be part of the leadership repertoire and to maximise opportunities to network, to advertise the EPS and to increase (as Covey [1989] suggests) the sphere of influence. Proactivity also means using the usual approaches to grow the service – open evenings, targeting the local Welsh schools for up and coming EPs/assistant EPs, sending those interested in learning Welsh on total immersion courses to develop Welsh within the team.

Maintaining Connection in Times of Change – Collaboration Within and Without

Connectivity (see Figure 10.4) has been the subject of discussion within the Wrexham team since the notable Welsh research and the resulting research paper by Professor Colleen McLauchlan (2015): The Connected School. This has arguably been one of the most influential pieces of work to come from Wales in recent years and has led to some introspection and self-evaluation within Wrexham EPS on the issue of connectedness. Very often these things don't happen by chance and the synchronicity of Professor McLauchlan's key concept with the guiding principles of the Wrexham team have led the whole team to engage, for example, in mindfulnessness training, to embrace some Buddhist principles in leading the team and delivering the service to Wrexham. Celebrating difference and enjoying our 'Gifts differing' (Myers & Myers, 1980).

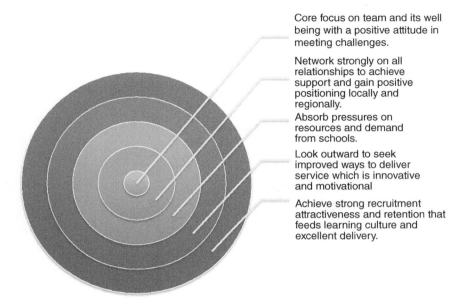

Core focus on team and its well being with a positive attitude in meeting challenges.

Network strongly on all relationships to achieve support and gain positive positioning locally and regionally.

Absorb pressures on resources and demand from schools.

Look outward to seek improved ways to deliver service which is innovative and motivational

Achieve strong recruitment attractiveness and retention that feeds learning culture and excellent delivery.

Figure 10.4 Connectivity.

The Connected School research document has as its central argument that:

> 'Everything is connected and that these connections matter greatly to education and to young people's development'. (McLaughlin, 2015, p. viii)

McLauchlan's (2015) central tenets of connectivity inform practice in Wrexham EPS and give a framework for service delivery based on these values and beliefs.

Maintaining connection within the team

This has to be a priority for team leaders with the nucleus of positive energy coming from a team committed to mutual support, respect and genuine acceptance of diversity.

As part of this necessary collaboration, we have decided to commit time to communication. This is not always an easy prioritisation when faced with the tasks in hand and the ever growing workload which will inevitably grow further with the advent of the new ALN Act (2017) and associated new responsibilities placed on the EP leadership in Wales. Inevitably, this leads to discussions about what is important to us which has led to the team activity of producing our one-page profile and we have connected this with the process of producing our annual team PATH (Promoting Alternative Tomorrows with Hope), which is also a visual reminder of our vision and our pledged objectives.

Our current Team Talk commitment can be seen in Figure 10.5.

To create a free flow of energy and maintain the well-being of the team, EPs are working together to maintain the building bricks of the Wrexham ethos. As with all organisations, these are built on rituals, routines, relationships and paying attention as far as possible, to the working environment.

Figure 10.5 Connected team.

Rituals

To support well-being at the team's core, paying attention to nurturing principles needs to be prioritised. Too often these are subjugated to completion of task and, of course, fulfilment of service development plan objectives is essential to maintain the momentum of positive change for children and families. In Wrexham this is achieved through binding rituals – Triads for example, where three members of the EP team on a rota basis meet to organise a surprise for each member of the team, once a term.

Routines

Routines are also written into the working week in order to bolster resilience and collaboration. As a part of the standing items of the weekly EP team meeting, 'celebrations' give all individuals a chance to share good news which means that the meetings begin with a noticeable feel good factor, which stands all in good stead when moving on to more challenging discussions such as time allocation and statutory assessments.

Multifaceted supervision

As mentioned previously, supervision is a key component of creating connection. A jigsaw of different supervisory opportunities gives us a spectrum of formats ranging from formal to informal. Formal includes the twice-yearly Performance Review and Development meeting with the PEP as leader, which is supplemented by half termly one-to-one meetings. The EP group make use of Kline's approach (2002) to developing the thinking environment in some of the meetings and use Kline duos as the basis for quality assurance partnerships to look at report writing casework quality. As a group, we make use of coaching in triads using the G.R.O.W. model (Whitmore, 2009) which serves the purpose of supervision and providing practice in keeping our coaching skills alive. Staff are also encouraged to ask for and to self-manage peer supervision.

Collaboration Without

Collaboration also means seeking to work with organisational partners in the wider system and again, making sure that time is spent on developing these important working relationships (Figure 10.6). A termly meeting with Education Inclusion officers allows liaison, to have some frank discussions about the challenges of inclusion, to update on mutual priorities and plan areas to work together in an efficient and effective manner. A joint approach to planning in schools, that is, joint visits at the start of the year, allows EPs and their counterpart Inclusion Officer to work together in a consistent way to support schools and allows for broader discussions of systemic needs and the resulting action plan for the year.

Weekly EPS team meetings also provide opportunities to network and connect, as well as to deal with internal issues. We will have regular visitor slots in team meetings so that all EPs increase knowledge of the organisation and the unique community which it serves. This will have a range of positive outcomes in many cases – a visit from the senior education social worker leads to stronger links between the teams, which leads to, for example,

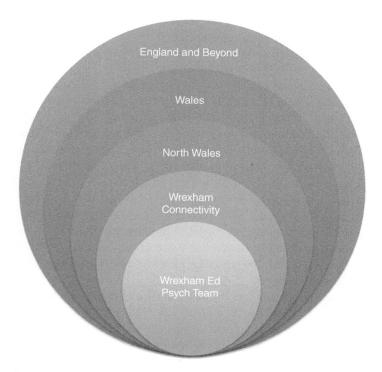

Figure 10.6   Circles of connectivity.

more effective joint working on issues relating to attendance and exclusion and collaboration on producing guidelines and training for schools on Pastoral Support Plans. An update visit from the Healthy Schools manager gives us the opportunity to plan a joint conference on the issue of well-being and to discuss sources of information and support within the area of sleep difficulties in children and young people and impact of gaming.

Close working relationship between EPS and the local Wrexham Child and Adolescent Mental Health team (CAMHS) continues to be a crucial one. There are regular meetings to share information, for example, on EPS training programmes. This allows EPS to signpost what we have to offer both to stakeholders and clients. It also ensures that the EPS is making efficient use of resources and not duplicating services. EPs participate together in a range of strategic groups focussing on the issue of mental health and well-being. This includes the "Five Ways to Well-being" strategic group; organise a weekly joint 'Drop In Service' for all professionals working with children and young people, ensuring that we record and evaluate on the spot, following each consultation and follow up with randomised phone calls to measure impact.

Leadership within a Rural Area

As a relatively small team of EPs, we work across two fairly rural authorities – Anglesey and Gwynedd, which are at the northwest corner of the country. With the two LAs showing the highest proportion of Welsh speakers in Wales in the 2011 Census, providing a bilingual Welsh/English EP service to the 26,000 school-age population and early years settings, their parents, and carers is essential. This raises recruitment and retention issues consistently. Areas of deprivation exist within both LAs with rural poverty and distance to services being a key factor.

With beautiful Snowdonia scenery comes travel (by car), varying school sizes and a feeling of being 'ships passing in the night' at times. From the rugged coastline of the far north of Anglesey, to the western tip of the Llyn and the River Dyfi in the south is an area of 1,259 square miles. This is second only to the LA of Powys, which is 2,000 square miles. The journey from Northern Anglesey to southern Gwynedd takes over 2 hours and has been done, over lunchtime, a few times (comparable to authorities such as Cornwall and Northumberland in England).

Following on from a strategic review, completed in September 2017, the EPS sits within an Integrated ALN and Inclusion Team (see Figure 10.7). This is a jointly commissioned service across the two LAs and is centrally funded. There is no traded aspect to the service apart from income generated from training that is additional to 'core' service and Emotional Literacy Support Assistant (ELSA) (Burton, 2004) training offered at cost. This is possibly a reflection of the wide range in size of schools.

Leading a small team within a large ALN and Inclusion Service is supportive, and the contribution of educational psychology is valued at a strategic level. Regular team meetings and supervision meetings are essential to ensure strong links within the team. The EPS is at the core of the service with the senior manager post and PEP post as one, and senior educational psychology (SEP) posts linked to each team with strategic responsibility. Working with two LAs with different strategic plans is challenging in terms of ensuring

Figure 10.7 Integrated ALN and inclusion team.

that the service provided is appropriate for both, and good working relationships are key. Schools are largely open to the service providing a varied range of input, from strategic projects, to consultation, to training and also specific interventions. Development of specialisms is advancing positively.

In looking at service delivery the strategic direction is provided by the host LA, which is Gwynedd. This has been adopted and developed with success. Other departments have established working practices which are in keeping with 'Ffordd Gwynedd' (loosely translating to the Gwynedd way of doing things') and the Education Department and ALN and Inclusion Service are now approaching this. 'Ffordd Gwynedd' has been developed using Vanguard Methodology (Seddon, 2005).

What is the Vanguard Methodology?

Vanguard Methodology was developed by Professor John Seddon (2005), following from the work of Deming (1982) and Ohno (1988), as a method of management which looks at systems management. It looks at identifying change and utilising intervention theory in terms of implementing and maintaining system change. It involves movement from traditional 'command and control' management, to viewing the organisation as a system (Seddon, 2005, 2008).

Seddon (2005) asserts that traditional methods of management teach people to manage people, money, resources and process in a top-down hierarchical way. Deming (1982) sees this method of command and control as an organisational prison (Seddon, 2005). In contrast Vanguard Methodology and Ffordd Gwynedd move toward a management style which considers how the organisation works as a system.

How the service is utilising Ffordd Gwynedd and Vanguard Methodology in order to improve service delivery

Potential uses are far reaching, both in looking at EPS processes and in supporting schools and other services to look at their own. Creating systems which add more value to the service users is always appealing and is in keeping with the ethos of the service and the approaches employed. The Ffordd Gwynedd six steps followed are briefly described here:

1) *Understanding the Demand*

   Looking at the type and frequency of our contacts with the service user gives information about the contacts that are valuable and the contacts that are not and highlights failures to provide. Gathering this information through looking at a sample of emails and phone calls to the service was extremely interesting in considering this.

2) *Defining the Purpose of the Service*

   Looking at what our service users need was quite simple and entailed stripping things back to the elements of what is required – this was achieved by discussing with frontline staff and also managers within the service. Our service users (who include the learners themselves, their families and school staff), from completion of step 1, want the correct service at the correct time. They want happy healthy learners who feel safe at school. Our 'back office' administrative processes do not feature in this need.

3) *Our Ability to Respond*

   Are our measures for efficiency of service management targets, or do our performance measures actually measure what the service user sees as important? This is a key element for the service as a whole. Many of our current measures relate to data such as use of resources, percentages of attendance, increases in the curriculum levels of learners, the number of practitioners we have trained and so on. Do we know, however, if our practices have made a difference to the whole child, how happy they are? Not to the extent we would like at the moment, but we are making steps toward this.

   Exploring service measures has taken us into the direction of use of Therapy Outcome Measures (TOM) (Enderby & John, 2015) as a tool which provides a framework for measuring effectiveness of intervention with a wider scope of assessment. We are currently exploring this as a measurement tool for measuring differences in the actual difficulties experienced, the level of activity or functionality that is observed, the ability of the individual to participate within their environment independently and also the well-being of the individual and those around them. TOMs is a tool developed for use within clinical settings and is exploratory in terms of application to an educational setting.

4) *Work Streams*

   Mapping the processes and pathways from planning to intervention, and other streams followed by administrative teams, highlighted steps within our processes as a whole which did not add value to the service user and those that did. The next stage is now obviously to look at how we work through the processes to remove steps that do not add value to the service user and make the system work better for them.

5) *Barriers*

Identifying restrictions along the way, both in terms of process, individuals, conventions and capacity, and how effective the service is in overcoming the barriers to change. This is of course a stage in the process which is of great interest to us as EPs.

6) *Beliefs*

This is a familiar and interesting stage - the final of the six. Here we explore the beliefs behind the barriers, managing change with groups and teams. Employing Kotter's eight steps to change (Kotter, 1995, 2007), Kübler-Ross' change curve (1969) and the Satir (Satir, Banmen, Gerber, Gomori, 1991) Model as our underpinning models. It is at this stage that the skill set of the EPS is crucial to the process.

Collaboration Across North Wales

Again, with the growing pressures of resource reduction, our outward-facing energies have led to close collaboration with our PEP partners in North Wales.

Once a term, the PEPs of Gwynedd and Anglesey, Conway, Flintshire, Denbighshire and Wrexham meet to share information, to discuss thorny issues such as capacity and recruitment and to support each other with solution focussed approaches and to plan joint work. This includes one of our current priorities which is using the British Psychological Society Division of Educational and Child Psychology (2019) guidelines for quality assurance to work in pairs on focussed issues. Another development of joint work has been collaboration and support with the Flintshire team (with whom we have a close historic relationship) on the Burton (2004) programme, which is now being delivered across Wales. Collaboration once a term gives us opportunity to compare our experiences, to discuss and resolve any difficulties and to plan for any future developments in joint working across the authorities. In the summer term, we will jointly host an ELSA celebration event with a joint planning team of members from both Wrexham and Flintshire teams. This event will be open to schools and other colleagues and will involve a number of ELSAs presenting their work, giving poster presentations, sharing resources and information about the programme across the two areas.

Joint professional development has been another successful collaborative venture. Experience shows that this is an efficient and effective way of acquiring continuing professional development as the cost can be split five ways and the whole experience of joint training gives us a shared language and further opportunities for joint working and setting up special interest groups. For example, initial training in cognitive behaviour therapy (CBT) is leading to current discussions on setting up a joint special interest group on EPs and therapeutic interventions. In recent years, we have organised joint training across North Wales on Coaching Psychology and EPs using CBT. In previous years, we have used different models of mixing external speakers with individual EPS presentations.

Collaboration also provides opportunities for peer supervision. Each half term, the first author meets with the Principal of Flintshire for peer supervision relating to a range of leadership issues. The current model used tends to be co-counselling with opportunity for active listening and the core Rogerian components. This supportive relationship, however, offers opportunity to try out alternative supervisory models including those from Nancy

Kline's (2002) Time to Think which allows for a time-bound partner role of noninterrupted listening, followed by feedback.

Within the termly NAPEP WALES meetings however, we have a different experience of group supervision using the Balint model (Bartle & Trevis, 2015) and facilitated by a tutor from the Cardiff University educational psychology doctoral course. The varied models of supervision allow for a responsive process of collaboration and a supportive and challenging experience. It also continues to forge our relationship with our Welsh doctoral course where we aim to develop close collaboration through traineeships, research and joint involvement in the recruitment and selection of new trainees. However, as a border LA, with easy potential access to other centres of learning and our neighbouring English LA services, we welcome the recent research article by Atkinson and Posada (2019) 'Leadership supervision for managers of educational psychology services'. In the interests of reaching out, and suggesting areas for future research in Welsh EPSs, we would say that EP leadership and PEP supervision within the Welsh context is a fertile ground for further research and would greatly benefit our future development, offer challenges and ongoing collaborative relationships.

References

Additional Learning Needs and Education Tribunal Act. (2018). Cardiff: National Assembly for Wales.

Additional Needs and Inclusion Division. (2008). *Statements or something better? Preliminary consultation on options for change to the framework for statutory assessment and statements of SEN: Summary of parental views*. Cardiff: National Assembly for Wales.

Atkinson, C. & Posada, S. (2019) Leadership supervision for managers of educational psychology services. *Educational Psychology in Practice, 35*(1), 34–49.

Bartle, D., & Trevis, A. (2015). An evaluation of group supervision in a specialist provision supporting young people with mental health needs: A social constructionist perspective. *Educational and Child Psychology, 32*(3), 78–89.

British Psychological Society (BPS). (2019). *Quality standards for Educational Psychology Services Division of Educational and Child Psychology*. Leicester: BPS. Retrieved from https://www.bps.org.uk/member-microsites/division-educational-child-psychology/resources

Burton, S. (2004). *Emotional literacy support assistants*. Winchester: Hampshire Educational Psychology Service.

Children, Young People and Education Committee. (2018). *Mind over matter: A report on the step change needed in emotional and mental health support for children and young people in Wales*. Cardiff: National Assembly for Wales.

Covey, S. (1989). *The 7 habits of highly effective people*. New York: Free Press.

Deming, W. E. (1982). *Out of crisis*. Cambridge: Cambridge University Press.

Donaldson, G. (2015). *Successful futures*. Cardiff: Welsh Government.

Enderby, P., & John, A. (2015). *Therapy outcome measures for Rehabilitation Professionals* (3rd ed.). Guildford: J & R Press.

Kline, N. (2002). *Time to Think – Listening to Ignite the Human Mind*. London: Cassell.

Kotter, J. P. (1995). Leading change: Why transformation efforts fail. *Harvard Business Review*, *73*, 59–67.

Kotter, J. P. (2007). Leading change: Why transformation efforts fail. *Harvard Business Review*, *85*(1), 96–103.

Kübler-Ross, E. (1969). *Death and dying*. New York: Routledge.

McLaughlin, C. (2015). *The connected school: A design for well-being – supporting children and young people in schools to flourish, thrive and achieve*. London: Pearson.

Myers, I. B., & Myers, P. B. (1980). *Gifts differing: understanding personality types*. Mountain View, CA: Davies-Black Publishing.

Ohno, T. (1988). *The Toyota production system*. New York: Productivity Press.

Satir, V., Banmen, J., Gerber, J., & Gomori, M. (1991). *The Satir model: Family therapy and beyond*. Palo Alto, CA: Science and Behaviour Books.

Seddon, J. (2005). *Freedom from command and control* (2nd ed.). Buckingham: Vanguard Education Limited.

Seddon, J. (2008). *Systems thinking in the public sector*. Axminster: Triarchy Press.

Social Services and Well-Being Act. (2014). Cardiff: National Assembly for Wales.

Office of the High Commissioner on Human Rights. (1989). United Nations Convention on Rights of the Child. Retrieved from https://www.ohchr.org/EN/ProfessionalInterest/Pages/CRC.aspx

Well-being of Future Generations Act. (2015). Cardiff: National Assembly for Wales.

Whitmore, J. (2009). *Coaching for performance: GROWing human potential and purpose: the principles and practice of coaching and leadership. People skills for professionals* (4th ed.). Boston: Nicholas Brealey.

11

Working in Different Leadership Teams with EPs and Others: Dealing with Tricky Situations

Harriet Martin and Melernie Meheux

Introduction

Over recent years the position of Educational Psychology Services (EPSs) in the structure of many Local Authorities (LAs) has changed, sometimes more than once. Principal Educational Psychologists (PEPs) are now often managing a range of services, including special educational needs and disability (SEND) assessment teams and advisory teachers. PEPs need to adjust to working with senior managers from very different professional backgrounds and consider how best to lead teams of nonpsychologists alongside educational psychologists (EPs). This scenario potentially increases the risk of conflict and tension between teams and team members. Teams may not necessarily share the same priorities and values and may not understand others' prime goals. They may not even be clear about others' skills and knowledge. Everyone may be uncertain as to how they fit within the wider organisation.

All LAs, and indeed other public sector services, are under huge financial pressure that has necessitated cuts and placed increasing demands on staff to deliver more for less and in less time. Many more people are now feeling anxious about job security and are likely to be more defensive and competitive with others. Staff may also be stressed and overwhelmed by the volume of work and the pressure to meet key performance indicators (KPIs) and legal time scales. The managing PEP is more likely to be spending a greater proportion of their time than before 'managing up' to support their teams and justify their existence. The likelihood of a 'tricky issue' arising is increased and, if it does, the level of stress already present in teams means that it may be harder to deal with and be more likely to escalate.

These 'tricky issues' nearly always involve a breakdown in relationships and understanding between people. Team members may get into conflict over, for example, a professional disagreement, or the individuals may come from teams that have different immediate priorities. An individual may end up becoming disgruntled because they feel unappreciated or that they are being excluded. Teams or individuals may blame each other for perceived failures or try to pass on responsibility in a situation that is getting difficult. People may feel that the workload is unfair or unreasonable. While it is not possible to ensure that these situations never arise, even in stressful times, the chances that they will arise can be reduced, as can the chances that they will escalate when they do emerge. This chapter will look at the atmosphere that is likely to lead to the most harmonious team working. It will

Leadership for Educational Psychologists: Principles & Practicalities, First Edition.
Edited by Julia Hardy, Charmian Hobbs and Mohammed Bham.
© 2020 John Wiley & Sons Ltd. Published 2020 by John Wiley & Sons Ltd.

also delve into how a PEP might manage difficult conversations if the necessity arises and give some illustrative examples.

Trust and the Team Ethos

An unpublished report by the Government Behavioural Insights Team[1] identified five styles and categories of behaviour that characterise effective public service leaders emerging from the literature. Three of these are particularly relevant in the context of this chapter. The first style (transactional) is one where the leader ensures clear expectations, rewards performance and monitors mistakes. The leader will ensure that team members have the resources they need, will establish clear team processes to manage time constraints and efficiency, and make sure that achievement is properly acknowledged. The second style (transformational) is one where the leader sets a shared vision and future direction whilst inspiring the team to achieve change. This includes developing individuals and teams and helping a team find meaning in their work. In the context of a PEP managing multiple teams that may have differing priorities or values it is important that all the teams are aware of and can sign up to the overall children's services' mission and values. If there are local disagreements it may help to refer to these. The third relevant style (ethical) is one where the leader embodies integrity and authenticity. This involves paying close attention to the intent and thinking of individuals in their teams, themselves showing honesty, trustworthiness, fairness and conscientiousness and, importantly vulnerability, taking time to know and manage themselves. A team or teams where everyone understands and has 'bought into' the organisation's mission, values and principles and where the leader walks the talk and is trusted is more likely to be effective and harmonious.

A related concept is that of the team mental model. A mental model is the structure we create in our mind to make sense of external reality. We need mental models to help us plan and solve problems (Markham & Gentner, 2001). The team mental model is the shared understanding that everyone in the team needs to achieve the team goals (Barrett & Martin, 2014). This includes understanding what others know, how they work and how the team or teams should work together. Research suggests that teams who share a mental model are more likely to work together effectively (Kozlowski & Ilgen, 2006). A clear team mental model is likely to reduce the instances of serious conflict as everyone should understand the principles underpinning their work and also have some idea of other individuals' motives and intents. Work to establish the team mental model will be time well spent as will time taken to understand the team mental models of those teams with whom a particular team works most closely. A PEP managing a number of teams is likely to find that fewer conflicts arise if they have taken time to arrange for teams to work together to understand each other and appreciate others' stresses and flashpoints.

Time thinking about the teams' cohesion and emotional needs is also important. Leaders should invest a reasonable amount of time attending to fears and feelings (Brown, 2018).

---

1 Centre for Public Services Leadership: Measurement was produced by the Government's Behavioural Insights Team. It discusses ways of evaluating leadership training.

Brown introduces the concept of 'rumbling with vulnerability'. This means being prepared to have discussions or meetings where participants are potentially exposed (become vulnerable) to arrive at a jointly agreed solution. A leader is not exempt from this. These kinds of conversations are never easy and require bravery and skill, for example, maintaining curiosity, an understanding of empathy and the effects of shame and genuine listening. However, if the PEP has worked with teams so that they feel able to have these kinds of conversations when necessary, and they are trusted to engage in them honestly, then the chances of conflict and tension getting out of control are reduced. These skills will also be useful in the event that a difficult situation does arise. If team members are used to behaving in this way at times of lesser conflict then they are likely to find it easier to engage if the situation becomes more serious.

Formal grievances, allegations of discrimination or bullying, harsh complaints about workload and social conflict often emerge writ large because the individuals concerned have felt neglected, unappreciated and not listened to for some time. This can be more acute for those managed by the PEP who are not EPs as they may feel that the PEP does not fully understand what they do or that the PEP favours EPs. It will, therefore, be worth investing time with all teams and continuing to keep on top of any emerging issues. PEPs should also take time to consider how they recognise and show appreciation of all their staff. Even a simple thank you demonstrates that someone has been noticed. All this contributes to a positive ethos and helps to prevent a build-up of resentment that can diminish the likelihood and severity, if they do occur, of difficult situations.

David Cotton (2014) provides a useful summary of the leadership role in reducing the likelihood of conflict. He cites lack of motivation as the key cause of 'difficult behaviour'. Difficulties within teams can be avoided if leaders create environments that contain and maintain a range of motivators.

Reduces conflict	**Leadership role**
Positive relationships within the team and with the leadership team	Facilitating good relationships within the team can greatly enhance working environments and staff well-being and reduce any difficulties. Allow team members to get to know one another in a way that isn't intrusive and is on their terms.
Having a range of work	Offering team members the opportunity to engage in a range of creative systemic and individual pieces of work enhances general feelings of job satisfaction. Carefully matching and sharing out work, evenly, to interested members and those who will benefit from further development illustrates the point that work is not simply delegated for it to be completed but also with the intent to help with individual career progression and best outcomes for team members.
	Times of austerity mean that some services are only able to carry out core work, however, within these services, a range of work within this can also be considered, for example, ensuring that staff work across the age phases and have access to statutory work that falls within most of the areas of need identified within the SEND code of practice (Department for Education & Department of Health, 2015).

Access to regular and good quality, management and case work supervision (distinguishing between the two)	The complexity of the work that EPs engage in means that they require support to step back and reflect on their work, within a safe supervisory space.
	Many services offer reflective team and peer supervision where team members take it in turns to present and listen to cases and offer a supportive framework to facilitate understanding of a specific issue or in addition to peer supervision, having regular and separate casework and management supervision can reduce any potential feeling of judgement or hierarchy on the part of supervisee. By keeping managerial issues separate from case supervision it can enhance openness and reflection, leading to feelings of containment. It also means that any managerial recurring difficulties can be explored and resolved safely.
	Some services have managed this by allocating team members two supervisors – one to carry out management supervision (typically the PEP or senior educational psychologist (SEP)) and one for casework.
	This applies equally to members of different teams.
Knowing that they will receive support from colleagues and the leadership team if needed; trusting others	Having an 'open door' policy ensures that members of the team know that they can approach the PEP when needed. This shows that leaders care and are available.
	When a leader is responsive, readily able to deal with things as they arise and protects the interest of their team members, it inspires a sense of loyalty and respect from the rest of the team.
	A supportive and warm response, in which leaders actively listen and hear team members, encourages team members to be open and share concerns before they become too big to handle.
Having a dedicated space to work in and an environment that the team wants to be in	Increasingly many teams are hot desking and remote working, in order to manage the demands of coping with restricted office space.
	However, despite the challenges, within these models it is possible to have designated 'areas' that the team work in or agree days/times that the team will all be in. It is also possible to be creative and punctuate these work functions with team lunches and/or working lunches to encourage the need to recharge, whilst also creating a continuing professional development (CPD) opportunity.
	Reducing isolation and enhancing the shared time that the team does have together leads to increased cohesion, a sense of belonging and general feelings of work satisfaction, which in turn reduces the likelihood of difficult situations within a team.
Knowing and understanding the vision of the service	Co-constructing the team vision, or regularly revisiting this for new team members ensures that every piece of work is understood in the context of the shared vision.
	This enhances understanding of desired outcomes and a strong commitment to carrying out the team functions.
Autonomy and flexibility as practitioners	Facilitating opportunities for team members to be autonomous and flexible in their practice, in line with ethical practice and Health and Care Professions Council (2018) and British Psychological Society (2017) guidelines, is essential to promote trust, staff satisfaction and retention.
	Allowing team members to find their own solutions and interventions in casework is essential. Micro-management and overinvolvement can make staff feel like they are not trusted and that they don't have the competence to manage work.

Rewards systems that are fair and transparent	Teams work best when their achievements and hard work are acknowledged and named. This needs to be fair and transparent and can be difficult to achieve.
	In one LA, the PEP developed a Recognition of Achievement Award (RAA) and asked team members to nominate each other following individual or whole team support given. In every team meeting this was prioritised on the agenda and the PEP would take the time to provide a certificate and feedback to nominated individuals, based on feedback within the team for things like 'supporting me with resources to deliver training' or 'taking the time to discuss a difficult case with me'. This developed relationships within the team and also meant that individual achievements were heard and valued by all.
Clear communication about any restructuring or changes within LA policy	Uncertainty can lead to tension and anxiety; thus any impending changes should be communicated.

What to Do When a Difficult Issue Arises

Unfortunately, challenging and difficult situations do occur at work even in the most harmonious of teams. These can arise within existing teams or following the arrival of new team members or leaders. Some models suggest conflict and challenge is necessary for the group to develop and function healthily. Psychologist Bruce Tuckman's forming-storming-norming-performing model describes this (Tuckman, 1965). However, in other circumstances conflict can be detrimental. Whatever the source of conflicts or tricky situations within a team or between teams, when the issue goes beyond healthy challenge and becomes an underlying and significant tension, if left unaddressed it can adversely affect team morale, emotional well-being and output.

Look at your own involvement

As a leader you need to model the behaviour you expect to see within the team. When you do not then you forgo the right to challenge or question. If you routinely send consultation summaries late or never meet your own statutory deadlines you cannot challenge team members on the same issues. Whilst this might point to challenges in workload and the need for a systemic piece of work around allocation and patches, you still cannot honestly admonish individuals. The answer would be to address the systemic issue rather than criticise the staff member. Always first ask yourself, is the presenting issue partly about me – or not? Always consider your own role and see if there is anything in your own behaviour that may have contributed to the perceived 'difficult behaviour' in the other person. If, on reflection, you can see how your own behaviour may have been a contributing factor, then the first step is to acknowledge this and work towards resolving it.

Check your lens

Burnham, Palma and Whitehouse (2008) originally developed the idea of the Social Graces to help practitioners monitor their own attitudes and biases when working with families and colleagues. They particularly encouraged practitioners to be aware of visible/invisible and voiced/unvoiced differences and how this might affect their formulation of presenting issues and problems. The Social Graces have since been expanded to the GGRRAAACCEEESSS (Burnham, 2011) and include:

> Gender (including gender identity), geography, race, religion, age, ability, appearance, class, culture, ethnicity, education, employment, sexuality, sexual orientation and spirituality

When an issue arises within your service it is important to be sensitive and respectful, ensuring that honest reflection on the GGRRAAACCEEESSS is undertaken and you consider any potential areas of difference between individuals and groups of people which can lead to discrimination.

Monitor

It is helpful to monitor and review the types of issues that arise in order to consider whether there is a systemic problem. For example, if a school frequently presents children with literacy difficulties, they might be supported by a whole school intervention focussing on literacy teaching. Similarly with challenging situations we need to look at patterns over time in order to identify any systemic issues or any apparently unrelated factors.

Simple differences in opinion

Whilst there are a number of strengths to working within multiagency teams, there are also obvious tensions and challenges. Working alongside other professionals presents a greater risk of differences in theoretical perspectives that can become destructive if not understood and addressed. Professionals, EPs included, are bound by shared values, ideals, objectives and ways of working which understandably mean that they may see things from a very different perspective. These differences may always be there and be manageable but can become problematic in specific situations.

For example, an EP and a special educational needs (SEN) caseworker had a difference of opinion about whether percentile scores were the best way of understanding the needs of a young person. The caseworker requested that the EP carry out an assessment so that the case could be reviewed quickly at the following meeting to help facilitate specialist placement. The EP queried whether a one-off assessment would capture the complexity of needs. There was much discussion about categorisation versus the use of a holistic approach taking into account all information collected over time. Whilst the SEN approach may have appeared 'quicker' with gentle exploration of desired outcomes and further explanation, the EP was able to encourage an alternative viewpoint. The EP also came to appreciate the time constraints facing the SEN caseworker and negotiated a suitable timeframe, offering to summarise all the presenting information alongside an assessment. The matter was, therefore, resolved sensitively and respectfully. This led to the best outcome for the child and a healthy ongoing working relationship where everybody felt listened to.

Trickier Situations – Structuring Your Approach

The following steps will help PEPs think about how they might structure their approach and any ensuing interactions and discussions, thus reducing conflict and the necessity of going down a more formal route.

1) Decide what your response will be

When faced with a potential difficult situation the first thing to do is consider how you will approach it. The Thomas–Kilmann (2010) model (Figure 11.1) identifies five basic conflict resolution responses, based on the combination of *Assertiveness* (the degree to which someone will try to satisfy their own agenda) and *Cooperativeness* (the degree to which someone tries to satisfy the other person's agenda). The model indicates that competing is assertive and not cooperative, and accommodating is cooperative and not assertive. Avoiding is neither assertive nor cooperative, whereas collaborating is both assertive and cooperative. Compromising falls in the middle on both dimensions.

2) Identify desired outcomes

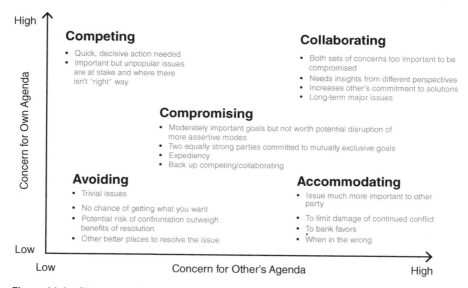

Figure 11.1 Diagram of Thomas-Kilmann (2010) model of conflict resolution.

After deciding what response to make Cotton (2014) suggests having Ideal, Realistic and Best (IRB) outcomes to help provide structure and generate the right questions before and during difficult discussions.

3) Have the discussion and apply your EP skills

Ideal	Ask yourself what would the ideal outcome be if I could get exactly what I want from this discussion?
Realistic	Realistically, what can I expect from this discussion, which would satisfy my needs, although it is not ideal.
Best alternative	What outcome would satisfy me and the other involved parties?

The actual conversation, although it can be anxiety inducing, is probably where PEPs are the most skilled! Using active listening, asking clarifying questions and summarising makes it more likely that we have heard narratives as they were intended. This approach, where we check our understanding rather than making assumptions about what the other person is saying, allows them to feel heard and understood.

Listening without assumption is an important and powerful tool, particularly if you have recently taken up a position that means you have taken on a new team. It is essential that whilst you listen to and are mindful of the experiences of the previous leader, that you set aside any judgement. 'Confirmation bias' is our tendency to look for the information that confirms the information we hold about a person or a thing. Thus if we have been told something specific about a team member, for example, that Malcolm is a very difficult team member, then we are likely to look solely for the examples of Malcolm being very difficult and fail to notice all the evidence that discredits this. In fact Malcolm may not be very difficult at all; the previous leader may have misunderstood him or possibly been very difficult themselves. For these reasons when taking on a new team or entering a new situation, take the time to meet each member of the team, get to know them and make up your own mind about their strengths, areas of need and the best way of managing and developing them. PEPs should not forget the skills that they use every day in consultation when working with their teams.

Giving feedback on a tricky issue

At times an issue may come to our attention that we need to discuss with team members – for example, a member of the team frequently turns up late or is absent from the team meeting – and it has an impact on their ability to keep up with important developments within the team. It is important to monitor and raise the issue if it occurs frequently, ensuring that you focus on the single issue which can be changed and that you do not introduce other topics of conversation. Give specific examples and dates of the behaviour that you have observed. Give the other person the chance to listen, reflect and respond, giving the opportunity to explain from their perspective. This can help shift perspectives for example if they explain that they have had an influx of Education, Health and Care Plan (EHCP) advices at their special school, which has necessitated additional visits, then you might respond in a different manner, for example by taking their name off the EHCP allocation list for a few weeks to reduce their workload. Whilst you need to be sensitive to the fact that the conversation might be upsetting, the message should be clear. Team meetings are an important part of the teams functioning and every member should attend.

Receiving feedback about a tricky situation

Sometimes team members will come to the PEP with a tricky situation. Cotton's DESC model (2014) is a helpful and focussed structure to apply, and one that allows each party to be heard and to speak. When using the framework you can explain the format first and invite each person to speak uninterrupted, as you would in a reflective team/peer supervision. The following example looks at a case of an EP who had a Structured Professional Assessment (SPA) point turned down.

Allow the employee to describe the situation as a single sentence **D**escribe the situation	The employee was able to say what he saw as being the cause of the conflict. For example, 'I have been working really hard for three years but when I applied for a SPA point I was turned down. I know people who have been here for the same amount of time have been awarded them when they have applied'.
Express how they feel	He said, 'I feel unappreciated and that my efforts haven't been recognised and that other members of the team are being rewarded. I'm also upset that I have been overlooked'.
Specify what they want	He said that he 'would appreciate us revisiting my application to see how I didn't meet the competencies for an award'.
Consequences	He felt that revisiting the application would help him identify what he needed to do in the future to help any future application and would also help his relationships with the leadership team.

This approach allowed the EP involved to express his thoughts and feelings without interruption and to alert the leadership team to his concerns. They were able to support him to reflect on his application and identify any gaps and also any strengths that were not recorded within the application, to help him make a future application. This helped the EP see that he was valued by the leadership team but also alerted the leadership team for the need to think about focussing on employee recognition within the wider team.

Tackling a tricky situation between two people

There will be times when differences emerge within or across teams. It's helpful on these occasions to meet with each party separately and get them to explain from their perspective what happened, with an emphasis on them doing so objectively and as rationally as is possible. After you have gathered separate accounts and established the facts and perspectives bring the two sides together. Collaboratively set ground rules, ensuring an emphasis on speaking volume, objective facts (not personal attacks) and a genuine desire to unpick the issue. Working within this space makes it more likely that each individual be heard and listened to equally and respectfully, with time to share fully any concerns and grievances they may have. Together come to a clear solution and reassure them that you will monitor and review the situation, and in so doing show that you are taking the issue seriously.

In such situations, record your discussions and agreed next steps, sharing the notes with all parties. This shows that you are not trivialising the situation and intend to review. However, this is also necessary for other purposes. Although the idea of bringing parties together is to resolve issues and avoid having to go down a formal disciplinary route, if difficulties arise later down the line it is important to have evidence of steps taken before.

Two colleagues from two separate teams got into conflict as a result of party A feeling she had been directed to do something by party B.

Party A felt disgruntled as they were equivalent in grade and that Party B could and should have carried out the task herself. The PEP got both sides of the story and noted that that the whole office was feeling stressed following a recent SEND inspection. On this particular day a director was coming to address the team and required a specific piece of IT to feedback the findings of the inspection.

From both accounts the PEP discovered that Party B had received a call from the director's office, asking if Party A was coming to collect the equipment. Party B had no knowledge of this and asked Party A if she was going to collect the IT equipment. Party A wanted to know why she needed to collect it and this led to an exchange of words in the office and culminated in Party A and B not talking to one another. As they sat together and needed to communicate regularly with one another, this would have presented a difficult situation for both teams if left unresolved.

Having had both accounts the PEP could see that in fact Party A wasn't aware that Party B had been directed by the director's office, to ask her to collect the equipment and that Party B wasn't simply directing her to get the equipment because she herself didn't want to get it. In addition, Party B wasn't aware that Party A didn't know anything about being assigned the job; otherwise she would have simply collected it herself.

The PEP invited them to meet with her. She established some ground rules and invited them to share their accounts with one another. In so doing Party A and Party B were able to reflect on the miscommunication that had happened and ways to resolve it going forward. The PEP was also able to share her perspective about the impact of the SEND inspection and recognise how difficult it had been for all of them. They agreed on some expected outcomes if they were communicating well together and the PEP emailed these, along with the general discussion, and got Party A and B to sign it. They agreed to meet in 2 weeks to review the situation, with the caveat they could meet earlier if necessary.

Miscommunication between others is common, and although the initial difficulty is often forgotten quickly, it can lead to continued and significant difficulties. In the case described here there could have been major consequences had the issue continued; for example, both team members had to share information and coordinate professional advice for statutory work needing to communicate frequently throughout the day. They would also answer one another's phones when the other was absent, which led to an efficient service for both teams and meant that all parental and professional queries were answered quickly. Had the issue continued and escalated it could have led to far-reaching consequences having an impact on the functioning of both teams and overall LA aims.

Disciplinary measures/formal procedures

Unfortunately, in spite of our best efforts, challenging situations can persist and we need to take more formal measures. This can feel like a personal failure for the PEP, however, it is a brave step and it is important that in addition to contacting the human resources (HR) department, that we seek out help and alternate perspectives. In these instances use the supervisory space and also discuss the issue with your line manager.

Supervision and line management support

It is important for PEPs to have a reflective space to fully explore the issues so they don't take a toll on you. Also ensure that you keep your line manager informed. Discuss situations with them in good time so they do not question why they have not heard about the situation earlier. Keeping your line manager informed is not a sign that you cannot manage situations, but rather, reassures them that they will always be the first to be aware of any difficulties and that they will not hear about them from outside the team. In addition, at times, it is necessary that somebody more senior needs to be involved to exercise some authority and to avoid further escalation. For example, during a multiagency joint project, with a team led by a clinical psychologist there were challenges in developing shared outcomes and a timeline, in spite of a number of meetings and discussion. The SEPs within the team tried a range of strategies to facilitate collaborative working and ensure that all perspectives could be heard, however, it was difficult to reach a consensus. The involvement of the PEP led to a shift in ways of working and the allocation of an experienced consultant PEP, external to both teams to lead the project.

Follow due process

However, sometimes in spite of applying all of the above, the situation still does not get resolved. In these instances it is necessary to take a more formal approach and initiate disciplinary proceedings. Each LA will have their own policy and procedures that sit within the UK legislative framework. It is important that as a leader you have been fair at all stages leading up to any disciplinary hearing and work within your LA framework and the law.

Are you in a position to start disciplinary proceedings?

Before you consider thinking about any process you need to ensure that you have:

- Kept all documentation following each meeting, with agreed minutes and actions so that there is no dispute over what has been said.
- Coproduced or agreed achievable targets with the employee in order to make changes.
- Given the employee a fair amount of time to meet targets before disciplinary proceedings.
- Remembered that it is important that an investigation happens quickly, whilst ensuring that the process will be thorough and robust.
- Kept all evidence of the way that you have handled the alleged misconduct/issue.

You will need to follow a more specific process once you have decided that you will proceed with a disciplinary route. The Advisory, Conciliation and Arbitration Service (2015) code of practice on disciplinary and grievance procedures will ensure that you do this properly. Use this alongside your council's HR guidance for managers.

It feels uncomfortable to get to this point but if we remain fair and reasonable throughout and document every stage, agreeing reasonable targets and providing enough time to achieve them, this can reduce difficult feelings.

Workplace bullying

If there are situations where a member of the team feels they are being victimised or bullied then these allegations need to be carefully investigated and treated seriously, in line with your council's HR policy. It is essential in such instances that you liaise with HR advisors closely and adhere to the council's policy to ensure that situations do not escalate any more than they need to. As soon as you are aware that there is an allegation of bullying, separate the accuser from the accused. Next, as in the previous section, ask the person making the allegation to record each situation in detail. It is important to try and stay impartial and be aware that just because you yourself may not have observed the reported behaviours, these incidents may still have taken place. Conversely it is also important to remain open to the fact that an accusation does not mean that bullying is taking place but could be down to different perspectives and interpretations or other factors. Instead of deciding whether the allegation is unfounded or true, leaders need to take every report seriously and work closely with HR to ensure that the correct processes are followed.

Summary

All PEPs will face a difficult situation at some point. Most are caused or exacerbated by a breakdown in communication and relationships. By taking time to foster a supportive, collaborative culture where team members understand others' mental models, intents and motivations PEPs can reduce the chances of such situations arising and, if they do, increase the chance of a good resolution.

It is worth remembering that when you are faced with a difficult situation it is easy to:

- take things personally
- ignore the issue and do nothing
- walk away
- be blindsided and not know what to do
- overreact

It is also important to remember that when a tricky issue arises, you need to consider the impact on the output and everyday functioning of the team as well as the individuals concerned. Differing perspectives may not necessarily be harmful but team members need to understand those perspectives and teams need to be able to adapt how they work to accommodate them. Remember when trying to sort out conflicting views:

- resist the urge to judge
- maintain a boundary between you and the persons(s) involved
- stop, think and act

- listen, really listen
- focus on the future
- learn to relax
- speak positively
- do not take things personally
- be aware of survivor guilt

PEPs already possess the necessary communication skills and psychological knowledge to manage tricky situations. This does not mean it is easy particularly if it makes the PEP feel vulnerable. However, being brave, listening and remaining respectful will go a long way.

References

Advisory, Conciliation and Arbitration Service. (2015). ACAS code of practice 1 on disciplinary and grievance procedures. Retrieved from http://www.acas.org.uk/index.aspx?articleid=2174

Barrett, E., & Martin, P. (2014). *Extreme; why some people thrive at the limits*. Oxford: Oxford University Press.

British Psychological Society. (2017). *Practice guidelines* (3rd ed.). Leicester: BPS.

Brown, B. (2018). *Dare to lead*. London: Vermillion.

Burnham, J. (2011). Developments in Social GRRRAAACCEEESSS: Visible-invisible and voiced-unvoiced. In I.-B. Krause (Ed.), *Culture and reflexivity in systemic psychotherapy: Mutual perspectives* (pp 139–160). London: Karnac.

Burnham, J., Palma, D. V., & Whitehouse, L. (2008). Learning as a context for differences and differences as a context for learning. *Journal of Family Therapy, 30*, 529–542.

Cotton, D. (2014). *Managing difficult people*. London: Hodder & Stoughton.

Department for Education & Department of Health. (2015). Special educational needs and disability code of practice: 0 to 25 years. Retrieved from https://www.gov.uk/government/publications/send-code-of-practice-0-to-25

Health and Care Professionals Council. (2018). Standards of conduct, performance and ethics. Retrieved from https://www.hcpc-uk.org/standards/standards-of-conduct-performance-and-ethics/

Kozlowski, S. W., & Ilgen, D. R. (2006). Enhancing the effectiveness of workgroups and teams. *Psychological Science in the Public Interest, 7*, 77–124.

Markman, A. B., & Gentner, D. (2001). Thinking. *Annual Review of Psychology, 52*, 223–247.

Thomas, K., & Kilmann, R. (2010). Thomas-Kilmann Conflict Mode Instrument Profile and interpretive report. Retrieved from https://shop.themyersbriggs.com/en/tkiproducts.aspx?pc=142

Tuckman, B. (1965). Developmental sequence in small groups. *Psychological Bulletin, 63*(6), 384–399.

12

Selling Educational Psychology Services
Julia Hardy, Jacqui Braithwaite and Rhona Hobson

Changing Contexts

Over the past few decades there has been a rapidly changing pattern of service delivery for Educational Psychology Services (EPSs). Prior to then the vast majority of educational psychologists (EPs) were employed by Local Authorities (LAs) to deliver psychological services to all children and young people within a geographical area as part of the LAs' centrally retained services. The concern within the profession about the increasing pressure on selling educational psychology services led the British Psychological Society's (BPS's) Division of Educational and Child Psychologists (DECP) to produce Ethical Trading: Guidelines for Practice for Educational Psychologists (BPS, 2013) and further changes to the trading landscape, especially within England (with a wider range of EPS commissioners) led to a second edition being produced (BPS, 2018b) as well as the DECP publishing a Guide for Commissioners of Educational Psychology Services (BPS, 2018c). There is still a debate within the profession as to whether the drive to sell EP services is inherently unethical; as Sudhir and Murphy (2001) note, any profit seeking is inherently unethical; and Werhane and Freeman (1999) write about 'the joke about business ethics' because 'it must be an oxymoron'.

Some EPSs are more comfortable with the demands of selling EPS; many prefer to uphold the principle of "buying into" the service rather than "buying out" through the use of agency EPs to build capacity. Most readers will agree with the reference in the introduction to Apter, Arnold and Hardy (2018) that the Children and Families Act (2014) is regarded by EPs as a necessary development but also a curate's egg with 'excellent parts'.[1] Certainly the increased statutory work is a huge theme for EPs working in England currently and yet there are still a wide range of scenarios in terms of pressures on EPSs, both with regard to their staffing capacity (see Chapter 9) and also on their ability to respond to the drivers to sell their services (Gibbs & Papps, 2017).

---

1 Cartoon in *Punch* by George du Maurier, November 9, 1895, titled 'True humility', and captioned Bishop: 'I'm afraid you've got a bad egg, Mr Jones'; Curate: 'Oh, no, my Lord, I assure you that parts of it are excellent!'

Leadership for Educational Psychologists: Principles & Practicalities, First Edition.
Edited by Julia Hardy, Charmian Hobbs and Mohammed Bham.

Preparing and Influencing Your Team(s)

Selling educational psychology services is a difficult and challenging task as a leader. Often, when Principal Educational Psychologists (PEPs) are asked to sell services this is done rapidly, with little warning. Usually this coincides with a reduction in the EPS budget and the related threat that if your income target is not met redundancies may be required. For new PEPs in particular, the threat to the services and the risks involved are anxiety provoking. Certainly one question that is often raised by EPs and their PEPs, is "how do we fit it all in?" as well as the questions about "where is the boundary between statutory and non-statutory work?" PEPs need to be prepared to take part in many team meetings where these tricky issues are discussed.

In one North East LA the PEP found out very late in the day that funding was being cut and had to run the lead into a traded service alongside redundancy proceedings just in case schools did not buy back. It was a shock to the team and they relied heavily on the psychology of change to plan the way forward and manage everyone's emotions. The team often mapped thoughts, feelings and behaviours onto the Kübler-Ross (1993) change cycle (see Figure 12.1) to check where they were and how they might respond to that.

One author has found that being clear about the service vision and mission and developing these as a whole team supports ownership of direction by the EPs within the team and allows for the model of delivery to create itself. Using a solution-focussed framework to create these made discussions about trading easier to manage. The expected outcomes were intrinsically linked to the vision.

As an example (Figure 12.2), one EPS team worked for a whole day to create a vision we could all buy into. The values underpinning this vision were cocreated. The mission was

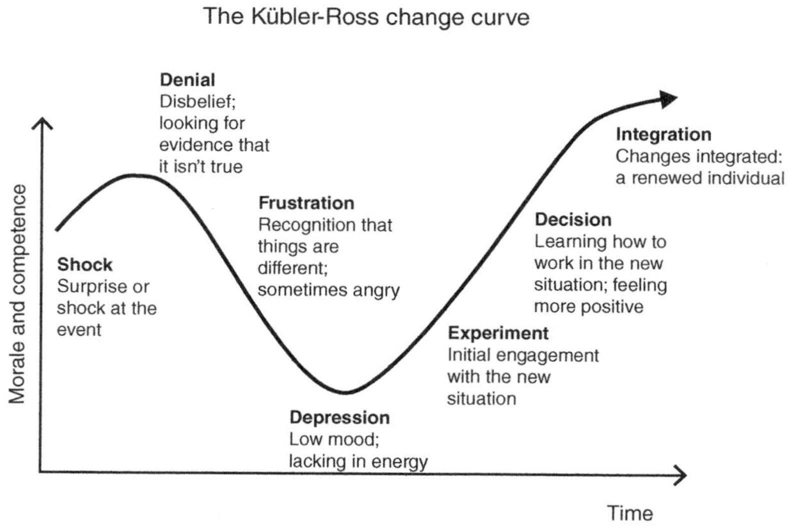

The Kübler-Ross change curve

Figure 12.1   The Kubler-Ross change curve (1993).

THE VISION	CORE VALUES
Opening and Changing Minds	EMPATHY –We seek to understand and share the feelings of others
	EQUALITY-We recognise the need to respond in different ways to individuals in order to promote fairness of opportunity
	INTEGRITY – We do what we think is right morally, ethically and professionally even when it is hard.
	RESPECT – We value and appreciate the views of others
	TRUST – We establish relationships based on confidence, honesty and hope
THE MISSION	PILLARS
Building relationships through meaningful conversations and a 'can-do' mind set to empower us all to be the best we can be	Child centred
	Scientist practitioner model
	Innovation

Figure 12.2 The vision.

democratically agreed, labelling clearly the pillars of the values required to support this. Readers will see that being an *innovation and science practitioner* is labelled explicitly as something we value. Giving permission for trying something out, sustaining the idea that learning and therefore mistake making is OK.

Selling EPSs raises emotional issues for all the team. Some staff may lack experience and confidence; it is a lot to ask an EP new to the profession to engage in conversations with headteachers or other commissioners about what needs they can meet and what services they can provide. Even if your service has the highest quality EPs imaginable, you will still need to plan for continuing professional development (CPD) to bring all EPs on board. This should include opportunities to learn from more experienced, confident colleagues who can demonstrate ways of convincing school leaders that they need to buy into the service and that the additional EP time will provide added value.

The EPS marketing strategy may already be part of the overall service vision and strategy, but even if it is there needs to be further service time devoted to agree how selling services fits with the EPS shared vision and values.

) Make About a 'Marketing Strategy'

..... une useful 4 Ps of selling: Product, Place, Price and People, known as the marketing mix (McCarthy, 1960), and subsequently revised by academics to the 8 Ps and 4 Cs (Khan, 2014). The 4 Cs were originally described by Bruner (1989) and then altered by Lauterborn (1991) who presented the elements of the marketing mix from the buyer's, rather than the seller's, perspective. The 4 Cs include Customer needs and wants (the equivalent of product), Cost (price), Convenience (place) and Communication (promotion).

Price. Usually, within LA EPSs, the price is not your decision, but that of someone higher up the organisation or taking a lead on all LA education trading. Nevertheless, it is useful to know what the charging rates are of your neighbouring EPSs, not to mention that of associate EPs working collaboratively with you or private EPs competing with your service. Some LA EPSs offer a graduated charging rate (charging less for more hours purchased) and some give incentives for agreeing to commit to buy back over the forthcoming years. If you have a choice, make sure that (a) the rate is easily remembered by all your EPs and (b) that you are consistent. Transparency is critical in being clear what is available free of charge and for the services being purchased, what does this include (e.g. administration undertaken away from the school site, follow-up liaison with special educational needs co-ordinators (SENCos)/parents/other professionals or even travel time).

Two of the trickiest issues in trading are firstly when private EPs try to 'poach' your LA schools, often by finding out what the LA EPS charge rate is and then attempting to undercut this. The second is when EPs leave the service to work as private EPs, sometimes taking "their" schools with them and invariably charging less than the LA EPS. When this happens it is important to have open and honest conversations with senior leaders within the school, talking about the benefits of purchasing from a whole EPS, where there is on offer a full range of expertise (mentioning the diverse individual strengths within the team) and easy access for the EPs to liaise with other professionals within the LA if needed. The DECP's Guide for Commissioners of Educational Psychology Services (BPS, 2018c) provides a useful reference document to give to headteachers when discussing the commissioning of EPSs. This document encourages EPs to help schools to be analytic in reflecting on EP work, for instance by undertaking the following activities:

- The EP service provider can carry out an analysis of referrals.
- They can have a yearly discussion about the balance and types of work and patterns of referral (e.g. area of need, year group, gender, ethnicity, etc.).
- They can then devise a clear plan to address any imbalances and evaluate future use of the service.
- This can be a helpful way of considering whether organisational factors are influencing individual referrals. There may be some work that could be done at a class or school level that would be more efficient and effective at resolving a problem than multiple individual referrals.

The focus of this analysis and subsequent discussion is on individual casework with children and young people. When selling services EPSs need to keep in mind and communicate with others that they work at a variety of levels: the Scottish Executive review of EPSs in Scotland (Scottish Executive, 2002) described how EPs work at three levels (the individual child or family, the school or establishment and the LA) with five core functions: consultation, psychological assessment, psychological intervention, training and research. The analysis described here should lead into conversations about schools' individual needs.

Place. Although the place is usually a school or early years setting, thinking about place helps the EPS to be creative in thinking about new opportunities. The DECP commissioned book on 16–25 (Apter et al., 2018) is full of examples of ways in which EPSs across the country have found new opportunities in delivering to different settings such as Further Education (FE) colleges. Likewise Soni (2017) demonstrates how EPs can deliver inspirational work in early years settings.

People. A PEP is always alert to ways to build on individual EP's strengths. For instance if one EP is already a Video Interaction Guidance (VIG) (Kennedy, Landor, & Todd, 2011) supervisor, then you can more easily offer VIG to potential new commissioners. One author has invested heavily in VIG within the team. For successful trading of new interventions in the service, placement of people within the system to pilot and demonstrate the benefits as well as being clear about what VIG can and cannot be within the context they are commissioning is vital. This can mean that you use an 'invest to save' type of argument with line managers, arguing that the intervention will eventually pay for itself. It is a long-term goal with some initial investment required. Time and expertise are the tradable commodities. Investing in the people so that an intervention such as VIG becomes something that the service can sell from intervention through to training and built-in supervision is the long-term goal. One author had a senior educational psychologist (SEP) who was interested in Guy Claxton's work, which led to a cluster of schools planning joint INSET on *Building Learning Power* (Claxton, 2002). What is crucial in the endeavour of engaging your service in trading is to consider the importance of all communications; to plan for and offer shadowing opportunities for less experienced EPs as well as to plan for the necessary service growth so that you can meet the growing demands, year on year. There are the inevitable risks in growing a service, but this is as much about predicting staff turnover and recruitment and retention issues more generally (see Chapter 5 on recruitment and retention) than it is about simply planning to increase service capacity to meet increasing buy-back demands.

Products. The term "product" can be off-putting to some working in LA settings. However, engaging your EPs in thinking about ways to plan new aspects of applied psychology to be offered is crucial if your service is to be successful in developing buy-back over the long term. The Boston Matrix is one way to think about the service offer (see The Boston Matrix, Figure 12.3)

You may have an established "product" such as Emotional Literacy Support Assistant (ELSA) training or coaching groups for school staff, which is not growing fast but has a good share of the offer to schools (a current 'cash cow'). You may be developing a new offer, such as running cognitive behaviour therapy (CBT) groups in schools, which will require an investment in initial training and on-going supervision for your EPs (a future 'star'). You may be committed to an area of offer that does not require buy-back and is unpredictable, such as critical incident school support (the '?' in Figure 12.3) which you want to offer as it is important that the EPS is available for school staff as the need arises. There may be other areas of the 'product'" portfolio that you rarely deliver, is not good use of service time, and so you may choose to remove from your service offer (the 'dog' metaphor in Figure 12.3). What is fundamental in the process of deciding what to offer in the

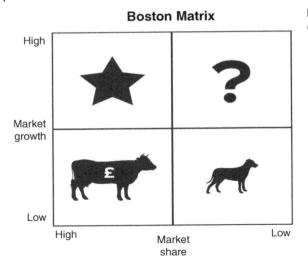

Boston Matrix

High

Market growth

Low

High   Market share   Low

Figure 12.3 The Boston Matrix (Henderson, 1970).

EPS portfolio is how do we seek to understand the local need? Once this is clear the EPS can plan to design, deliver and evaluate different packages and approaches. Frameworks are always useful in structuring our planning; the Currie framework (Scottish Executive, 2002) of the range of EPS activities (consultation, psychological assessment, psychological intervention, training and research and evaluation) helps us reflect on how balanced we are in the approaches on offer to improve schools and other settings to maximise the benefits to children and young people.

Necessity Is the Mother of Invention! The Story of One EP Team's Rapid Move to Buy-Back

Our EPS found out very late in the day that funding was being cut and we had to run the lead into a traded service alongside redundancy proceedings just in case schools did not buy back. We found that the traded model evolves over time, as all the partners gain trust in each other. Where you start is not where you will finish but it is important to start with the principles, the nonnegotiable red lines that will not be crossed in the name of trading. The whole team was involved in this. We were very clear that whatever we did it was about improving outcomes for the children in our LA and not about keeping ourselves in jobs. We started with open and honest discussions with the headteachers and SENCos. We wanted our schools to fully understand the situation and make an informed choice about what was right for them (back to our principles, we wanted to work with not do to). We drew up a simple grid outlining the advantages and disadvantages, as we saw them, from various options of EPS delivery. The options ranged from buying into our LA service, working as clusters of schools and employing their own EP to pay-as-you go options from private EPs. The schools overwhelmingly bought into our principle of 'local services for local people' and opted en masse to buy into the LA EP Team. We really believe that LA EP teams are best placed to provide integrated support with colleagues from health, social care and the voluntary and community sector and the schools agreed with this.

Once we knew we had the support of schools we wanted to be very clear from the outset and to start as we meant to go on. We did many presentations to school leaders, SENCos and governors outlining the fledgling model. The most important message we gave was 'he/she who pays the piper does not necessarily call the tune'. We were clear we would continue to offer challenge to schools and we were clear we would only act in the best interests of the child. We were also clear about costs and started at a realistic price. If a traded service was going to work it had to break even straight away without any subsidy. It was a bitter pill for schools to swallow, paying for a service that up until that point had been fully funded by the LA; however, a realistic price meant they only had to do it once. They soon got used to it and because it only went up with inflation rises, schools could budget accordingly. At each service level agreement (SLA) renewal schools quickly started to ask to buy more and more.

We needed to be alert to the practicalities: uncertainty breeds anxiety and all partners had to know exactly where they stood. For that reason the model of traded services was buying time by the day. The schools agree to a number of days for the financial year as part of the SLA. They cannot spot purchase within year. That way schools know exactly what time they have at their disposal, the PEP can budget for a level of staffing required for the year and individual EPs know exactly what buy back time they have to deliver across the year. Schools are required to use the time proportionately across the year; they are not allowed to save it for a rainy day! As the model has developed schools now buy into 2-year SLAs to help with recruitment and retention of EPs. Every school pays the same rate per day. In keeping with our principles of accessibility and equality of opportunity we do not have a system where schools with a lot of money who can buy a lot of time can get a cheaper rate than smaller or less advantaged schools that have the same level of need but less budget. We charge the same rate whether the person delivering the service is an experienced senior at the top of the scale or a trainee educational psychologist (TEP). We are transparent about this with commissioners. Schools understand our model of service delivery with TEPs linked to SEPs and they trust in the quality of the service.

As part of the SLA schools buy into 'cluster time' which provides the flexibility everybody needs. This means that clusters of schools buy additional time that they use both proactively for training and development according to cluster needs and responsively according to urgent need. If a school does not have enough buy-back time and there is an urgent need they negotiate with their colleagues to access the cluster time. It is much easier to build cluster time into the model in a planned way rather than squeeze in spot purchases when the capacity is not there. Another principle: let's all work collaboratively and with compassion for the good of us all.

Another part of managing expectations has been emphasising that schools are buying into a service not a particular EP. Schools are not allowed to ask for the EP they prefer any more than a parent can demand their child be with a particular class teacher. The key is high-quality staff and a high-quality service so that schools have confidence regardless. We understand that relationships are very important and every school has their own link EP; however, we work to a strengths-based approach so if it is better for another EP to lead on a particular piece of work, whether it is training or casework, then this is negotiated between EPs. In this way all of our schools are getting to know many more of the EPs within the service and so when a change of EP is required then schools manage the transition better, as the chances are they already know the EP.

Managing the expectations of the LA is also incredibly important from the outset. It is vital that the director of children's services and assistant director for education fully understand the role of the EP (not just the statutory function) and support the trading of services as much as possible. The attached models highlighting both the 'vicious' cycle and 'virtuous' cycle (see Figures 12.4 and 12.5) really helped senior leaders in the LA understand their EPS and in maintaining confidence in the system. On the basis of this, and as trust has grown in the model over the last 7 years, we now have the ability to make temporary contracts permanent and set a budget with generous income generation targets which were not possible in the early days. Also our LA took part in Gibbs and Papps' (2017) research Identifying the Costs and Benefits of Educational Psychology: A Preliminary Exploration in Two Local Authorities and this helped senior leaders in the authority to understand the links between early intervention from EPs and statistics such as number of statutory assessments and number of pupils permanently excluded from school.

As the EP team have become more explicit about what they can do in terms of consultation, psychological assessment, psychological intervention, training and research and evaluation, a wider range of commissions has been sought and successfully delivered. The EP team will only seek/accept funding if the project will further enhance the direction of travel of the EP Team/LA – funding is not just for funding sake as this could distract from the key focus points within the EP development plan. Examples of funding sources have included:

- The Clinical Commissioning Group (Autism and Emotional well-being work)
- Health Education England (workforce development regarding emotional well-being)

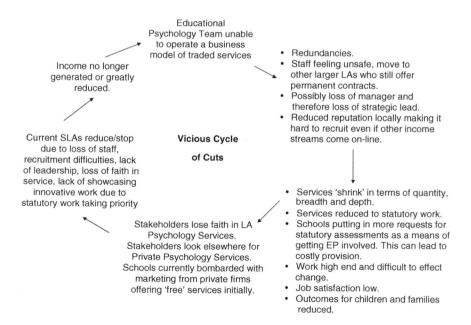

Figure 12.4 The vicious cycle of cuts.

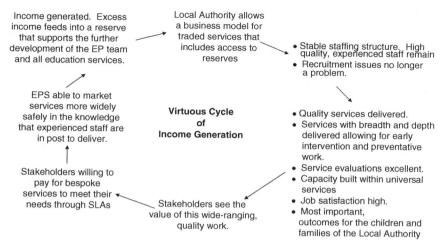

Figure 12.5 The virtuous cycle of income generation.

- Social Care (work with Troubled Families Programme, Looked After Children, Virtual School, Early Intervention Team and the Edge of Care Team). Social care work tends to be a mix of training, group supervision/joint problem solving, person-centred planning with a clear voice of the child as well as acting as care coordinator for complex casework
- School Improvement (projects on transition, boys' learning and resilience)
- Mainstream post-16 work (mainly building capacity in the workforce to cope with greater mental health difficulties and support with transitions of vulnerable young people)
- Other LA departments, for example, working with human resources (HR) and corporate services on staff well-being
- Voluntary and Community sector (they are able to bid more widely than the public sector but often value our expertise in the delivery of the projects)

This case study of the implementation of buy-back in one EPS has attempted to demonstrate the importance of Capacity, Communication and developing the Confidence and Competence of the EPs: a version of the 4Cs which works for us in reflecting on the process of selling educational psychology services. Communication with everyone involved (headteachers, SENCos, governors, EPs, LA leaders, other commissioners) has been paramount throughout. The capacity issue is built into the model, schools buy up-front (including planned responsive time via cluster time) and EPs know exactly what is expected of them at the start of the year. The collaborative teamwork, CPD programme and strengths-based approaches means that the confidence and competence of the team are high.

Building Relationships with a Range of Commissioners

EPSs throughout England are increasingly being commissioned by others within the LA (such as Public Health funding towards the Sandwell Well-Being Charter Mark [n.d.]; Social Care; and Youth Offending Teams) as well as others (e.g. Clinical Commissioning Group). Relationships are key in developing trust, so that the PEP becomes one of the first in mind

nmissioners begin to think about whom to ask, to whom to go. One author has
exp   ce of this taking significant periods of time. Commissioners within the LA had
already held and developed views about what the EPS offered as the model of service delivery, which significantly differed to the views of the PEP when she took up her new post. This
prevented commissioners from even considering that the EPS could add value towards their
Key Performance Indicators (KPIs). Sharing with others, the EPS's service vision and mission with underpinning values and how this forms the basis for service delivery was vital. It
is important to learn a commissioner's language. They often use different terms and one way
to support them to realise what can be offered is to learn *commissioner speak* – linking into
the Local Transformation Plans, KPIs and SLAs, for example. The DECP has recently produced guidance for commissioners of EPSs (BPS, 2018c) which is extremely helpful for commissioners, especially schools that are increasingly approached by private EP providers.

Ethical Practice

In discussing the topic of EPs selling services over the years, one recurring theme is the
issue of inequality. This may be to do with some schools choosing to buy large amounts of
EP time (such as a day a week) compared to others where there is no buy-back. In one sense
we can argue that it has always been this way: schools have usually been the ones choosing
what their priorities are; the buy-back of EPSs just exacerbates this. Our task as EPS leaders
is to find ways into schools, so that we can help to influence their choices. One key way to
do this is to use data effectively (see Chapter 13, Whitehead & Gillum), sharing the pattern
of EP consultations/involvement in a school with their staff, discussing their whole school
issues and patterns of needs, in order to help them think about how EPs can assist them
through consultations, training and evidence-based approaches.

Another issue for PEPs and service managers is how to conduct yourself when you are
working alongside other services that are not required to trade. This is another tricky issue;
if the PEP has responsibility for both a traded EPS and other services, it may be useful to
designate a SEP/deputy EP as lead for EPS buy-back so that the PEP is seen as attending to
all those diverse services for which they may be responsible (see Chapter 11 for further
discussion of tricky issues in line management).

As an increasing proportion of EP work is directly commissioned the concept of fair
practice becomes more complex. For example, EPs are less able to control access to their
services and will, therefore, need to reflect more carefully on their broader responsibilities
to the vulnerable and the 'unsponsored child'. EPs continue to express concern that with
selling EP services, there is no longer equity of access. This is indeed the case; although in
the past, before EPS trading, one could argue that the equity of access still depended on a
range of factors, such as the size of the EPS and the LA, the particular priorities of headteachers and SENCos in determining priorities for EP work. The recently updated DECP
Ethical Trading Guidelines reminds us to address the range of ethical dilemmas and to use
the previous Code of Ethics and Conduct (BPS, 2018a) framework for considering ethical
dilemmas with all members of your EPS.

In one author's Local Authority, what has been helpful has been the creation of the
social, emotional and mental health portfolio. This, alongside the guide for professionals

regarding how the EPs delivers service and why we choose to deliver in this way has been fundamental to challenging long held beliefs about our role. When we created this portfolio we were very clear that this was NOT a menu that schools could buy from but rather a set of examples of work that the EPS could be involved in from a whole system perspective right down to the individual child level. We provide evaluation data with outcome and impact measures for interested parties. We have been clear that this is not an exhaustive list of things that we can engage with and that any engagement has to be indicated as appropriate from formulations created during consultation with key staff in schools.

The EPS team are not all trained in all of the interventions and we are clear with schools and other partners that if it is indicated as appropriate it may be that a different EP delivers the work. This has meant that we must be flexible with the time allocation. We have had to build in pooled time that is held by us to use appropriately. This has also allowed us to operate in an under promise and over deliver manner within the traded remit. Consultation clusters that deliver the core time have given added flexibility whilst maintaining a core offer to all schools within the LA.

The portfolio is freely accessible to all people working within the authority and has allowed for a broadening of the work that EPs can be involved in. It has also facilitated joint working and a shared understanding across team members increasing support for one another. This has also allowed for the premise that the service is bought in as a whole. We will allocate the best person to deliver that particular piece of work ensuring high-quality interventions are delivered across the service. It is important to make this clear with schools and then they appreciate that they are getting the best the service offers making it inherently more valuable.

Our portfolio details interventions that are not readily available with other nontraded partners and the passion with which the EPs sell these interventions (due to the ownership they have of them) means that they are in high demand.

Conclusions

In managing a high-quality EPS that is involved in trading, it is important that you are principled in leading this endeavour. For instance, if you resist schools that try to choose a certain EP, arguing that they are buying a service not an individual, you will be respected for this. The phrase 'what we permit we promote' says it all; if you are strong and principled, are seen to be fair and consistent, you will be respected by EPs and commissioners alike. During a recent training course on leadership, PEPs and SEPs suggested ways to "Speculate to Accumulate", for example, offer trials for free, piloting new offers, take a 'can-do' approach and extending the institutions that you work in (such as post-16/colleges). One author stresses the need to be aware of the 4 Cs of trading: have you got 'Capacity'? Are your staff both 'Competent' and 'Confident'? Are you communicating effectively both within the service (e.g. sowing the seeds through service CPD and peer-to-peer reference groups) and externally (through leaflets and the analysis of evaluations)? All that we do comes back to relationships within the service, the LA, schools and other commissioners. We need to ask ourselves are we visible and do we take up the opportunities as they arise? These opportunities may arise out of the EPS/School planning meetings, or they may be serendipitous.

Develop a 'no idea is a bad idea' in your team. What may seem strange or unusual, different or off tangent often can have something of merit and individuality. Do not be afraid to try new things as a pilot. One of the authors has bought into a number of different CPD programmes for EPs allowing them to follow their interests (as much as is sensible and possible – it does not affect service delivery), this includes VIG, Zippy's friends, emotion-focussed therapy, narrative therapy, positive psychology courses and solution-focussed therapy. The rationale for this approach is that passion for something most often translates into action and growth. When something has a strong evidence base and when those who deliver it believe it in, it becomes more desired and easier to sell.

Being a "buy-back" service is no easy matter. There are difficult times, such as when temporary staff "poach" schools from the LA EPS, or indeed when new approaches required from EPs result in valued staff leaving the service. That said there are possibilities and opportunities in trading EP services that, if well managed, can lead to enhanced services and improved outcomes for children and families as well as improved job satisfaction for the EP. The EPS described in the case study now finds itself with a LA budget reduced by two thirds in the last 9 years and yet the size of the team has tripled, the work is more varied than ever, statutory assessments remain fairly static (approximately 10 per year per full-time EP) and recruitment and retention are currently not an issue. With principles and applied psychology trading can work for some teams.

References

Apter, B., Arnold, C., & Hardy, J. (Eds.). (2018). *Applied educational psychology with 16–25 year olds: New frameworks and perspectives for working with young people.* London: UCL and IOE Press.

British Psychological Society (BPS). (2013). *Ethical trading: Guidelines for practice for educational psychologists: Division of Educational and Child Psychology.* Leicester: BPS.

British Psychological Society (BPS). (2018a). Code of ethics and conduct. Leicester: BPS.

British Psychological Society (BPS). (2018b). *Ethical Trading. Guidelines for practice for educational psychologists: The Division of Educational and Child Psychology* (2nd ed.). Leicester: BPS. Retrieved from https://www.bps.org.uk/member-microsites/division-educational-child-psychology/resources

British Psychological Society (BPS). (2018c). *Guide for commissioners of educational psychology services: the Division of Educational and Child Psychology.* Leicester: BPS.

Bruner, G. C. (1989). The marketing mix: Time for reconceptualization. *Journal of Marketing Education, 11*, 72–77. Retrieved from https://www.bps.org.uk/member-microsites/division-educational-child-psychology/resources

Children and Families Act. (2014). Retrieved from http://www.legislation.gov.uk/ukpga/2014/6/contents/enacted

Claxton, G. (2002). *Building learning power.* London: TLO Ltd.

Gibbs. S., & Papps, I. (2017). Identifying the costs and benefits of educational psychology: A preliminary exploration in two local authorities. *Educational Psychology in Practice, 33*(1), 81–92.

Henderson, B. (1970). *The Boston Matrix.* Boston: The Boston Consulting Group.

Kennedy, H., Landor, M., & Todd, L. (Eds.). (2011). *Video interaction guidance. A relationship-based intervention to promote attunement, empathy and wellbeing.* London: Jessica Kingsley Publishers.

Khan, M. T. (2014). The concept of 'marketing mix' and its elements (A conceptual review paper). *International Journal of Information, Business and Management, 6*(2), 95–107.

Kübler-Ross, E. (1993). *On death and dying.* London: Taylor and Francis.

Lauterborn, R. (1991). From 4Ps to 4Cs. *Advertising Age, 61*(41), 26.

McCarthy, E. J. (1960). *Basic marketing: A managerial approach.* Homewood, IL: R. D. Irwin.

Sandwell Well-Being Charter Mark. (n.d.). Retrieved from http://www.sandwell.gov.uk/info/200343/well-being_charter_mark/4225/about_the_sandwell_well-being_charter_mark

Scottish Executive. (2002). *Review of provision of Educational Psychology Services in Scotland.* Edinburgh: Education Scotland.

Soni, A. (2017). Distinctive experiences of children in the early years: Evaluating their provision. In J. Hardy & C. Hobbs (Eds.). *Using qualitative research to hear the voice of children and young people: The work of British educational psychologists.* Leicester: BPS.

Sudhir, V., & Murthy, P. N. (2001). Ethical challenge to business: The deeper meaning. *Journal of Business Ethics, 30*(2), 197–210.

Werhane, P. H., & Freeman, R. E. (1999). Business ethics: The state of the art. *International Journal of Management Reviews, 1*(1), 1–16.

13

Using Evaluation to Deliver Effective Psychology

James Gillum and Juliet Whitehead

Introduction

If Educational Psychology Services (EPSs) are to flourish, and enable children and young people to do likewise, we need robust systems of evaluation which enable us to recognise our strengths and limitations, plan for improvement and drive change.

In the shifting cultural, political and educational landscape of the United Kingdom (UK), this is more important than ever as, over the past decade, leaders within educational psychology have seen some weighty developments within the field of special educational needs and disability (SEND). These have included:

- The introduction of Local Area (SEND) inspections to measure how well SEND duties in the Children and Families Act 2014 are being implemented. The inspections provide impetus for all public agencies working across a local area to evidence not only their effectiveness but their ability to work together to improve outcomes for children and young people.
- A growth in the market for EPSs, with Local Authorities (LAs), community interest companies, academy chains, private conglomerates and sole traders all now offering services. This increased competition makes it important for services to measure and communicate their impact for service users.
- A squeeze on budgets and a renewed interest from school finance officers and LAs in obtaining best value for money.
- An expansion in digital communication, leading to an expectation that services engage in a continued dialogue of evaluation and improvement with service users.

The combined effect of these changes has been not only to make evaluation more important than ever but also to increase its scope and complexity.

This chapter sets out the decisions that were faced by a senior leadership team from an LA EPS, as they designed, developed and implemented a new evaluation strategy. Each section concludes with some key questions, designed to help other leadership teams wishing to develop or renew an evaluation strategy for their service.

Leadership for Educational Psychologists: Principles & Practicalities, First Edition.
Edited by Julia Hardy, Charmian Hobbs and Mohammed Bham.
© 2020 John Wiley & Sons Ltd. Published 2020 by John Wiley & Sons Ltd.

Who Is Being Evaluated?

The first task when planning an evaluation policy is to select the services that will fall within its scope. This was particularly pertinent in this case, as the EPS formed part of an integrated SEND Support Service, which itself had links to other services within the LA and the local National Health Service (NHS) trust. It was necessary to decide whether the policy should evaluate the EP team, the wider SEND Support Service, or the provision of SEND services across the local area.

For the sake of expediency the scope of the evaluation was initially limited to the educational psychologist (EP) team. However, from the outset, consideration was given to the evaluative systems already in place across the LA, in particular:

- Opportunities for joint data gathering including, for example, the possibility of using a single survey to gather information about multiple SEND teams (e.g. support teachers specialising in autism and sensory needs)
- The strategic priorities of the LA and how the EP team could work to address them
- Ways in which data relating to multiple teams could be aggregated to provide a broader, cross-service perspective
- Opportunities for improving the efficiency of data analysis including, for example, shared use of the LA's business services team

As a result, the team was able to prepare a policy that would complement and enhance the evaluative work completed by other LA teams and address the higher-level strategic objectives of the LA.

Key questions

- *Which services and organisations make up the wider ecosystem within which the EPS operates?*
- *Which services fall within the scope of the present evaluation?*
- *Which services and organisations does the present evaluation need to link with?*

What Is the Purpose of the Evaluation?

The next task is to agree the principles that will underpin the evaluation and its broad purpose. The senior leadership team chose to define evaluation as 'a collaborative and iterative process through which members of the EPS and the EPS Senior Leadership Team (EPS SLT) reflect upon practice, identify strengths and areas in need of development and agree actions for improving the quality of service delivery'. In so doing, evaluation was framed as a shared task, rather than something done unto the EPs within the team. Three reasons for undertaking evaluation were also agreed.

1) *To maintain and improve outcomes for all service users*
   The leadership team agreed that the primary function of an EPS is to improve outcomes for the children and young people, particularly those who are vulnerable or who have

SEND. Consequently, self-evaluation should focus firstly on this group of service users by asking how well EPs apply psychology to improve outcomes for children and young people with SEND.

It was also recognised that through working with children and young people, the EPS also aims to support parents and carers, teachers and support staff and other professionals and that outcomes for these groups should also be considered as part of the self-evaluation process.

2) *To enable service members to continually develop their practice*

The leadership team also recognised and valued the contribution that members of the service make toward improving outcomes for children and young people and were explicit that the evaluation process should help ensure that the EPS provides a positive and supportive working environment which facilitates psychological practice. This would include, for example, providing access to high-quality continuing professional development (CPD), supervision and opportunities to develop professional interests.

3) *To ensure professional guidelines are followed*

Finally, the leadership team recognised that EPs are required to follow professional guidelines provided by the Health and Care Professions Council (2018) and should have regard to the quality standards provided by the British Psychological Society (BPS, 2019) and the West Midlands Regional Association of Principal Educational Psychologists (PEPs). Self-evaluation was viewed as one way of ensuring that these guidelines were followed and that the service continually develops its practice.

Key questions

- *How will evaluation be defined?*
- *What is/are the purpose(s) of the evaluation?*

What Is Being Evaluated?

It quickly became apparent to the team leaders that in order to evidence the delivery of a high-quality EPS, it would be necessary to demonstrate two things: (a) that the service provided an environment from within which the practice of high quality psychology could flourish and(b) that the application of psychology leads to improved outcomes for children, young people, families and teaching staff.

Delivering on only one of these outcomes would be insufficient. If high-quality psychology were applied without any associated improvement in outcomes for children and young people, then the effectiveness of the psychology service would need to be questioned and alternative models for supporting children and young people considered. Conversely, if a service were able to evidence its effectiveness but not demonstrate that its application of psychology is sufficiently robust, then service commissioners could rightly question whether the expense of employing practitioner psychologists could be justified. In order to evidence an effective psychology service, it would be necessary to gather information and evidence both.

Key questions

- *How can the provision of high-quality psychology be evidenced?*
- *How can service effectiveness be evidenced?*

How Can the Quality of Psychology Be Measured?

The BPS Quality Standards for Educational Psychology Services (BPS, 2019) serves as an effective measure for EPs to self-evaluate and promote the highest quality and consistency of the service provided by an EPS. This tool was first developed in 1997 and has been revised several times since to ensure that the measure continues to be relevant and reflect best practice within the profession.

A further draft revision of the document was made available in 2018 following feedback from the West Midlands Regional Association of PEPs and a revised version has just been published by the DECP (May 2019). This provided, in the first instance, the opportunity for a member of the SLT in the local authority EPS to pair with another member of the SLT in an external service within the same region and that served a similar population. In the first instance, each member of the SLT familiarised themselves with the document before commencing the self-assessment process in relation to 10 areas of service functioning. These were:

1) Professional Practice
2) Leadership
3) Service Structure and Staffing
4) Induction
5) Continuing Professional Development
6) Professional Supervision of Assistant Educational Psychologists
7) Professional Supervision of Trainee Educational Psychologists
8) Appraisal
9) Supervision
10) Ethical Practice including Trading and Commissioning

Evidence was gathered from a range of sources including service evaluations, satisfaction surveys, policies, performance data, and service user feedback. Following the independent self-evaluation, it was a helpful process to discuss the perceived strengths and limitations of each area of service functioning within the individual EPSs with the member of the SLT from the external EPS. It provided a platform to discuss best practice being employed, areas for improvement and most important scope for reciprocal learning. This regional collaborative learning experience took place in a respectful manner and confidentiality was agreed and maintained. It contributed to the creation of trust which underpinned the confidence to share vital information in a nondefensive manner.

Following these initial discussions each of the areas of service functioning's subsections were rated on a scale of 1 to 4 (1 being outstanding and 4 being weak and in need of immediate action). These scores were recorded within the document along with the source of evidence to justify the score. The average of the subsection scores was calculated so that each section was allocated a score. Completing this section in conjunction with an external service promoted increased reliability and accuracy, as justification for each score was provided. The scores were recorded on a summary sheet and these served to highlight areas of overall strength within each EPS and opportunities where each service could focus upon improvement. The process took place over several meetings. The quality standards document proved useful in identifying the strengths of the EPS, these being the EPS's continued professional development offer and professional supervision of trainee educational psychologists. There were some areas for development which were identified and subsequently addressed including the scheme for induction for new employees. The EPS had a clearly defined induction process for EPs new to the EPS which included time frames and reference to service documents. However, the associated documents referred to were not electronically saved together and thus not easily accessible.

This initial process enabled a first-time user of the BPS quality standards document (BPS, 2019) to have a fuller understanding of how to utilise this tool effectively before introducing it to the EPS. At the annual EPS development day the document was introduced to the wider service and the process was repeated within small groups, generating scores for the separate sections. This provided further accuracy and reliability in the score-generating process. The internal judgements informed through service documents and EPs' observations of service life generated rich and honest discussion amongst the team. Along with the feedback sought from the member of the SLT within an external service, a representative overview was generated which reflected similar strengths and weaknesses of the service. This informed the strategic plan for the year ahead and will be reviewed at the next annual service development day.

What Are the Key Indicators Against Which Service Effectiveness Will Be Measured?

Once satisfied that the BPS quality standards (BPS, 2019) would provide an effective means of securing the quality of the psychology delivered by the service, the leadership team began to consider how best to measure effectiveness.

We began by considering two key national publications, the most recent of which was The Handbook for the Inspection of Local Areas' Effectiveness in Identifying and Meeting the Needs of Children and Young People Who Have Special Educational Needs and/or Disabilities (Ofsted, 2016) and also the Quality Standards for SEN Support and Outreach Services (Department for Children, Schools and Families, 2008).

Whilst neither document was written specifically for EPSs, an approach based on these documents had the advantage of being aligned with government policy and that of the national inspectorate. The leadership team were acutely aware that both documents focussed foremost on the impact that SEND services had on individual children and young people but were confident that the full range of EP work could still be evaluated as part of the wider approach to evaluation.

From these two documents, four key performance indicators (KPIs) were developed to address the range of work undertaken by EPs with regard to individual children and young people.

1) EPs help the LA, schools and others identify SEN and provision in an efficient and appropriate manner.
2) Consultation with parents and teachers is used to agree challenging yet achievable outcomes for children and young people.
3) Consultation review ensures that agreed outcomes are achieved and new targets are set.
4) Service users report a high level of satisfaction with the service provided. Feedback from service users is used to develop the service.

The first three KPIs aligned closely with the key inspection questions outlined by Ofsted and the Care Quality Commission (CQC) but were adapted to reflect the fact that consultation was the model of service delivery used by EPs.

One of the reasons that national guidance features strongly in the present example is that the service being evaluated operates within a LA context. Services that work independently of a LA may find that a different relationship with national guidance is needed to meet their needs.

Key questions

- *What national frameworks and guidelines should influence the development of KPIs?*
- *How, and to what extent, should national frameworks and guidelines be adapted to reflect the mode of working within the service?*

Which Sources of Information Will Be Used for the Evaluation?

Once KPIs had been identified and agreed, the leadership team considered the range of sources that could potentially hold information about service performance. Initially, the team sought to identify all possible sources of information, regardless of how easy or difficult it would be to gather data from them. Three broad types of source were identified:

1) Stakeholders, whose views could provide evidence of a KPI being met or failed. For example, parental satisfaction was identified as a key part of evidencing progress toward KPI 4.
2) Large-scale data sets. For example, records of the dates that Education Health Care Advice were due and provided were used to help evidence KPI 1.
3) Gaps in data, where a new system or way of recording would be needed. For example, a need to develop a means of quantitatively recording progress toward outcomes was needed in order to fully evidence KPI 3.

Once a list of sources had been compiled for each of the KPIs, a smaller group of sources were selected for inclusion in the evaluation plan. The leadership team then considered the method through which information was to be gathered from the source. For example, the team chose to gather information from parents about their level of satisfaction with the service using both questionnaires, shared by EPs following consultation meetings and through focus group interview.

In deciding which sources to include, the leadership team sought to strike a balance between developing an evaluation plan that was manageable and efficient and gathering enough information to enable valid and reliable analysis. Wherever possible, a source of information was used to gather information to facilitate judgements about more than one KPI. For example, a parent questionnaire was devised to gather information with reference to KPIs 2, 3 and 4.

The validity of the evaluation was strengthened through the triangulation of data and a peer moderation process was built in to strengthen reliability.

Key questions

- *Which sources of information will best inform judgement about progress toward KPIs?*
- *How can data be gathered from these sources in a way which is valid, reliable and efficient?*

How Will the Information that Is Gathered Be Used to Judge Whether KPIs Are Being Met?

Finally, the leadership team agreed a set of criteria which, if fulfilled, would indicate that a KPI was being met and similarly, a set of criteria that would indicate a KPI was being missed. An example of this can be seen in Figure 13.1 which shows how data are gathered

Source of evidence	Method for data collection and analysis	Evidence of good performance	Evidence of the need for improvement
Consultation and Consultation Review Records	Twice-annual review of EPs' consultation records (1 per EP) undertaken by line managers during supervision.	Consultation records include detailed outcomes which are appropriate to the needs of the child and which move them forward from their current situation.	Targets are vague, and/or are not relevant to the needs of the children and young people.
Assessment and Reporting Policy	Annual review of five random, anonymised consultation records within the service by an EP reference group to check that records are written in line with policy and guidelines.	Consultation records include strategies/actions to be undertaken by parents/teachers and the child themselves where appropriate.	Consultation records lack clarity regarding strategies/actions and who is responsible for carrying them out.

Figure 13.1 Information source, data collection method and performance criteria.

from one source, in relation to KPI 2 'Consultation with parents and teachers is used to agree challenging yet achievable outcomes for children and young people'.

The leadership team agreed that evidence gathering, impact assessment and service development are continuous, year-round processes but also recognised the importance of undertaking periodic summative evaluation to inform service development planning. The team elected to formally evaluate practice once every 2 years.

Key questions

- *What criteria will be used to judge good and poor performance?*
- *How will evaluation be used to inform service planning?*

Summary

Within the shifting cultural, economic, political and educational landscape, leadership within our profession is more important than ever. Leadership encompasses the evaluation of the delivery of services on offer to ensure practice can be adapted where necessary and to ensure the best outcomes for children and young people with whom we work. This chapter explores key aspects to be considered when evaluating an EPS and will, it is hoped, benefit those leadership teams carrying out a similar task. Such considerations include identifying who is being evaluated, especially for those EPSs existing within the broader context of a local authority. Attention has been given to addressing the purpose of evaluation and identifying *what* is being evaluated; that is, both the quality of psychology employed and its effectiveness. Examples of tools employed to achieve a comprehensive evaluation process have been documented. It is hoped that the sharing of evaluative approaches by EPS leadership teams will benefit the profession as a whole and ensure that we benefit those with whom we work to the best of our abilities.

References

British Psychological Society. (2019). *Quality standards for Educational Psychology Services: Division of Educational and Child Psychology*. Leicester: BPS. Retrieved from https://www.bps.org.uk/member-microsites/division-educational-child-psychology/resources

Children and Families Act. (2014). Retrieved from http://www.legislation.gov.uk/ukpga/2014/6/contents/enacted

Department for Children, Schools and Families. (2008). Quality standards for SEN Support and Outreach Services. Retrieved from https://dera.ioe.ac.uk/8552/

Health and Care professionals Council. (2018). Standards of conduct, performance and ethics. Retrieved from https://www.hcpc-uk.org/standards/standards-of-conduct-performance-and-ethics/

Ofsted (2016) The handbook for the inspection of local areas' effectiveness in identifying and meeting the needs of children and young people who have special educational needs and/or disabilities. Retrieved from https://assets.publishing.service.gov.uk/government/uploads/system/uploads/attachment_data/file/790834/LA_SEND_inspection_handbook_290319.pdf

14

Support Mechanisms for Educational Psychologists in Leadership, Keeping It Going, and Managing Your Well-Being

Julia Hardy and Mohammed Bham

This concluding chapter reminds readers that in order to keep all the inspirational ideas going leaders must first attend to themselves. As Covey (1989) described, when writing about his seventh Habit, this involves looking after yourself (your physical, mental, social and emotional and spiritual self); if you don't attend to those four dimensions then you are less able to maintain all the good work that you and the team have put in place.

One way to attend to your well-being is to identify a coach or peer mentor, who can help you check out on those aspects of a leader's well-being. Effective leaders inevitably focus on their team, the service's priorities, and the strategic direction of the organisation. Educational psychologists (EPs) are also constantly focussing on the well-being of others: the children and young people within our local area, as well as the schools, school staff, parents and colleagues with whom we work. How often, while we are doing this, do we also reflect on our own personal needs and priorities? With an identified coach or mentor with whom we meet regularly, the questions around how we look after ourselves can be addressed.

The educational psychology literature is full of publications about coaching; especially the importance of applying a coaching model within schools; to support teachers and others to reflect on their priorities, their strategies and how to promote the well-being of all those within the school community (Adams, 2016a, 2016b; Gus, Rose, & Gilbert, 2015).

One of the early authors on coaching (Grant, 2001) defined personal or life coaching as:

> 'A solution focused, result-orientated systematic process in which the coach facilitates the enhancement of the coachee's life experience and performance in various domains (as determined by the coachee), and fosters the self-directed learning and growth of the coachee'. (p. 8)

There have been considerable developments in understanding of coaching over the last decade, from Hudson (1999) who emphasised a facilitation approach to coaching: 'a coach is a person who facilitates experiential learning that results in future-oriented abilities' (p. 6) to Grant (2011):

Leadership for Educational Psychologists: Principles & Practicalities, First Edition.
Edited by Julia Hardy, Charmian Hobbs and Mohammed Bham.
© 2020 John Wiley & Sons Ltd. Published 2020 by John Wiley & Sons Ltd.

'Coaching psychology is a branch of psychology that is concerned with the systematic application of the behavioural science of psychology to the enhancement of life experience, work performance and wellbeing for individuals, groups and organisations. Coaching psychology focuses on facilitating goal attainment, and on enhancing the personal and professional growth and development of clients in personal life and in work domains. It is not aimed at directly treating clinically significant mental illness issues or abnormal levels of distress'. (pp. 88–89)

Grant (2005) also summarises a Tripartite Meta-Typology of Coaching, which distinguishes between skills, performance and developmental coaching.

There is now a British Psychological Society's (BPS) Special Group in Coaching Psychology that was set up in 2004, which aims to 'promote the development of coaching psychology as a professional activity and clarify the benefits of psychological approaches within coaching practice' (BPS, n.d.)

The Institute of Coaching (n.d.) describes five basic skills required to engage in coaching conversations:

- Active listening to assure the listener that you are hearing what they are saying
- Three levels of listening and the benefits of operating at the higher levels
- Recognising the saboteur and eliminating your limiting beliefs
- The appreciative inquiry (see Chapter 8) approach to improvement which builds upon the positive as opposed to starting from a premise of what is wrong
- Championing – showing that you believe in the client and his/her abilities

Although EPs will understand and have been trained in the aforementioned skills, our question is how often do EPs apply a coaching methodology for their own benefit and if so how?

Augustijnen, Schnitzer and Van Esbroecka (2011) applied grounded theory methodology to elicit a model for executive coaching, which they discovered included four phases related to the development of the coaching process:-

1) Defining formal organisation-bound objectives between coach, coachee and employer
2) Self-reflection
3) Self-awareness
4) Changes in behaviour and personal changes

Augustijnen et al. (2011) also identified two central variables: (a) the relationship based on trust between coach and coachee; and (b) openness to coachee introspection.

Pant (2011) in writing about work with experts, identified four key principles underpinning how experts learn:

1) Practice
2) Feedback
3) Reflection
4) Coaching

Pant argued that 'reflection is not cognitive, but it is, well, a reflex' (p. 9) and that experts encouraged participants to strengthen the reflex of reflection. With coaching, this includes helping others to be clear about their goals and how they will see them through. In the leadership courses that we have designed we have encouraged the use of a reflective log as a journal to think about your progress as a leader.

The Use of a Coaching Model for Groups of EPs

There are a multiplicity of models and frameworks applied within coaching that EPSs could utilise. The first author applied a coaching model within her last two EPSs in order that individuals could bring work-related issues to a 'consultant' with the support of a small reflecting team. The stages in this process are as follows:

1) Allocate roles within the team

   Agree the 'consultant' and 'consultee' roles. The consultee volunteers to bring a priority issue for them to the coaching group. The group is usually 5–8 people, with a process facilitator (who prompts others, especially the consultant, to follow the model). Sometimes a timekeeper is also allocated.
2) The consultation
   * Understanding the situation
   The consultee describes the scenario with the consultant prompting for clarification about the issues. The consultant may ask the following:
       – Who is involved?
       – Who is concerned?
       – What is causing concern?
       – How long?
       – Patterns of interactions around the concern?
       – Beliefs that seem enacted in the behaviours?
       – Have the people concerned expressed their feelings about the scenario?
       – What has been tried?
       – What have the effects been?
       – What expectations have there been of the EP?
       – How have the expectations been explored/addressed?
   * Analysis
   The reflecting team reflects with each other in an appreciative fashion on what they noticed during the consultation about what the consultee has been thinking, feeling and doing in relation to the issue described. The aim at this stage is to further explore the narrative account and thereby facilitate for the consultee the exploration of new possibilities/options. *The aim is not, therefore, to offer advice.* It is important here that the reflecting team talk amongst themselves and do not fall into the trap of advising the consultant.
   The consultee and consultant listen to the reflecting team.
   * Generating alternatives and action planning
   The consultee reflects with the consulting colleague on what they have heard and how this adds to their narrative about the concern and the alternative possibilities and possible courses of action. The session usually ends with the consultee summarising what action, if any, they have decided to take.

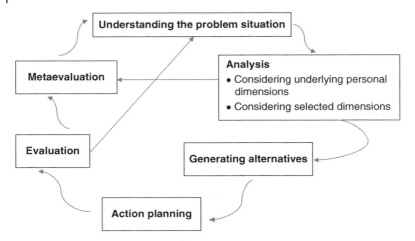

Figure 14.1   The coaching model for Educational Psychology Services.

- Evaluation
The consultee and then other group members reflect from their individual perspectives, on the *issue discussed* and how they might use any of the ideas.
3) Metaevaluation
The whole group reflects on the whole coaching process and how they might use this approach further within their work. This phase also includes specific, appreciative comments about the way the consultant applied psychological questioning to help the thinking process.

Where Does a Coaching Model Used Within an EPS Fit Within the Range of EPS Activities?

One of the questions that one of the author's services asked was where does coaching fit into a service time allocation model? After some discussion it was agreed that this coaching was a part of the service continuing professional development (CPD) time, with the facilitator being responsible for keeping a record of the rota in practice relating to who took up which roles (consultee and consultant), as well as a note of attendees and the topic area. Clearly if EPSs categorise this as part of the CPD time, the individuals volunteering to be consultant and consultee would keep their own personal records for their CPD records as to how this met their individual learning objectives. So, for example, if an EP had learnt to improve their open questioning style, following feedback from a reflecting team, they would record this either within the EPS's own CPD format or use the BPS's suggested one (https://www.bps.org.uk/psychologists/professional-development and log in for "My CPD"). Alternatively, if a newly qualified EP had during their induction prioritised improving their confidence in having conversations with headteachers about buying into the EPS, and this was then a topic they had taken to coaching, this would be recorded as a CPD activity in line with their individually agreed priorities.

What Other Approaches Could Be Used While Undergoing Coaching?

The coaching model described here has been used for the past 15 years as a significant part of whole-day leadership courses. In addition to this model, other 'creative' approaches have been applied as well. These have been more visual and imaginative, with the aim to use different approaches; encouraging creative rather than our default analytic responses. Some of the approaches will be familiar (e.g. 'Viewpoints' where the group consider the issues from different stakeholder positions; or 'Wishful thinking', identifying fantastic or even outrageous solutions to the topic under discussion; this discussion will then trigger new ideas).

Strange links

Another approach is to quickly list a set of objects or words at random (perhaps around a common theme). After this follow these steps (see Figure 14.2).

- Identify the features and attributes of each object or word in turn
- Think about how to make a connection (through one or several links) between the object and its features and the problem you are attempting to solve
- List the links and the ideas generated as they occur
- Evaluate and select ideas generated

Analogies

This encourages the issue holder to think about possible analogous systems as follows (see Figure 14.3)

- Describe some features of the system
- Identify an analogous system which has similar features
- Think about the implications if the system operated like the analogy

Figure 14.2 Framework for strange links ideas.

My system	Analogy	Implications
Ideas:		

Figure 14.3 Framework for analogies.

- Note down ideas and issues as they occur
- Evaluate and select ideas generated

Reversals

Another approach is to think of the opposites to the situation under discussion as follows:

- Describe some key features of the existing situation
- Turn the key features back to front
- Think about the implications
- Note down ideas and issues as they occur
- Evaluate and select ideas generated

KJ method

This method, originally described by Kawakita Jiro in the 1960s (also referred to as the Affinity diagram, see Scupin, 1997) is designed to discuss an issue together within a group. Essentially it starts with defining the issue.

- **Step 1 Label making:** A group write down any thoughts, ideas, facts, or concepts related to the issue.
- **Step 2 Label grouping:** Participants then discuss any of the labels and whether they can be put together.
- **Step 3 Label Naming:** Here those involved agree a label that could be given to each group of ideas.
- **Step 4 Chart Making:** All the ideas, grouped together with agreed summary labels, are then put on a chart and participants then discuss and agree whether there is a **cause and effect** shown by → **an interdependence** shown by ↔ a connection shown by or a **contradiction** shown by >—<.
- **Step 5 Explanation:** A group facilitator describes the chart verbally, revising what is said after discussion with the group.

When this method is used in leadership courses the person who raised the issue takes the chart away with them, with all the details and their record of the explanation.

How Else to Look After Yourself as an EPS Leader

Principal Educational Psychologists (PEPs) are often subject to a deluge of demands, by others in the organisation as well as from schools, parents and other outside bodies. Senior EPs (SEPs) are likewise pressurised, and they also may have the issue of feeling 'in the middle', with demands from EPs as well as from their PEP. SEPs may have conflicting priorities and loyalties, not to mention all the other demands of their work within schools and communities. Apart from ensuring that there is someone who is there for them (it might be a line manager but it could also be a coach who they choose to go to for support), leaders within EPSs need to be mindful of how they prioritise (see Covey's [1989] third habit, 'Put first things First').

Time has been a key topic of discussion amongst EPs and the debate about the relative value of a time allocation to schools and other areas of work has been there for decades. Imich (1999), in his research of the areas mentioned that are not about direct work, identified the only aspect of looking after yourself as an EP was peer consultation which some services found time for in the holidays. The EP profession has come a long way since then, perhaps helped by BPS Practice Guidelines (BPS, 2017) with supervision now written into our professional guidelines. The Division of Educational and Child Psychology (DECP) (BPS, 2010) guidance on supervision mentions that supervision is 'a psychological process that enables a focus on personal and professional development and that offers a confidential and reflective space for the EP to consider their work and their responses to it' (p. 7). This document includes a supervisory competency framework structured within the following six areas:

- Training
- Values
- Context
- Knowledge
- Skills
- Evaluation

We should be mindful of the importance of those offering supervision to others (such as SEPs) such that they too should have protected time to reflect on how well they are delivering supervision. They need their own space as a consultee to bring such issues to a confidential space to reflect on their role as a supervisor (see Kline, 2009, p. 41), including a consideration of the differences in beliefs, power and lifestyle that can be reflected upon using the Social Graces (GGRRAAACCEEESSS) acronym (Burham, 2012). As Kennedy, Keaney, Shaldon and Canagaratnam (2018) suggest, EPs should apply their knowledge of robust psychological theories, including their familiarity with the wider systems and systemic lenses, to their experiences of supervision.

Time Management

Time is one of the most frequently cited issues mentioned by EPs in describing work pressures. There is a wealth of literature on time management but one simple and useful approach is to apply a time management framework to external demands (see Figure 14.4), asking of these requests: Is it important and Is it urgent?

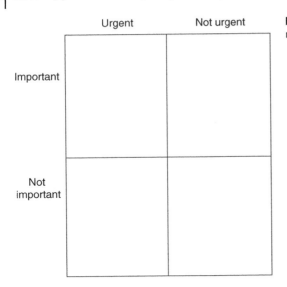

	Urgent	Not urgent
Important		
Not important		

Figure 14.4 The time management matrix.

This framework helps us think about all the continuous demands upon us and how to set priorities that work for us. Covey's (1989) third habit 'Put first things first' (combined with 'be proactive' and 'begin with the end in mind') combine to bring about a 'Private Victory'. How often is it that EPS leaders feel that they are inundated with unpredictable demands, and even if they apply the time management matrix to help them decide which demands to undertake first, they also need to have a way to develop their perspective on relating to stakeholders.

You need to reflect on (a) how much power certain stakeholders have to influence the functioning of your EPS but also (b) how much interest have they in your service, and is this something that you need to work on to develop? Apply the Stakeholder Analysis (see Chapter 7, p. 106) to help you decide on your priorities.

Being a Resilient Leader

As the Roffey Park paper (Lucy, Poorkavoos, & Thompson, 2014) suggests 'everyone has a degree of resilience or they certainly would not be employed in a leadership position' (p. 6). Lock (2014) gives a working definition of resilience as 'adapting well to volatility, uncertainty, complexity, ambiguity and adversity' and 'learning to grow not crumble, through adversity' (p. 3).

Look back at a time in your promoted position in an EPS when you needed to be resilient. Tell your story of that time. Identify what helped you through. This will remind you that you have already accessed resources both inside and outside of yourselves to get through a tough time and can call upon these resources again. This exercise helps counteract the learned helplessness that it can be easy to develop in challenging times.

Lucy et al. (2014) developed a research-based model on the key factors that make for a resilient leader:

- **Perspective**: recognise that perceptions and the way we think about challenges drives feelings, not the situation. Practice *uncovering and challenging negative beliefs*, empowering new, more positive beliefs.

- **Emotional Intelligence**: Acknowledge your own feelings and express them appropriately. An easy way to say this is: *Feel it, name it, express it!*
- **Purpose, Values and Strengths**: Take some time to reflect on the following questions: What is your purpose at work? What one thing could you start doing/do more of that would help you focus on your purpose at work? How does your work fit/not fit with your personal values? What are your strengths? How could you use more of your strengths at work?
- **Connections**: Invest time in mutually supportive relationships; Social support is multifaceted, and it is worth thinking about both who is in your support network and what types of support they offer.
- **Managing physical energy**: Manage boundaries between work and home life. Find ways to switch off; get enough sleep, eat healthily and exercise regularly.

You may wish to consider completing Roffey Park's free online Resilience Capability Index (RCI) questionnaire and compare your scores to others in a relative norm group: https://www.roffeypark.com/resilience-capability-index/.

Leadership Supervision

Within a world of work which is more pressurised, it may not be possible to take the pressure off. Instead PEPs in their leadership role require supervision to help reframe negative experiences as well as opportunity to regulate and not suppress their emotions. Supervision is an essential tool to support psychologists at all levels within a team, to respond to the Health and Care Professions Council's (2015) standard of proficiency: 'to be able to manage the physical, psychological and emotional impact of their work'.

Atkinson and Posada (2019) found that there has been little focus on the supervision of EPS leaders. They found that although PEPs received supervision, a lot of this was reported to focus on the hierarchical managerial or human resource (HR) type of support regarding deploying resources. Instead PEPs would prefer supervision to be focussed on maintaining and developing professional competencies as psychologists, including a focus on affective factors, within a reflective space to be open and honest about their clinical practice and systemic issues. To counteract their limited access to appropriate professional supervision, they found PEPs were undertaking professional development in supervisory skills and forging links with other PEPs.

Organising and Shared Leadership

In order to sustain yourself as a leader and to ensure continuity and succession for the EPS, a team leadership structure is required based on relationships creating mutual commitments to work together. Relationships can be built as a result of one-to-one meetings (such as supervision of leadership team members by the PEP) and small group meetings (for instance, regular meetings between members of the senior leadership team facilitated by the PEP), which can create the foundation of a leadership team and establish roots in commitments people make to each other. Good organisation therefore requires the investment of our hearts (motivation), our heads (strategy) and our hands and feet (action). These skills of motivation, strategising and collective action can be taught and learned, and are critical leadership skills for whole system development and building.

Over the past 15 years in promoted posts, the second author has experienced being part of and establishing leadership teams with PEPs/SEPs, senior school improvement advisers, senior specialist teachers, project managers and senior officers. Although not all have been psychologists, all have shared the narrative of human rights and responsibility to promote equalities and inclusive education within the community. Leading within the public sector at times of austerity has reinforced the importance of structured leadership teams, as the leaders' role is to encourage stability, motivation, creativity and accountability to meet:

- Standards of those they serve (e.g. directors of Education and Children's Services)
- Learning how to be more effective at meeting outcomes over time (e.g. reducing exclusions of pupils)
- Enhancing the learning and growth of individuals on the team (e.g. adoption of evidence-informed interventions; data analysis to target action; etc)

Leaders of leadership teams are required to co-ordinate and empower others to take on leadership, which requires delegating responsibility (rather than just tasks) and holding others accountable for carrying out that responsibility.

Drawing on the work of Marshall Ganz, Harvard University and modified by Abel R. Cano (2016), the following are 'key organising and leadership practices' required of the leader, that is, the PEP and head of service:

Disorganisation →	Leadership →	Organisation
Divided	*Build relationships*	Community
Confused	*Interpret*	Understanding
Passive	*Motivate*	Participation
Reactive	*Strategise*	Initiative
Inaction	*Mobilise*	Action
Drift	*Accept responsibility*	Purpose

Figure 14.5 Key organising and leadership practices.

Telling Our Stories

Within public sector EPSs, we are not always able to recruit leaders (PEPs, SEPs, Heads of Service for Inclusion) from the outside, therefore a good leader organises to reach out and find leaders within your community who can help co-ordinate others well. Organising is rooted in shared values expressed as public narrative. Stories help to bring alive motivation that is rooted in values, highlighting each person's own calling, our calling as a people and the urgent challenges to that calling we must face. Values-based organising invites people to escape their silos and come together so that their diversity becomes an asset rather than an obstacle. It is because values are experienced emotionally that people can access the moral resources– courage, hope and solidarity – that it takes to risk learning new things and explore new ways. Each person who learns how to tell their own story, a practice that enhances their own efficacy, creates trust and solidarity within their 'leadership campaign' or initiative, equipping them to engage others far more effectively.

Each of us has a story that can move others to action. As we learn this skill, we will be learning to tell a compelling story about yourself, your community and the need for urgent and hopeful action. In addition, we will gain practice in listening and coaching others to tell a good story. The following frameworks may help get you started with making your 'implicit' story explicit:

Figure 14.6   Public narrative.

Developing your story of self

Think about the challenge, choice and outcome in your story. The outcome might be what you learned, in addition to what happened. Try drawing pictures here as images to help shape understanding of you and your calling.

Challenge:	Choice:	Outcome:

Developing your story of us

Your story of us may be a story of what you have already done together (common experiences), challenges you have already faced and outcomes you have achieved. Or it may be a story of some of your shared heroes, challenges they faced and outcomes they have achieved. Hearing how challenges have been met in the past gives us hope that we can face new challenges. As a leadership group, work through the following questions:

- Which meaningful experiences have you shared with this leadership team? (events that your team feel connected around)
- What *specific* shared values are being expressed in these moments?
- What were the *challenges* in the/these stories?

Developing your story of now

A story of now communicates an urgent challenge that you are calling your leadership team or community services to join you in acting on now. The story of now focusses on a challenge to your service or community demanding action now, a source of hope and the choice of a pathway to action you call on others to join you in taking.

Story of Now

What change do you want to see in the world? In what cause do you care deeply about, might you call upon your leadership team or community leaders to join you?

Finally, We Can Make a Difference

First we have to step up to leadership and be there if we are to make a difference. Think strategically and plan for a marathon, not a sprint. Remember to keep ourselves safe, motivated, supported and resilient.

Be clear about the additionality you bring, your authentic self and your leadership style. Be ready for challenges and opportunities. Weave a compelling narrative for change – culturally competent and different ways of leading and learning.

Remember to also help others to get into leadership roles and positions. Although we may spend time thinking of those we follow or those that move on, we must always think about those behind us with the hope that we can inspire others to become leaders in educational psychology!

And finally, leadership is about 'for all of us'. Presenting a new psychology of leadership that is the result of two decades of research inspired by social identity and self-categorisation theories, Haslam, Reicher and Plato (2010) argue that to succeed, leaders need to create, champion and embed a group identity in order to cultivate an understanding of 'us' of which they themselves are representative. It also shows how, by doing this, they can make a material difference to the groups, organisations and societies that they lead.

A key value in British EPSs is about group success and this is a result of everyone sharing a sense of 'us'. Although it is easy to imagine our services being led by great individuals with personality, vision and drive to change the world, it is through leadership teams, regional networks and national associations such as National Association of Principal Educational Psychologists that we are 'leaderful'.

References

Adams, M. (2016a). Coaching psychology: An approach to practice for educational psychologists. *Educational Psychology in Practice, 32*(3), 231–244.

Adams, M. (2016b). *Coaching psychology in schools. Enhancing performance, development and wellbeing*. London: Routledge.

Atkinson, C., & Posada, S. (2019). Leadership supervision for managers of educational psychology services. *Educational Psychology in Practice, 35*(1), 34–49.

Augustijnen, M.-T., Schnitzer, G., & Van Esbroecka, R. (2011), A model of executive coaching: A qualitative study. *International Coaching Psychology Review, 6*(2), 150–164

British Psychological Society (BPS). (2010). *Professional supervision: Guidelines for practice for educational psychologists: Division of Educational and Child Psychology*. Leicester: BPS.

British Psychological Society (BPS). (2017). *Practice guidelines* (3rd ed.). Leicester: BPS.

British Psychological Society (BPS). (n.d.). Special Group in Coaching Psychology. Retrieved from https://www.bps.org.uk/member-microsites/special-group-coaching-psychology

Burnham, J. (2012). Development in Social GRRRAAACCEEESSS: Visible-invisible and voiced-unvoiced. In I. B. Krause (Ed.), *Culture and reflexivity in systemic psychotherapy: Mutual perspectives* (pp. 139–160). London: Karnac.

Cano, A. R. (2016). *Leadership, organising and action: Organising workshop participant guide*. December 12–14, Marrakesh, Morocco. Retrieved from http://communitylearningpartnership.org/wp-content/uploads/2017/01/Ganz-Marrakesh-training-guide-.pdf

Covey, S. R. (1989). *The 7 habits of highly effective people*. London: FranklinCovey.

Grant, A. M. (2001). *Towards a psychology of coaching*. Position paper. Coaching Psychology Unit, School of Psychology, University of Sydney.

Grant, A. M. (2005). What is evidence-based executive, workplace and life coaching? In M. Cavanagh, A. Grant, & T. Kemp (Eds.), *Evidence-based coaching Volume 1: Theory, research and practice from the behavioural sciences* (pp.1–12). Bowen Hills, QLD: Australian Academic Press.

Grant, A. M. (2011). Developing an agenda for teaching coaching psychology. *International Coaching Psychology Review, 6*(1), 84–89.

Gus, L., Rose, J., & Gilbert, L. (2015). Emotion coaching: A universal strategy for supporting and promoting sustainable emotional and behavioural well-being. *Educational & Child Psychology, 32*(1), 31–41.

Haslam, S. A,. Reicher, S. D., & Plato, M. J. (2010). *The new psychology of leadership: Identity, influence and power*. London. Psychology Press.

Health & Care Professions Council. (2015). Standards of proficiency for practitioner psychologists. Retrieved from https://www.hcpc-uk.org/standards/standards-of-proficiency/practitioner-psychologists/

Hudson, F. M. (1999). *The handbook of coaching*. San Francisco, CA: Jossey-Bass.

Imich, A. (1999). Educational psychologists and the allocation of time. *Educational Psychology in Practice, 15*(2) 89–97.

Institute of Coaching. (n.d.). About coaching. Retrieved from https://instituteofcoaching.org/coaching-overview/about-coaching

Kennedy, E. K., Keaney, C., Shaldon, C., & Canagaratnam, M. (2018). A relational model of supervision for applied psychology practice: professional growth through relating and reflecting. *Educational Psychology in Practice*, *34*(3), 282–299.

Kline, N. (2009). *More time to think.* Pool in Wharfedale, UK: Fisher King.

Lock, A. (2014). *The resilient leader Debunking the myths and building your capabilities.* Horsham, UK: Roffey Park Institute. Retrieved from https://www.roffeypark.com/wp-content/uploads2/The-Resilient-Leader.pdf

Lucy, D., Poorkavoos, M., & Thompson, A. (2014). Building resilience: Five key capabilities. *Research report.* Retrieved from http://www.roffeypark.com/wp-content/uploads2/Building-Resilince-Report-with-covers.pdf

Pant, P. N. (2011). Leadership and judgement. Why leaders know more than they think they do. INSEAD Faculty and Research Working Paper. Retrieved from https://papers.ssrn.com/sol3/papers.cfm?abstract_id=1750100

Scupin, R. (1997, June). The KJ method: A technique for analyzing data derived from Japanese ethnology. *Human Organization*, *56*(2).

Index

a

absence rates, sickness 62
academisation of schools 35
academy chains xi, 91, 189
accountability 35, 36
  financial 36, 45–46
  and management 18
  models of 15, 17, 27
  public sector organisations 18
  results 17
action research 17, 56, 62
  appreciative inquiry *see* appreciative
    inquiry (AI)
  practitioner 55, 56
activity theory 55, 89
additional learning needs (ALN) xi
  coordinators 147
  legislation 145–147
  services 147, *155*
Additional Learning Needs Act (2017) 145
Additional Learning Needs and
  Education Tribunal
  Act (2018) 146, 148–149, 151
Affinity diagrams 202
Ainscow, Mel 60
Alban-Metcalfe, John 68, 74–75
Alimo-Metcalfe, Beverley 66, 68, 74–75
ALN Act *see* Additional Learning Needs
  Act (2017)
Ancona, Deborah 23
Anglesey, UK 147, 154–157

appreciative inquiry (AI) xi, 5, 17,
  115–132, 198
  assumptions 115, 117
  case studies 115, 121–130
  criticism of 115
  definitions 116
  evaluation 121, 125–126, 129–130
  four-D cycle *see* four-D cycle of AI
  interview questions 122–123, 128, 132
  origins 116–117
  principles 117, 132
  process 117–119, 121–126, 128–130
  structure 115
  theoretical influences 119
  and working relationships 120–121
Apter, Brian 175, 179
Archer, Margaret S. 40
Argyris, Chris 88
Association of Educational Psychologists
  (AEP) xi, 15, 81
Atkinson, Cathy 43, 76, 158, 205
Augustijnen, Marie-Thérèse 198
austerity 4, 58, 163
  see also public spending cuts
authorising environments 18–19
autonomy 57, 58, 62

b

Balint model 158
Bandura, Albert 36
Barker, Pat, *Silence of the Girls* 70

Leadership for Educational Psychologists: Principles & Practicalities, First Edition.
Edited by Julia Hardy, Charmian Hobbs and Mohammed Bham.
© 2020 John Wiley & Sons Ltd. Published 2020 by John Wiley & Sons Ltd.

Printed and bound by CPI Group (UK) Ltd, Croydon, CR0 4YY
10/11/2021

03091408-0001